HANDS AROUND THE GLOBE

Alan Parry, president of the World Council, holding the chain of office, 1997. (COURTESY OF WOCCU)

HANDS AROUND THE GLOBE

A History of the International Credit Union
Movement and the Role and Development of
World Council of Credit Unions, Inc.

Ian MacPherson

Horsdal & Schubart Publishers Ltd.
and
World Council of Credit Unions

Horsdal & Schubart Publishers Ltd., Victoria, BC, Canada

Cover design by Denise E. Knudsvig, WOCCU, Madison, Wisconsin.

This book is set in American Garamond Book Text.

We acknowledge the support of the Canada Council for the Arts for our publishing program.

We also acknowledge the assistance of the Province of British Columbia, through the British Columbia Arts Council.

Printed and bound in Canada by Printcrafters Inc., Winnipeg, Manitoba.

Canadian Cataloguing in Publication Data

MacPherson, Ian
Hands around the globe

Co-published by: World Council of Credit Unions.
Includes bibliographical references and index.
ISBN 0-920663-67-2

1. Credit Unions—History. 2. World Council of Credit Unions—History.
I. World Council of Credit Unions. II. Title.
HG2035.M32 1999   334'.22'09   C99-910411-X

Printed and bound in Canada

DEDICATION

This book is dedicated to all those credit union people, in their great variety, who have contributed to the development of the international credit union movement and who have helped build the World Council of Credit Unions.

FOREWORD

THE INTERNATIONAL CREDIT UNION MOVEMENT HAS A long and deep history. It can be seen, to some extent, as emanating from those informal mutual-aid traditions that, in many parts of the world, go back as far as anyone can remember. More narrowly, it can be seen as an important descendant of the community co-operative banking tradition that started in Europe in the middle of the nineteenth century. From yet another perspective, it is a movement with a thousand beginnings, one for each of the local, regional and national movements that today make up the international credit union family.

The subject of this book is the international credit union movement. It is a vast subject that could have filled several volumes. Indeed, one of the great credit union challenges is to understand and appreciate the diversity of the international movement. Credit unions must function effectively in the market place as businesses and, in that perspective, they are similar one to the other. Beyond that, though, they are profoundly different — and should be different. They reflect the societies in which they function; they meet the varying needs of their memberships.

This book continually reminds the reader of how credit union members and leaders ultimately shape their own institu-tions by the kinds of decisions they make; understanding how that happens around the world is a challenging and exciting task. In an age when people use the word "globalization" easily and frequently, it is nevertheless incredibly difficult to actually think globally.

Some powerful leaders of credit unionism are discussed in this volume — people like Desjardins, Filene, Bergengren, Gartland, Bailey, Shipe, Glen, Morgan and Arneil. Because of the limits of space, the author could not describe in detail the contributions of thousands of credit unionists who made it possible for the movement to prosper. The international movement would not have developed if there had not been tens of thousands of people in communities all around the world who shared the dream of the possibilities of commu-nity-based co-operative banking; who saw how credit unions could enrich their lives — socially and economically. Their names may not be recorded in this book, but they provided the foundation upon which the international movement has been built.

Alan Parry
President
World Council of Credit Unions

CONTENTS

Acknowledgments

When I started this project, I envisioned a rather simple book. As it unfolded, it became a steadily more demanding master. It demanded packed hours during afternoons, evenings and weekends snatched from all the other things that crowd into a life. At times, it became an obsession; at others, it was frustrating because of the magnitude of what it demanded. Whatever else, though, it never became dull.

The book took longer than I expected, and I am very grateful to the board and management of the World Council of Credit Unions for their remarkable patience. I would particularly like to thank Chris Baker and Tod Manrell for their support and understanding.

The book forced me to try to think from a global perspective, never easy but always rewarding; never fully accomplished but always engrossing. The lens the credit union movement provides for understanding the world is a revelation only partly suggested by what follows on these pages; it is a vista that one has to observe for oneself before the possibilities are fully grasped. I hope others will pick up the glass, find new perspectives, explore the many corners not examined in this study, and help create more complete understanding. The possibilities are endless: few other international institutional frameworks have the capacity to reveal and reflect so much; few others are so deeply rooted in the lives of so many people.

It is difficult for me to list all those who assisted in researching into, and reflecting upon, this subject. I benefited from long sessions with Chris Baker, Paul Hebert, Paddy Bailey, Al Charbonneau, Tony Schumacher, Dale Majers, Selma and Jack Dublin, Percy Avram, Gordon Hurd and Lorrell Bruce. I had shorter sessions with many others. In total, I was in touch with people who had more than 250 years of credit union experience.

Both in preparing this study and during the years I was involved as an elected person within credit unions, I had the opportunity to meet with countless credit unionists at several conferences, in many different parts of the world. Less obviously, but not less importantly, those encounters have helped shape this book.

Several individuals contributed directly to this volume and I am very much in their debt. Paddy Bailey, Ken Miller, Al Charbonneau, Jim Murphy and Paul Hebert read portions or all of the manuscript, as did Kecia Doyle. I am indebted to them for their comments, which made this study more complete and accurate than it otherwise would have been. As for the interpretations, correct or incorrect as they may be — they are my own; I had complete freedom to reach my own conclusions.

I appreciate very much the people at the World Council who contributed directly to the book by helping to locate information, by providing photographs, and by facilitating the publication process. I am particularly indebted to Kecia Doyle, who shepherded the project through its last days, to Melanie Tavera for her assistance in the WOCCU library, to Gabriel Kirkpatrick for her assistance in the CUNA resource centre and to Nancy Zarada for all her efforts. I would also like to thank Gayle Stevenson and Tom Gies of Credit Union Central of British Columbia for their help.

I am indebted to Marlyn Horsdal and her colleagues, Heather Graham and Bridget O'Reilly, for their careful copy-editing, and to Michael Schubart for his skill in preparing the book for publication.

Finally, I would like to express my gratitude to my family and my colleagues — particularly Elizabeth MacPherson and Donna Trenholm — for giving me the mental and physical space to prepare this study, even when other demands were pressing. Their patience and understanding are deeply appreciated.

Ian MacPherson
Victoria, British Columbia
Canada

THE DYNAMICS OF CREDIT UNIONS

WHY ARE CREDIT UNIONS ORGANIZED? HOW ARE they created? How do they generally develop? What are the common patterns in their development? What are their priorities? Do those priorities change as they grow? What are the trends they tend to follow as they develop over time?

These questions are not as easy to answer as people unfamiliar with credit unions might think, and this book explores them, albeit in a preliminary way. The underlying point of view of this study is a theory about the dynamics of credit unions that emphasizes four interrelated dimensions of the movement's history: three perspectives within which the movement generally can be situated; five spheres within which credit unions operate; three cultures typically found within credit union organizations; and three stages through which they typically go.

My understanding of these four dimensions, which started to take shape in an earlier history of the British Columbia credit union movement, became more important as the research for this book progressed. I came to see that all four helped in comprehending what had happened in credit union history; they assisted me in explaining why there were certain kinds of persistent tensions within credit union movements. Perhaps most importantly, reflecting on the four dimensions helped me to understand credit unions today; to explain some of the issues with which their leaders grapple; and to appreciate the differences that exist in credit unions around the world.

Amid the remarkable diversity that is the international credit union movement today, there are still powerful echoes of past events and earlier debates; there are certain kinds of issues that do not disappear; there are problems that constantly reappear, albeit in different guises; there are some ideas that deserve to be remembered and reapplied. These factors are all better understood through the lenses provided by broad perspectives, spheres of activities, institutional cultures and stages of development.

Cumulatively or individually, the patterns that emerge from considering the four dimensions, however, do not create "iron laws" governing the development of any specific credit union or credit union movement. In the end, there is too much diversity, too many unique circumstances and too many dynamic individuals for any single mode of understanding. Movements make choices, they often reflect contending priorities, and they rarely fit conveniently into any preordained category. In my view, at least, while there may be tendencies, there is no necessary progression through any of the four dimensions.

I. PERSPECTIVES

The history of the international credit union movement can be viewed from at least three broad perspectives that are not so much competing frameworks as overlapping yet distinctive ways of understanding where credit unions fit into the sweep of history.

1. CREDIT UNIONS — AN ADAPTABLE FRAMEWORK

Credit unions can be seen as a form of organization that is more culturally empowering than it is culture bound. This perspective emphasizes the capacity of the credit union (and co-operative) form of organization to adapt to local circumstances and to be shaped by them. It means that credit unions are essentially representative of local conditions: that they are a flexible form of organization animated by the needs, ambitions and cultures of people around the world.

From this viewpoint, this book is the story of a malleable kind of institution that absorbs, with unerring accuracy, the main trends in a steadily growing number of countries and societies; it is more a matter of diversity than it is a North American or European phenomenon writ large. This somewhat ahistorical perspective, most readily found outside North America, encourages the pride that people in other countries have in their own movements and helps explain some of the unavoidable tensions within the international movement. It also reflects in both obvious and subtle ways indigenous traditions of mutual aid and self-help.

2. THE TRADITIONS OF BANKING CO-OPERATIVES

The history of credit unionism can be situated within a tradition of community-based co-operative banking with roots customarily traced back to Germany in the middle of the nineteenth century. From this perspective, credit unions are part of an international co-operative movement that has typically found its strongest supporters in countries experiencing rapid modernization, particularly societies being transformed by industrialization.

For over 150 years this kind of co-operative endeavour has grown steadily, albeit in somewhat different forms around the globe. Its success is a remarkable testimony to the efficacy of the co-operative approach to economic and social organization, the capacity of democracy (no matter how imperfectly practised) to operate in the marketplace, and the ability of human beings to work together. The contemporary extent of this wide and diverse kind of human activity suggests that credit unionists should reflect upon how associations with this wider and historic "family" might be fostered and expanded; much of their future may be inherent in their past.

3. THE NORTH AMERICAN BACKGROUND

The third perspective emphasizes the North American background of the movement, a story that emerges primarily from the United States and, to a lesser extent, Canada. Following the pioneering work of Alphonse and Dorimene Desjardins in Quebec at the turn of the twentieth century, the movement spread to the United States where it gained remarkable strength, initially serving the needs of working people and then other groups in society. Beginning in the 1930s the movement spread to English-speaking Canada, which developed a movement similar to the one that had emerged in the United States.

From an international perspective, the three movements were essentially shaped by the experiences and values of northern North America. They were individually and collectively taken outward from the two countries to many other parts of the world; in particular, the experiences and leadership of the American movement did much to shape the movement around the world.

The global expansion of credit unions, therefore, can be seen as an aspect of the rise of North American society in the twentieth century. Inevitably, it transmitted the values and assumptions of that society even if, in some ways, it was critical of aspects of life in the United States and Canada. In the curious way in which many co-operative experiments are both critics and proponents of the societies in which they function, the credit union movement carried much that was good but also much that was questionable from the North American homelands.

This perspective on credit unions is most naturally held by North American credit unionists, who are justifiably proud of what their movement has accomplished. They have been anxious to share that experience — and the lessons derived from it — with the rest of the world. At the same time, they have sometimes been insensitive to the different ways in which credit unionism has been absorbed into other societies.

This study suggests that there is merit in remembering all three of these perspectives, even if they sometimes create different understandings of what has happened. As in the case of so much historical enquiry, the best views are not found on only one mountaintop; rather, they are found in trying to make the best sense of what several perspectives have revealed. The results of that kind of enquiry can be awkward and less definitive than some would like, but they may provide a more acceptable explanation for what has occurred.

II. SPHERES

1. MEMBERS

This study suggests that credit unions can be understood by thinking about how they operate within five spheres of activities. The first, the way in which they relate to their members, is a complex and changing sphere of activity, related to the size of the credit union, its stage of development, the technology it employs, the nature of its management, and the amount of resources it has available at any given time.

In their origins, most credit unions had a remarkably clear idea of membership: they were "ordinary" people, for many years captured perfectly by the symbol of "the little man under the umbrella", protected from the rain of "hard times, sickness and financial distress" by his credit union. As much as it represented protection, however, "the credit union idea" also meant an affirmation of the capacity of ordinary people to control, and thus to shape, their own destiny.

In the original configuration of this idea, best associated with the work of Edward Filene, Roy Bergengren and Moses Coady, the focus of credit union activity was the working class, both urban and rural. The message to the members of that class made several points: thrift would ultimately permit more prosperity than could readily be appreciated; the study of economics and the operation of credit unions was a significant form of empowerment; the credit union movement was a form of education as much as a tool for economic betterment; and people working together locally, regionally and internationally

could create a fairer world. It was no less than an agenda for the "emancipation" of the working class.

As the years went by, the focus on the working class became somewhat blurred, particularly in the more economically developed countries. The movement reached out to many different kinds of people and some groups — for example, those in the public service and teaching — had achieved economic stability, if not high financial status. As a result, "emancipation" became narrower and more nuanced and credit unions sought out more financial "products" that would help members better understand and manage their own economic affairs. It was an important and often difficult transition.

2. COMMUNITY

Credit unions have deep and abiding connections to the communities in which they exist, based upon bonds of association which can be either "closed" or "open". Closed bonds refer to credit unions with memberships restricted to those who work in a specific organization (private company or government department) or who belong to a specific church or ethnic community. By their nature, these bonds promote a notion of community of like-minded people who share a considerable portion of their lives in one way or other. As a result, the webs holding their credit unions together can be strong and intricate, especially since they are reinforced by the need to understand their members well in order to extend credit.

The community credit union, with the looser bonds of open association, is based on geography, often at a neighbourhood level when it begins. As they grow, such credit unions tend to serve people in a town, even a city, and the role of community becomes less clearly focused, though not necessarily less important. Community credit unions rely for their success upon vibrant communities, and, as social institutions, they usually recognize a responsibility to enhance the lives of those who live within them.

3. STATE

Credit unions are organized under regulations provided by state/provincial or federal governments. From the earliest period in American credit union history, credit unionists have placed great emphasis on the importance of good legislation for at least four reasons: it defines the governance structure of credit unions; it stipulates many of the relationships between credit unions and government officials; it normally establishes the fiduciary responsibilities of directors; and it often affects the taxation position credit unions enjoy.

More subtly, credit unions are potential providers of all kinds of services, and many consider them agents of economic and social change. Thus they have a need to be at least well informed about government policies, and they need to be heard as governments and their citizens seek to shape the future. They should not be simply organizations destined to act as niche players in locations and circumstances that the really important financial institutions leave unattended.

4. STRUCTURE

The fourth sphere of activity involves the ways in which credit unions associate with each other at local, national, regional and international levels. This has always been, and will always be, a difficult issue for organizations built upon the principle of member control and traditions of local responsibility. Without exception, every national movement has to struggle regularly with the most effective way in which to organize its affairs. They have to cope with differences caused by widely varying sizes of institutions, competing managerial groups, cultural differences and, occasionally, political disagreements.

Similarly, national movements often found it challenging to work out appropriate structures for continental or regional associations. Although desirable for both philosophical and business reasons, unity requires continuous deliberation and conformity with the general purposes of credit unions at the local level.

5. MANAGEMENT

The continual search for better management practice is a pressing priority for credit unions in all stages of their development; without careful attention to it, they will not survive. In the early stages, the emphasis is on educating volunteer leaders so that they can carry out their responsibilities in running financial institutions. The emphasis then turns to training secretary-treasurers or managers and, subsequently, to the integration of a series of financial specialists, such as accountants and professional lenders.

"Management" is always a vital sphere because it is central to how the contending interests within a credit union are balanced. There will always be different priorities for those who are essentially savers and those who are primarily borrowers. There will always be a tension between democratic impulses and the need for efficiency, between individual and community priorities, and between present needs and future requirements. Accommodating these different interests becomes a perpetual challenge for credit unions, and their success in meeting it is the true, best test of their efficacy as credit unions.

The management sphere is particularly complex, because it requires not only absorbing the "best practices" followed by managers in private industry but also finding the best ways to apply credit union/co-operative principles and methods. Nor is it a matter simply for employed managers: it demands the attention of the elected leaders who, in ways distinctive to co-operative structures, have their own responsibilities and accountabilities. It also should reach out to members of credit unions — they too have their stewardship responsibilities.

Put another way, the sphere of management is particularly challenging because it is the sphere within which the activities of the other spheres typically become concentrated on a daily basis. Its further complexities can be seen when one realizes that credit unions typically are dominated by cultures that continually struggle within organizational practices and structures, cultures that change as credit unions go through different stages of development.

III. CULTURES

In addition to the three perspectives from which the history of the international movement can be seen and the five spheres of activities in which they typically operate, there are also three kinds of institutional cultures that typify the historical development of credit unions. It is important to note, however, that there is no necessary progression from one culture to another; individuals, credit unions and credit union movements can choose their culture — as long as the consequences of that decision are clear, affordable and acceptable.

1. THE POPULIST CULTURE

The first kind of culture — first, because chronologically it tends to be first — can be referred to as "populist". The term "populist" fits because it refers to credit unions with deep commitments to the practice of direct democracy: the kind of democracy historically associated with Athens, the democracy in which all citizens are directly involved in all key decisions. An inevitable corollary of that emphasis is a general suspicion of delegated democracy and domination by professionals. Characteristically, populist credit unions evince an abiding commitment to their communities, however that might be defined — by geography, association or employment. That emphasis means a strong commitment to the social dimensions of credit unions: support for education, sponsoring of entertainments, concern for youth, and care for the unfortunate. As for growth, the standard response from credit unions dominated by this culture is the creation of new credit unions, usually serving small numbers of members.

The vitality of a populist institutional culture typically depends upon small groups of enthusiasts who create the credit unions, attract the support of government, and develop associations and institutions (typically leagues) geared essentially to the promotion and support of new credit unions. They are deeply committed individuals, often greatly influenced by religious or political beliefs that make them willing to undergo great sacrifices for the movement.

In most instances, work within populist credit unions is exciting and invigorating, particularly for those engaged from the beginning of the formative period. The challenges and sacrifices inevitable in mobilizing people, creating enthusiasm, struggling against adversity, and meeting the specific and pressing needs of particularly deserving members create the traditions which often later sustain the movement.

Credit unions steeped in the populist culture almost invariably emphasize their capacity to emancipate "the little man" from the bondage of economic deprivation; it is an emphasis that adds an abiding emotional dimension to the movement. It creates a powerful vision that is not necessarily just a passing phase: several credit union movements, most notably in Ireland, Sri Lanka and the Philippines, retained their populist perspectives even when their movements became large and sophisticated. Smaller closed-bond credit unions, even in the most market-sensitive environments, frequently retain a deep sense of member ownership and responsibility; they often rely extensively upon volunteer labour.

2. THE MANAGERIAL CULTURE

The second kind of culture applies to credit unions in which managerial issues dominate the operations and purposes of the organization. Almost invariably, credit unions reflecting this culture place increased emphasis on the managerial sphere of their activities; in fact, unless the members, elected leaders and managers are careful, credit unions caught up in managerial preoccupations can ignore their commitments to help members, as opposed to turning them into customers to be manipulated — they can forget the communities that once gave their organization meaning and focus.

The emergence of strong managerial groups in credit unions also tends to create issues around leadership, resource allocation and voting structures within central organizations, such as leagues or centrals, issues that often prove to be particularly divisive, even debilitating. Ultimately, too, the increased emphasis on the "managerial sphere" challenges original assumptions about democracy and requires innovative thought and action that conform with the basic values upon which credit unions, like all co-operatives, should be based.

3. THE STRUCTURALIST CULTURE

The third kind of culture refers to credit union organizations that are strongly committed to the growing integration of credit unions within state/provincial, national, regional and international structures. While this goal is always present within credit union movements, it is a culture that frequently competes with the values of populist and managerial cultures; indeed, those struggles underlie many of the continuing tensions and issues discussed in this book.

The problem of how best to create a culture that fosters the national, regional and international integration of credit unions has bedevilled leaders for generations. The issue in the past has generally been how to create structures that are cost-effective, will meet the needs of different kinds of credit unions, and can enlist the support of leaders who often do not work together easily. The issue, as the twenty-first century approaches, is how best to construct an international movement, enlisting the support of similar organizations, so that financial services based on democratic control can survive in an age when technology and capital concentrate power, even more than in the past, in the hands of the few.

IV. STAGES

There are at least three stages through which credit union movements typically develop.

1. THE FORMATIVE STAGE

During the earliest stages of their development, credit unions have to rely upon the support of patrons, other institutions, government departments or funding agencies; despite common mythologies, they are rarely able exclusively to "pull themselves up by their own bootstraps". They also have to utilize networks provided by such institutions and groups as churches, farm organizations, other co-operatives, trade unions and professional associations.

The organizing networks provide the means whereby movements reach out to communities of people already drawn together for a purpose. They can also provide leaders with legitimacy in communities and among their peers; legitimacy is essential in the development of any financial institution, but especially one built on common bonds.

In time, though, these networks can inhibit development once credit unions are up and running. In many instances, the leaders provided by the networks may have a very specific set of goals, and they can also tend to be paternalistic, depending upon their motivation. The result is that necessary managerial and technical changes may be inhibited by the "founders": revered individuals who have made great contributions but who, as they age and the institution they helped found develops, may hold back necessary change and new generations of leadership.

During the formative stages, credit unions do have a limited set of needs that can be met by central organizations. They require education and training programmes, public education or promotion, lobbying of government to secure good legislation, some interlending activities, the provision of insurance services and the procurement of inexpensive supplies. Typically, therefore, credit unions with populist cultures tend to be very common within movements in the formative stage of development.

2. THE NATIONAL STAGE

The second stage of development occurs as credit union movements form state/provincial and national organizations. It is the result of increasing sophistication among a significant number of credit unions. The existing state/provincial and national institutions are required to undertake more activities related to the expanding economic activities of the credit unions; typically, these new or enhanced activities are related to changing technological requirements, more complicated and riskier lending practices, new financial "products", enhanced marketing programmes, and higher degrees of technical competence.

This transition usually brings about periods of intense debate over such issues as funding formulae, control systems, the roles of members and volunteers, relationships among different sizes and types of credit unions and, a frequent by-product of all the others, managerial competence. On occasion it can lead to serious fragmentation: the creation of rival groups of credit unions, and credit unionists. To some extent, the debate can be seen as the result of differences of opinion between credit unions steeped in populist cultures and those exhibiting the characteristics of managerial cultures.

The second stage of credit union development, however, is a particularly creative stage. Normally, it is the time when credit unions reach out to larger constituencies, provide more services to their members, and begin to have a significant impact on the general economy.

3. THE INTERNATIONAL STAGE

It is a paradox — but an understandable one — that international organizations, which may be seen as the top of the hierarchy, have the most difficulty in gaining authority and influence. A simple explanation is that credit unions, like other co-operatives, have a primary commitment to local communities and groups: they delegate sparingly and question authority regularly.

Thus, although internationalism has been evident in the history of credit unionism from its beginnings, and a universal view is deeply entrenched in credit union/co-operative thought, the road toward a strong international presence has been long, slow and arduous. In fact, it is a stage that arguably is just beginning: in an age when the concept of globalization has a particular resonance, it will surely reshape the credit union world.

A PEOPLE'S MOVEMENT

Three different perspectives, five spheres of activity, three institutional cultures, three stages — such are the warp and woof of credit union history. The colours and patterns, however, flow from the efforts and convictions of people struggling to control their economic destiny. The details and texture of the history result from the specific realities that preoccupy ordinary people; not even in credit unions whose size and sophistication may delude their leaders into thinking they do not have to listen to their members can that connection be completely severed. In the final analysis, credit unions are a movement of and for the people, or they have little reason for being. Amid all the perspectives, spheres of activity, institutional cultures and stages of development, there must be a continuity of values and purpose. There is a set of responsibilities and a particular kind of dignity that emanate from that simple fact.

CHAPTER ONE

THE ORIGINS ARE DIVERSE

Unquestionably the "credit unions" originated in Germany, but they now belong to all the people. They are now a part of the birth right of each one of us — just as is the warm sunlight.

Luigi Luzzatti

A credit union is not an ordinary financial concern, seeking to enrich its members at the expense of the general public. Neither is it a loan company, seeking to make a profit at the expense of the unfortunate. ... The Credit Union is nothing of the kind; it is an expression in the field of economics of a high social ideal.

Alphonse Desjardins

MUTUAL-AID AND WEALTH-SHARING ORGANIZATIONS are called different names in different parts of the world. In China they are "*lun-hui*"; in Ethiopia, "*ekub*" and "*neklondis*"; in Benin, "*ndjonu*"; in Egypt, "*gameya*"; in Sudan, "*sanduk*"; in Liberia through Zaire, "*esusu*" or "*osusu*", sometimes "*cha*" and "*adish*"; in South India, "*nidhis*"; in other parts of India they are referred to as "*chitty*" or "*chit*" or "*chit funds*". In Belize, they are "*syndicate*"; in Sri Lanka, "*cheetu*"; in Lesotho and Cameroon, "*djanngi*"; in Jamaica, "*partner*"; in Uganda, "*kwegatta*" or "*chilemba*" (sometimes spelled "*chilimba*"), a name also used in Malawi, Zambia and Zimbabwe; in Pakistan, "*bisi*"; in Thailand, "*len chaer*" or "*bia huey*"; in Ireland, "*meitheal*"; in Japan, "*mujin*", "*hootoku*" and "*ko*"; in Nepal, "*dhikuri*"; in the Philippines, "*paluwagan*"; and in French-speaking Africa, Malaysia and Singapore, "*tontine*" or "*kootu*", the latter a name also used by Tamil peoples. In Scotland, credit unions were called "*menages*" in Celtic times, and in England, "slates". Some West African people call them "*sou sou*", as they do in Trinidad; in Indonesia they are called "*arisan uang*" ("*mapalus*" in North Sulawesi); in Mexico and Puerto Rico, "*cundina*" or "*tanda*"; in Antigua, "*box*"; in Guinea, "*boxi*". Bahamians use the name "*asue*"; Koreans call them "*kei*", "*kae*" or "*kye*"; Fijians, "*kerekere*".

People have used these informal savings and lending associations for centuries to help each other through difficult times, to educate children or to finance special occasions such as weddings or funerals. They work in somewhat different ways around the globe, but in their most common form, individuals who join the organization make regular deposits to the person responsible. Contributors can then borrow from the accumulated pool, typically on a rotating basis, for such purposes as the purchase of consumer goods, the payment of medical expenses or the construction of housing. For the most part, these organizations meet the needs of their members or participants well, but, in their traditional forms, they are also unregulated and transitory: typically, they last for only one season and are used only when other ways to avoid disaster cannot be found.

In some ways, credit unions echo these older, traditional methods of sharing resources. They are manifestations of a desire to find communal means to protect and enhance the ways people shape their lives. Indeed, it is difficult for someone to understand the ease with which credit unions took hold in various parts of the world, but particularly Africa and Asia, without realizing how important these age-old institutions were. From that perspective, credit unions are continuations of an ages-old impulse to band together for the common good and individual advancement. It is a dimension of human history often ignored or ridiculed in the ideological confrontations and power struggles of the last two centuries. It is a perspective that may take on new meaning as the theories of metahistory, that desire to see human history in the longest sweep of time, take shape and give it greater significance.

Credit unions, however, are also formal financial co-operatives: they are legal institutions, incorporated under provincial, state or national legislation. Their legal status is what primarily distinguishes them from the informal mutual institutions which have helped make organized human existence possible since before the beginnings of recorded human memory. It also helps differentiate them from other financial institutions, and usually from other co-operatives.

As institutions, credit unions can be seen as having their origins in the 1840s, when the organized co-operative movement began to emerge. It was a tumultuous decade for much of the world and, in European history, a time when many people in most countries suffered as the result of severe economic depression, social dislocation and political unrest. In Ireland, a famine still recalled in awed tones over a century later killed thousands and ultimately forced the exodus of millions of people to the Americas, South Africa and Australasia.

In Great Britain, the negative consequences of the Industrial Revolution became evident in industrial slums, disrupted family life and class warfare. Those problems cumulatively formed what generations of social activists, religious leaders and political leaders would call the "Social Question" — how to resolve the problems of extreme poverty and social dislocation created by industrialization and rapid urbanization, problems paradoxically linked to the unprecedented economic growth and prosperity of the times.

Urban centres had been part of human existence for centuries, but the industrial cities of the nineteenth century seemed very different from anything before. The factories of the new industrialization reshaped work relationships dramatically. The needs of steadily larger factories for armies of workers created ghettos of poorly paid workers while simultaneously draining the surrounding countryside of its surplus, and sometimes essential, labour force. Children went from working within the household to workplaces with badly supervised conditions that could be abusive. Women took their labour to sweatshops, even to mines, where the demands of the workplace made it impossible for many of them to fulfil satisfactorily their traditional roles of wife and mother.

Just as importantly, the new urban circumstances challenged the existing ideas of an appropriate social ethic. Families, clans, parishes and communities that once had provided subtle, interwoven forms of self-help and mutual aid found it difficult to create the kind of security they had once known. Liberals and conservatives alike could agree that the fabric of the social order was in disarray even as they argued about what was wrong and what the basis for a new civil society should be. Powerful social, religious, political and economic movements appeared as a result, competing for the right to define a new order.

The growth of industrial cities also had a profound impact on the British countryside, as it ultimately did on most of the European rural areas. That impact was simultaneously positive and negative. On the positive side, the new cities offered farm people immense potential for the sale of farm produce. As long as rural producers could amass sufficient capital and the requisite scientific and technological knowledge, they could enter profitably into the rapidly expanding market systems for crop and animal production and processing. In many instances, they organized co-operatives to take advantage of these opportunities. It was a story that would be repeated frequently as industrialization and urbanization spread around the world from the early nineteenth century to the present day; only the location of the essential story would change.

On the negative side, the expansion of the cities and industrialization could create serious problems for the countryside. From the beginning it meant that young people left family farms in alarming numbers; the securities of older landed aristocratic structures and established milling systems were undermined, often at bewildering speed. The web of generally permanent, settled agrarian communities was torn asunder. Adjusting to the new realities was not easy for most farm families and, among the various problems they faced, one of the most difficult was finding the funds with which to improve the quantity and quality of what they produced.

The European nineteenth-century context is important, because it is within that context that co-operative banking, and especially co-operative community banking, took shape. It was also very similar to the kind of context within which credit unions would emerge in the next century. The same kinds of pressures on urban and rural peoples in Africa, Asia and Latin America would elicit similar reactions. Industrialization, whether manifest in the cities that harboured it or in the rural areas that fed it, would become the natural home of "credit unionism" and the institutions that it created.

The nineteenth-century heritage was also important because it shaped the distinctive ideological perspective that guided credit union development. That heritage is not easily discerned because it had to exist in societies where other, more aggressive, ideologies struggled for dominance and gained wider audiences.

In 1848, a series of revolutions swept several countries, particularly France and Germany. The revolutions were profoundly important because they crystallized ideological confrontations over a wide range of difficult issues: monarchy versus republicanism; democracy versus authoritarianism; cultural diversity versus national conformity; the involvement of the state versus private initiative; and the general good versus private benefit.

The same year as the revolutions, in fact, Karl Marx published *The Communist Manifesto*, the first major statement of an ideology that would challenge much of the world for generations. At the same time, the ideas of anarchism were becoming more popular, largely through the writings of Pierre Joseph Proudhon; a series of even more powerful writers would make this option more potent in the future. More importantly, the writings of Adam Smith and Jeremy Bentham, soon to be joined by those of John Stuart Mill, would raise the possibilities of classical liberalism in both its economic and political manifestations. The modern era was struggling to be born, promising and delivering much in terms of expanded production and distribution, but exacting a heavy price in the form of redistributed economic costs, increased social uncertainties and, for too many, abject poverty.

The co-operative movement was among the great ideologies that emerged during the 1840s — even if its ideological claims are not as well recognized some 150 years later. The roots of co-operative thought (or co-operativism) can be found in the eighteenth century, in the writings of the Philosophes and in the popular thought associated with the French and American Revolutions.[1] Its original organizational manifestations included a wide range of informal and formal co-operative or quasi co-operative structures evident everywhere in early and mid-nineteenth-century Europe. There were, for example, several kinds of savings and building societies as well as "friendly societies" and mutual associations in most European countries. While strictly speaking not organized as co-operatives, they provided traditions and experiences upon which co-operatives could be built.

The growth of interest in co-operatives can be traced through the writings of a large number of enthusiasts, including such figures as Robert Owen, Henri Saint Simon and William King. It was manifested in widespread experiments with co-operative communities, consumer co-operatives and worker co-operatives. The movement's founding model, though, did not appear until 1844, when a group of workers opened a co-operative store in Rochdale, an industrial community near Manchester, England.

The Equitable Society of Pioneers, as the Rochdale association was formally called, was primarily concerned with providing good-quality consumer goods at fair prices to its members. It was also concerned with the accumulation of capital. Indeed, the society needed extensive surpluses if it was to carry out its original central objective of building new co-operative communities. As the years went by, however, the Rochdale society reduced its objectives and became more preoccupied with developing an integrated consumer co-operative system that would include production in factories and on farms as well as sales in co-operative stores — all of them linked together in the interests of the consumers through a powerful wholesale society. These activities became so successful that many came to believe it would be possible to organize the entire economy on the basis of consumer control of the factors of production through co-operative organizations. It was an attractive vision that profoundly affected the British movement, similar movements in Europe and the international movement generally when it took form at the end of the nineteenth century.

The problem of capital, however, would not disappear — for Rochdale or for any other kind of co-operative. Most obviously, it was a vital issue because capital was essential for most kinds of economic activity. The "capital issue", in fact, led inevitably to the raising of several important questions and some very complicated debates both within and outside the co-operative movements of the time and later. Who, after all, should control capital? For what purposes should they control it? How should capital be raised? To what extent should it be rewarded? How could more people gain access to it?

Although not always debated as directly as they might have been, such questions were at the heart of the great ideological confrontations of the nineteenth century — as they would be in more subdued forms in the century that followed. They were among the most difficult issues that all kinds of co-operative organizations, but particularly financial co-operatives, would face from the beginnings of their history.

It is not necessary, and probably impossible, to decide which European country had the first co-operative bank organized on a community basis. The permanent beginnings of co-operative banking occurred in Germany, which, for many reasons, was fertile ground for the relatively speedy and easy organization of such banks. Its urban residents possessed a strong sense of identity derived from the continuing bonds of guild systems, which had only begun to disintegrate in the early nineteenth century. Moreover, extensive industrialization would not occur until later in the century, meaning that there was considerable social cohesion and class identity upon which co-operative banks could be based, even in most urban locations. And, in the rural areas, villages typically possessed populations of about a hundred people, and their traditions of communal cohesiveness lent themselves readily to the formation of co-operative banks.

In 1846 a famine swept much of the German countryside. Many peasants had little to eat other than small potatoes, chicory broth and sauerkraut. In the following year, the economy improved, but the need for credit became critical as farm families tried to achieve a semblance of economic security. It was within the specific context of that economic crisis, as well as the unrest associated with the 1848 revolutions, that the German co-operative banking movement took shape.

While the German movement quickly grew far beyond their initial efforts, three leaders were particularly important in shaping its basic characteristics. The first was Victor Aimé Huber, a physician who rarely practised his profession, preferring to travel extensively in France and England from the 1820s until the 1860s. He became an enthusiast for all the great co-operative traditions then emerging in Europe: the communitarian tradition espoused by Robert Owen and Saint Simon; the Rochdale consumer movement; and the French worker co-operative movement associated with Philippe Buchez and Louis Blanc.

Huber became an important if somewhat iconoclastic advocate for all kinds of co-operative endeavour in Germany. Most importantly, he published a series of tracts recommending co-operative banking, in which he argued that financial co-operatives, if extended to all classes of people, would improve their living conditions. He stressed the value of ownership of property, seeing it as essential for self-support and self-respect, but he realized that many people could own and cultivate land only if more credit was available. He believed in the social value of people of different classes associating for their mutual benefit, and he speculated on the kind of management necessary for the operation of successful co-operative banks. Huber also possessed a deep moral sense: he was a devout Lutheran for most of his life. He believed that co-operative banking should have an ethical purpose, and encourage the ethical and religious improvement of its members.[2]

Hermann Schulze, the second major early leader of the German movement, was drawn particularly to the practical side of Huber's writings. Schulze came from the village of Delitzsch in an area that would become part of Prussia. A lawyer by training, he entered the public service as a local magistrate and was elected to Parliament in the wake of the

1848 revolution; there he took the name Schulze-Delitzsch so that he could be differentiated from all the other Schulzes in the legislature.

While Schulze-Delitzsch was preoccupied by general political issues for much of his life, his main work was the creation of people's banks. He focused on the needs of city dwellers, particularly craftspeople, shop owners and traders. They were people experiencing considerable change as the government legislated the guild system out of existence, despite strenuous opposition. The resulting unease was a significant factor in the 1848 revolutions and, along with the uncertainties associated with emergent industrialization, provided the framework that made Schulze-Delitzsch's banking activities possible.

Schulze-Delitzsch was a liberal with a pragmatic, secular interest in economic matters. He did not encourage the members of his banking co-operatives to devote their time or their organization's resources to social issues. Most of the business of the Schulze-Delitzsch co-operatives was conducted by an executive which was chosen by a twelve-person general committee elected by the members at the annual meeting. The directors of Schulze-Delitzsch's banks were paid for their services, and the membership could be large and diverse, two characteristics that made them different from other kinds of co-operative banks.

Schulze-Delitzsch was a remarkable organizer in three respects. First, he was very effective in travelling throughout Germany encouraging the formation of local co-operative banks. By the end of his life he had organized 1,900 such banks, with 466,000 members. Second, he was adept at creating an intricate superstructure of regional and national banks; indeed, most of his time between 1860 and his death in 1883 was devoted to this task. Third, Schulze-Delitzsch ardently pursued the passage of legislation for co-operative banking, a difficult struggle because of opposition from other banking institutions and political foes. In 1867 he successfully introduced legislation on co-operative banking into the Prussian legislature, and it essentially became the basis for the German law that was passed in 1871.[3]

Meanwhile, in the countryside, Friedrich Wilhelm Raiffeisen was leading the organization of a co-operative banking movement that would meet the distinct needs of rural people. A deeply religious and conservative man, Raiffeisen was alarmed by the poverty he saw in and around the various Rhine Valley cities in which he lived during the 1840s and 1850s. He witnessed that poverty first when he served consecutively as *burgermeister* of Weyerbusch and Flammersfeld from 1846 to 1852; he was confronted by it even more dramatically in the latter year, when he became mayor of Heddesdorf.

Throughout the mid-1850s Raiffeisen was preoccupied with the growing issue of extreme poverty in the cities and especially their hinterlands. In May 1854, he helped start the Heddesdorf Welfare Association to alleviate the needs of the growing numbers of impoverished citizens.

This association originally had many purposes, including the education of neglected young people, the creation of jobs for the unemployed, and the establishment of a public library as well as the meeting of members' financial needs. By 1864, when Raiffeisen started a distinctly credit co-operative in Heddesdorf, all of the broader purposes had been abandoned, and the association became exclusively a co-operative banking

Hermann Schulze-Delitzsch. (Courtesy of CUNA)

facility with the main elements of the kind of co-operative banking to which credit unions would belong: each member had one vote; only members could deposit and borrow; and character was the most important security for loans. By the time of his death in 1888 Raiffeisen had started 423 local institutions, all of them loosely federated into a type of co-operative bank owned by the institutions.

A kind of mystique came to envelop Raiffeisen during his life, and it seemed to grow after his death. From the height of his career to the present, he has been revered not only in the extensive Raiffeisenbank movement he directly founded, but

Friedrich Wilhelm Raiffeisen. (COURTESY OF CUNA)

also in the credit union movement that he profoundly influenced. His obvious commitment to ethical and religious values endeared him to generations of similarly motivated credit union enthusiasts, many of whom were also devoutly religious. His early preoccupation with the health of communities and his intelligent interest in general economic and social issues meant he would be widely quoted in several languages for generations. His emphasis on self-reliance and self-responsibility made his thought attractive to pragmatic credit union leaders even a century after his death. His critique of the increasingly dehumanizing effects of the new economic trends of his day would resonate among credit unionists facing similar situations in other times and places. For generations of credit unionists, his work long remained both an intellectual source and a pragmatic model.

The successes of the Schulze-Delitzsch and Raiffeisen systems were widely publicized both within and outside Germany during the later nineteenth century. They were directly imitated in several countries, including Belgium, the Netherlands and France. In Italy, Luigi Luzzatti, an economist and eventually prime minister of Italy, started the Peoples Bank of Milan, an adaptation of both German systems; within a short time, over 3,000 such banks had been organized in the industrializing regions of the country. Shortly afterward, Leone Wollemborg introduced a modified Raiffeisen system into rural Italy; by the early years of the twentieth century, over 2,000 of these banks had been organized. The Italian system became well known in other European countries, as well as in North America, and would play an important role in defining the nature of credit unions when they emerged in North America.

Co-operative banking also spread to central and eastern Europe. Within central Europe, it was championed by Germans who had settled in the area, and it became common among the Czech, Slovak, Austrian and Polish peoples. In southeastern Europe, Serbs and Bulgarians created strong movements. Within the Russian Empire, co-operative banking made remarkable progress as one of the most effective ways in which serfs could amass the necessary capital to control their own future to at least some degree.[4]

One of the most enthusiastic and effective publicists of the German experiments was Henry W. Wolff, an iconoclastic but widely respected English co-operator. He wrote widely circulated books on co-operatives and did his best to promote the cause of community-based co-operative credit societies during the formative years of the International Co-operative Alliance (ICA). It was not an easy cause for him to champion, however, because it could conflict with the emphasis on consumer co-operation so evident in the British movement. Nevertheless, between the late 1880s and his death in 1930, Wolff tirelessly promoted community-based co-operative banking movements in Europe and on other continents.

While these experiments in community-owned co-operative banks were emerging, other kinds of co-operatives, notably consumer, worker and agricultural co-operatives, started their own banking systems. The English consumer movement began this trend in the 1870s when it organized its Co-operative Bank through a series of administrative steps; most of the co-operative wholesaling societies in the other European countries soon followed suit. Toward the end of the century, agricultural marketing co-operatives, many of them with the assistance of government, developed banking facilities in order to play a greater role in the production, processing and distribution of agricultural products.

Such banks were more like subsidiaries of the large co-operatives that started them; local ownership was indirect — through the boards of those organizations — and they quickly became large and influential institutions in their own right. These were distinctly different kinds of banking enterprises, however, from those in the community bank tradition. They were created as servants to other interests, usually based on the needs of consumption or production, and they lacked the community bonds and deep sense of membership control that characterized the two German movements and their successors, including credit unions.

Among the millions of people who left Europe from the middle of the nineteenth century onward were many who took the traditions and understanding of the organized co-operative movement with them. Wherever they went — the United States, Canada, Australia, Latin America, Africa — they arrived with knowledge of, and experience in, co-operative undertakings. Many British immigrants demonstrated in their new homes an abiding commitment to co-operative stores; thus, in Australia, the United States and Canada, wherever there were large concentrations of English or Scottish settlers, co-operative stores were commonplace. Many of these stores would become the organizing frameworks for co-operative banks and credit unions in later years. People from central and eastern Europe, from Russia, Poland and the Ukraine, established informal financial co-operatives in their new homes. German settlers, especially those who went to Argentina, Chile and Uruguay, established co-operative banks in the traditions of Raiffeisen and Schulze-Delitzsch.

The establishment of co-operative banking by Europeans in other parts of the world, however, was not just a by-product of the immigration process. Toward the end of the nineteenth century and at the beginning of the twentieth century, the major European powers introduced co-operative banking into their colonies, especially in Asia and Africa. They did so for many reasons. Most commonly, they saw co-operatives as effective ways to mobilize agricultural production, particularly cotton, coffee and cacao. Thus, in Africa, Asia, the Caribbean and South America, the British, French and German imperial masters passed co-operative legislation reflecting their somewhat different national co-operative traditions. In general, the administrators tended to favour adaptations of the Raiffeisen approach when they started co-operative banks, although they carefully avoided the full implementation of the democratic features of that model; overcoming the results of that lack would be a major problem for credit union organizers trying to restructure them or build upon what was left of them decades later.

Many imperial civil servants and some politicians saw co-operatives as a way to reform the social and economic systems they found in the colonies. One of the more celebrated and influential experiments occurred in India. Several British administrators, public servants and religious leaders became alarmed at the parasitical role of moneylenders in Indian society in the 1880s and 1890s. Following a government report in 1895, advocating the promotion of Raiffeisen co-operatives, legislation was introduced over the next few years in several Indian states. One of the better known experiments took place in Bengal under the leadership of William Robert Gourlay, the registrar.[5]

Like many imperial bureaucrats in later generations, Gourlay saw the co-operative banks he helped start as an effective way to introduce European concepts of work and thrift as well as democratic theory and practice. His views would be shared by many: over the next fifty years, administrators in nearly all the British colonies — in Asia, Africa, the British West Indies, the Pacific islands and South America — introduced legislation to encourage co-operative banking. Thus, when credit unions emerged in those countries, even as late as the 1940s, 1950s and 1960s, they had to situate themselves within the legislative frameworks and traditions of this older, government-led form of co-operative banking.

The emergence of co-operative banking in North America is a somewhat different story, largely because it relied less upon government initiatives. Its roots can be seen in the numerous self-help and mutual assistance programmes used by virtually all immigrant groups to ease the process of immigration. In the United States it was influenced by an extensive array of building and loan societies that emerged in the nineteenth century, some of which were inaccurately called "co-operative banks". It can be associated with the informal co-operative techniques — from building bees to joint purchasing schemes — common on the settlement frontier and in agricultural districts. It was related to the numerous benevolent and friendly societies upon which working-class and farm families relied in times of adversity. It cannot be divorced from a long history of utopian communities in American and, to a lesser extent, Canadian society during the nineteenth century. The point is that, despite the subsequent mythic emphasis on individualism, the continent was opened and built on substantial communal and co-operative effort; in some ways, credit unions were a continuation of that effort.

Banking issues were particularly evident in rural areas as the nineteenth century came to an end. In the United States, Mexico and Canada, the problems farm families faced in trying to enter the market system, especially those living in newly settled areas, were immense. In all three countries powerful agrarian revolts emerged partly out of these problems, and those revolts raised generally the issue of inadequate sources of credit and the spectre of usury.

The banking history of the United States in particular was dominated by periodic outbursts from people unhappy with the traditional banking system. The massive Progressive revolt of the 1890s, under the leadership of William Jennings Bryan, can be seen essentially as a rebellion against the existing financial structure, and it was so powerful that it shook the national political system to its roots. The emergence of co-operative banking was not a minor aspect of the continent's history; it was a natural and significant consequence of the way in which North America was developed.

To the north, in Canada, several farm groups explored the possibilities of co-operative banking from the 1860s onward, but it was in Quebec that the movement gained its first large body of adherents. Many French-speaking residents of that province were desperately in need of financial services during the later nineteenth century and afterward. Generally less well off than their English-speaking neighbours, and restricted in their opportunities to enter into commerce, they did not have financial institutions that were sufficiently numerous or flexible to meet their needs.

One of the families that encountered financial difficulties was that of Alphonse Desjardins. Desjardins was a native of Levis, a small community across the St. Lawrence River from Quebec City. He grew up in a family left struggling economically by the premature death of his father. He retained a sympathetic concern for the poor throughout his life, a concern that was deepened by his strong commitment to Catholic social activism. In 1887, while working as a translator in the House of Commons for the Dominion government, he observed a debate over usury. At those meetings Desjardins became aware of the great difficulties experienced by most Canadians — the large majority with limited financial resources — in gaining credit.

Deeply troubled, Desjardins spent much of the rest of his life searching for ways to alleviate the poverty that characterized the lives of many of his countrymen. His search led him first to the writings of Europeans, most importantly Henry W. Wolff and Luigi Luzzatti, on the development of co-operative banking institutions. Enthused by what he read, he promoted the idea of community co-operative banking in his own parish of Levis. The system he developed was a combination of the concern for young people that would become instilled in the *caisses populaires*/credit union movement.[6]

The Levis *caisse* grew steadily in the first seven years of its existence. It accumulated $80,000 in assets and made 2,900 loans, totalling $350,000, without incurring a single loss. It even forced three unincorporated moneylenders, who had been doing a thriving business, to close their doors.[7]

From its original base in the Desjardins home in Levis the movement spread slowly but effectively through the parishes of Quebec and into Francophone communities in other provinces. Before his death in 1920, Desjardins had organized 175 *caisses* in Quebec.[8] He also played an important role in the beginnings of the genuine co-operative banking movement in the United States after 1907. His work was publicized in the

Alphonse Desjardins, the founder of the caisse populaire *movement and pioneer of co-operative banking in North America.* (COURTESY OF SOCIÉTÉ HISTORIQUE ALPHONSE-DESJARDINS)

Dorimene Desjardins, whose volunteer labour contributed to the success of the first caisse populaire *in Levis, Quebec.* (COURTESY OF SHAD)

ideas of Raiffeisen and Luzzatti. With the assistance of his wife Dorimene and several neighbours, Desjardins formed the Levis *caisse populaire* on December 6, 1900. Desjardins invested the first ten cents in the bank; all told, he, his wife and his neighbours raised $26.40 at their first meeting.

One of the primary goals of the founders of the Levis *caisse* was the encouragement of thrift among the society's members. They placed emphasis on members regularly saving from their income and spending prudently. They also believed it was important to train people in the habits of saving and careful expenditure from an early age: within a year of starting their movement they had established a *l'épargne sou* or "penny savings" programme for children; in time, it became a school savings programme. In the process, they started a tradition of

New England states by word of mouth among the hundreds of thousands of Quebec immigrants who poured over the border in search of employment in the factories of the region. It was also reported upon in the French newspapers of the area.

One of those who read of Desjardins's work was Monsignor Hevey of St. Mary's Church in Manchester, New Hampshire. In 1908 Hevey contacted Desjardins and invited him to Manchester to explain his banking system to members of the parish. His trip was a success, and leaders of the congregation organized a co-operative credit society in November 1908. Five months later, the New Hampshire legislature passed a special act to provide statutory authority for what they had done and make it possible for other parish-based financial institutions to open their doors.[9]

The creation of the Manchester financial co-operative took place during a time when banking was a major issue in American political life on two fronts. At the national level, state and federal governments were searching for ways to expand credit facilities to assist farm families in purchasing the land, seed, livestock and equipment they needed to enter profitably into the market economy. These efforts, which ultimately led to the development of government-sponsored farm credit programmes, also exposed rural people to the possibilities of co-operative credit, particularly by publicizing the European efforts.

More importantly for the development of credit unions, the existing banking system was not meeting the needs of the urban poor. One of the cities where this problem was particularly evident was Boston, which had a large immigrant population, extensive workshops and considerable social unrest. One of the most important of several Bostonians concerned about this problem was Edward A. Filene, member of a very successful Boston merchant family. Filene's father, then known as Wilhelm Filehne, left Germany amid the disruptions of the revolutions of 1848 and settled in Massachusetts, starting his first store in Lynn in 1852. He married Clara Ballin, with whom he had five children, one of whom he named Edward in honour of the visit of Prince Edward, the British heir apparent, in 1860.

Edward Filene was an unusual character. When he was five years old he suffered an injury that left him with a severe limp that he overcame only after years of lonely, determined effort. This struggle, along with a severe periodic problem with eczema, made him shy, even reclusive, in his personal life. He remained single, "his family, in a very real sense [becoming] society as a whole".[10] Filene developed a deep social conscience shaped by the difficult history and rich intellectual traditions of the Jewish people during the late nineteenth and early twentieth centuries and by the excesses of poverty and social

Edward A. Filene, the great benefactor of credit unions in the United States.
(COURTESY OF CUNA)

dislocation he saw increasing all around him as the new century was born. Particularly appalled by war and class struggle, he devoted much of his time and considerable financial resources to the cause of peace. From 1880 until his death in Paris in 1937, he toured Europe frequently and read widely in European thought; in particular, he became thoroughly conversant with the European co-operative experience.

In many ways, though, Filene was always, as he repeatedly said, a "shopkeeper". Under his direction and that of his brother Lincoln, the store they inherited from their father flourished. It featured a basement sales room in which good quality merchandise could be purchased at "bargain basement" prices. It catered to the needs of working-class men and women, particularly the clothing requirements of women. In helping create this innovation — in effect, a merchandising revolution — Filene learned about the immense potential of the economic power of the working classes, if only their accumulated purchasing power could be directed toward the common good.

As the years went by, Filene focused primarily upon "the causes of poverty, disease, and social distress".[11] In doing so, he corresponded with a wide variety of the leaders of his time, including Woodrow Wilson, Georges Clemenceau, Lenin and Gandhi; he also became an influential advisor to Franklin Delano Roosevelt, especially when he was governor of New York State, but also, to a more limited extent, after he became president. Closer to home, in working with his brother in the operation of the department store, Filene was an enlightened employer for his time. He installed staff lounges and a cafeteria, promoted a staff savings fund, provided free medical care, and encouraged an employees' association to set working hours and determine holidays.[12]

Filene was far from alone in showing concern for his employees. The period after the Civil War in the United States — the so-called "Guilded Age" — was characterized by the rapid rise of the modern corporation. That rise produced severe confrontations between capital and management, on the one hand, and workers and their struggling unions on the other. Strikes and riots became an all too common feature of American cities and industrial towns. A generation of social critics, headed by Thorstein Veblen and Lincoln Steffens, savagely attacked the new American system and pilloried the "robber barons" who manipulated the "new" economy for their own exclusive benefit.

In reaction, some business leaders, including Edward Filene, sought to ameliorate the conditions of their employees. In 1892, employees of *The Boston Globe*, with the encouragement of their employer, formed the Globe Savings and Loans Association in order to save and lend each other money. Four other loans associations were organized in the Boston area over the next decade, including one promoted by Filene among his employees. They spread to other cities as well, manifestations of employer paternalism or social concern, depending upon one's viewpoint. They could also be open to abuse if employers provided funds for the associations and then charged exorbitant interest rates for advances on pay or loans made to employees. It was nevertheless a tradition of workplace banking from which the credit union movement would benefit.

In 1907 Filene embarked upon a worldwide tour in search of effective ways in which to resolve important contemporary social and economic issues.[13] One of the countries he visited was India, where he was appalled by the poverty in both the cities and the rural areas. By accident he met William Gourlay while touring the country and learned about Gourlay's banking activities. As a result, he undertook a tour of co-operative banks to see how they helped peasants to escape the control of moneylenders.

Like many other credit union pioneers, Filene had a particular hatred for usury, believing that it robbed people of a fair reward for the work they did. Just as perniciously, it removed vast amounts of purchasing power from the market system. Moreover, he saw usurious systems, including those in Boston, as differing only in degree around the world. He saw the same social evil in the Philippines, on the way back to the United States and, once home, recommended co-operative banking for that country to President Teddy Roosevelt. The trip in 1907 was the beginning of a passion for co-operative banking that would come to dominate much of the remainder of his life.

Filene's interest in helping working people save and borrow wisely was shared by several Bostonians, including a number of prominent Jews alarmed by urban problems and resentful of the tendency to lay the blame for them on "Shylocks". These individuals, including Louis Brandeis, Abraham Cohen and Felix Vorenberg, would play important roles during the succeeding twenty years in sponsoring credit union initiatives in New England. Initially, they were helped significantly by a key public servant, Pierre Jay, the state commissioner for banks.

Jay was a perceptive government official whose reports reflect a compassionate mind and, even nearly a century later, careful research. As he went about his work he became aware that the existing banking system did not adequately provide small loans for low-income people. In his annual report on the banking situation in Massachusetts for 1908, Jay advocated the passage of legislation to allow for the incorporation of co-operative banks that would serve people bound together "in small places or among other favourable units of population".[14]

Jay's motivations were clearly mixed. There is no doubt that he wanted financial institutions that could meet the needs of low-income people. There is equally no doubt that he was concerned about ethical issues. He believed that co-operative banks could inculcate the highly desirable quality of thrift among their members. He also approved of their possibilities as:

> effective moral and educating agencies: moral, because no one [would be] admitted except after a careful scrutiny of his honesty and industry, thereby affording an object lesson of the value of these traits of character; and educating, because they teach the value of saving in small amounts and the necessity of prompt payment of obligations. Furthermore, the fact that the purposes for which a loan is desired must be stated to the credit committee exercises an important influence, for by this means improvident and thriftless borrowing is effectively prevented. [15]

Like Filene and Desjardins, Jay had read the works of Henry J. Wolff; in fact, his reading of Wolff in 1906 led him to explore North American experiments in co-operative banking and brought him into contact with Desjardins. In the summer of 1908 Jay visited Desjardins in Canada and reviewed the structure and provincial legislation under which the Levis *caisse* had been organized. Later that year, he took advantage of a visit by Desjardins to New England to arrange a meeting in Boston with several economic and social leaders, including Filene.

Early in 1909, after collecting information on the thrift associations promoted in several Boston-area businesses, Jay, with Desjardins's help, prepared legislation for the incorporation of co-operative savings institutions. In the process, the decision was made to use the term "credit union", because the words "co-operative bank" had been used indiscriminately by building and loan associations in Massachusetts. There does not seem to have been much (if any) discussion of the possibility of "people's banks". Years later, Filene, who developed a rather undignified tendency to demand recognition for many things, declared that he had chosen the name. In a 1936 memorandum attested to by Roy Bergengren, Filene wrote:

> The name "union" was opposed strongly in 1908 when I decided to adopt it (and for yrs [*sic*] afterward). I decided on this name because I believed that I could help the just cause of labor if I could make the name of "union" as used by the labor union also apply to employee organizations that were not condemned by almost all employers at that time. The march of events as to credit unions has I feel fully justified the purpose in naming credit unions so as to incidentally help social justice.[16]

Jay may have played a greater role than Filene was later prepared to acknowledge. In corresponding with Desjardins in March 1909, Jay suggested that they could hardly "do better than 'Credit Unions' as a name. It is important to have something both brief and dissimilar to any name now in use by banking institutions".[17]

Whoever was responsible for the selection of the name, the Massachusetts Credit Union Enabling Act, passed in June 1909, articulated a clear understanding of what they would be like. The Board of Bank Incorporation would allow seven or more citizens of the Commonwealth of Massachusetts to organize a credit union if it was "satisfied that the proposed field of operation was favourable to success and that the standing of the proposed members was such as to give assurance that its affairs would be administered in accordance with the spirit of the credit union act".[18] This rather judgmental basis for membership reflected the concerns of Jay, Desjardins and Filene that credit unions encourage the values of thrift and the wise use of money.

The Massachusetts act defined a credit union as a co-operative association formed for promoting thrift among its members. It could receive the shares and deposits of its members, make loans to members on reasonable terms, and undertake "other activities germane to its purpose".[19] Each member had only one vote, and proxy voting was not allowed. Loans were made by a credit committee elected by the members at the annual meeting, and the interest charged would be "at a reasonable rate". The day-to-day activities were directed by a supervisory committee, also elected by the members at their annual meeting. Directors were not to receive any remuneration, but they might authorize remuneration for any officer they appointed. At the end of each fiscal year the members were authorized to distribute surpluses accumulated during the year, although 20 percent of any surplus had to be assigned to a guaranty or reserve fund.[20]

It is possible to exaggerate the importance of the beginnings of credit unions in Massachusetts. After all, the first credit union in the United States was organized in New Hampshire — in a parish, by a priest, with the help of Alphonse Desjardins, even before there was enabling state legislation. There were experiments in other states as well. The Jewish Agricultural and Industrial Aid Society, for example, established eighteen credit unions in New York, New Jersey, Connecticut and Massachusetts at about the same time.[21] Similarly, numerous groups around the United States and in Canada were simultaneously exploring co-operative credit. The subsequent development of credit unions was made possible, at least in part, by this widespread interest.

The Massachusetts experience, however, was significant because it came to be accepted as the start of the organized movement in the United States. It was also a useful, early manifestation of "the credit union idea" and, in fact, became a model for legislation elsewhere for many years. It is important to reflect on the credit union idea in its early North American manifestation because it was a powerful concept, one that would be changed in different contexts over time, but would have a profound impact for many people in the twentieth century.

The first point is that even at its birth, the credit union idea reflected a long tradition that reached back for more than half a century into North Atlantic history. Its antecedents were diverse; they stretched over several cultures and reflected a complex history reaching deep into the European experience. What had happened in Germany thirty and sixty years earlier was important and formative, and so were the experiences in more recent times in other lands. Second, the idea was, in its essence, international, meaning it would be adapted to the American experience, but that experience would never be the summation of the idea. Third, the idea was interpreted largely by practical people concerned with basic economic issues; it was, therefore, an idea that would be immediately applied to existing realities, with all the uncertainties, debates and logical imperfections that that would mean. Fourth, the idea was predicated on an optimistic faith in the capacity of most people to understand their circumstances, evaluate possibilities, make good decisions, and operate effectively what could be complicated organizations. Fifth, the idea emphasized character and individual self-worth — not a simple premise in societies on the verge of domination by the various kinds of materialism to be found on both the left and the right of conventional political ideology.

Moreover, the credit union idea as fashioned by Filene and Bergengren in the early years of the twentieth century had at its core a populist culture: it placed great emphasis on democratic process and volunteer involvement. It had an immense appeal then and in subsequent decades among people anxious to improve their lot and empower their lives. It also had some characteristic problems. What were the best ways to ensure appropriate legislative frameworks for credit unions in various jurisdictions? How could the necessary training be provided so that independent credit unions would be able to administer their affairs satisfactorily? How could effective organizations be developed at the state and national levels? How should the movement respond to the attacks that inevitably would come? Answering such questions would not be easy, and for a growing number of people the credit union alternative would become the main work of their lives.

CHAPTER TWO

CREATING A MOVEMENT
1909-1941

We are in a new age, and it is the age of the consuming masses. We have practically solved the problem of production; for we have learned how the good things of life may be produced so abundantly that everybody can theoretically have an abundance. Our problem is to get that abundance to everybody; and it is an urgent problem because, if it is not solved, our whole wonderful machine falls into disuse and everybody suffers.

Edward A. Filene

If finally any biography of myself is written, or any attempt made to evaluate the work I have done or tried to do, I want it to be borne in mind that I have, almost from the first, planned to do preventive work; i.e., work that will prevent the social and political and economic wounding and killing of great groups of our citizens.

Edward A. Filene

THE PASSAGE IN 1909 OF THE MASSACHUSETTS CREDIT Union Enabling Act did not immediately usher in a Golden Age of credit union development. Not even in the United States, where the most extensive development would occur, was it a simple or easy matter to launch the movement. The few credit unions created in the decade following 1909 were the result of further visits by Desjardins or the enthusiasm of a local leader, usually a priest. They were not the result of a mass movement suddenly taking fire.

One of the reasons for the slow progress was that the movement in the early years did not have a resourceful, continuing champion. Pierre Jay moved on to become vice-president of the Bank of Manhattan shortly after the Massachusetts legislation was passed. Although he retained an interest in credit unions, he counselled slow development and probably inhibited the work of his successor, Arthur Chapin. The only other possible champion was Edward Filene, but he was following a circuitous route to the greatest cause of his life.

From the 1880s onward, Filene's interests ranged broadly over the world and across a wide range of contemporary issues. Even as he was building the family business with his brother, he was devoting increasing amounts of his time and thought to social and economic problems, or, as he put it, "the causes of poverty, disease, and social distress".[22]

In the late 1890s Filene became involved in the Boston manifestation of the urban reform movement then beginning to reshape many North American cities. His immediate concern — one shared by Louis Brandeis, the future Supreme Court justice who would be a close colleague for forty years — was the increasingly dangerous influence exerted over municipal politics by transportation and electric companies. His interest broadened in the new century to include the generally worsening conditions of the city, obvious in increased social unrest, the growth of ethnic ghettos, the deterioration of public health, the escalation of crime rates, the cultural exclusion of many people, and the "flight to the suburbs" by the city's increasingly self-centred wealthier citizens.

In 1909 Filene invited Lincoln Steffens, the celebrated author and "muckraker", to Boston to help address the city's problems. Together they created "Boston 1915", a poorly conceptualized but well-meaning programme of "public improvement". Its approach was typical of the methods Filene liked to employ in his community activities: it established the facts of urban decay through a survey; it gathered representatives from the concerned community to reach a consensus on the nature of the problems; and it developed a practical programme, involving the best minds of the city, to solve the problems.[23] The premise of the project, which would also come to typify his approach to credit unions, was simple:

> The Boston 1915 movement is based upon the fact that it should be possible for a willing worker earning an average amount to live, himself and his family, healthfully and comfortably; to bring up his children in good surroundings; to educate them so that they may be truly useful, good citizens; and to lay aside enough to provide for himself and wife in their old age.[24]

Steffens, already controversial because of his investigative reporting on corporations and wealthy America, was not well received, especially among the prominent Bostonians Filene hoped to enlist in his project; nor did Steffens prove to be an effective organizer. Those problems, along with the fact that the goals of Boston 1915 were never well defined, meant that the project accomplished little. Its premise, however, was important to Filene, as were some of the investigations it undertook. Those investigations, and several coincidental studies produced by the Russell Sage Foundation,[25] demonstrated the plight of working people who did not save regularly or who were unable to secure loans at reasonable interest rates. The picture of poverty and helplessness they presented, coupled with an understanding of what control over money could mean, even for the poor, became fundamental to Filene's later extensive support of credit unions.

Filene did offer encouragement for the development of credit unions in the years immediately after the passage of the 1909 act. For the most part, he did so through efforts among prominent people in the Boston area. One of the successful ventures he assisted was the Industrial Credit Union, sponsored by the Women's Educational and Industrial Union of Boston; it was important because it invited men and women "of known honesty and integrity" in the greater Boston area to join.[26] Its success in attracting some prominent Bostonians, as well as people from other classes and minority ethnic groups, meant it subsequently became an example of what credit unions could accomplish.

In 1914 Filene joined with a number of business leaders, many of them Jewish, to form the Massachusetts Credit Union Association (MCUA). Its membership included both individuals and credit unions, and its objectives were to promote the movement by assisting credit unions and by making loans when local credit unions could not do so. It was the first attempt at creating an institution that could systematically develop credit unions.

The MCUA hired an attorney, William Stanton, as its first organizer, but it made slow progress, despite continuing support from Jews as well as growing support from Irish and French Catholics in the state. One of the problems the MCUA encountered was that, even among the fifty credit unions in existence in the state by 1919, there was uncertainty over their distinctive qualities, always a significant issue whenever legislation was being created or new people became interested in forming them.

As a result, Filene, with the help of Stanton and the bank commissioner, drafted a statement of principles. Its main points were the following:

> credit unions must be organized on a co-operative basis;
> they were associations of people not shareholders;
> they should "rigidly exclude thriftless and improvident borrowing";
> they should admit only "honest and industrious men and women";
> they should "restrict operations to small communities and groups";

they should make only small loans to be repaid frequently and promptly through regular partial payments;

and they should lend on the basis of character and industry.[27]

This statement of principles became important in defining the credit union idea for Americans and others, even seventy-five years later;[28] perhaps as well as any list, it describes "populist" credit unions.

For the next four years the Massachusetts Credit Union Association carried on, but it made slow progress. Few employers were receptive to its appeals, those concerned about employee welfare preferring other kinds of savings programmes. Many people were suspicious because the idea was still new. A new "people's bank", in reality a private initiative started by Arthur J. Morris, competed for low-income depositors with considerable, albeit short-lived, success. Perhaps more importantly, the state bank commissioner became less supportive because he did not believe the existing credit unions were sufficiently businesslike, a concern echoed in the Massachusetts legislature.

Like many of the credit union movements that would emerge in other states and countries, the Massachusetts movement did not develop without difficulties. This is an important point that North Americans, even many decades later, should recall when they help new movements in other lands. What Massachusetts credit unions experienced in the 1910s and 1920s was similar to what English-Canadian credit unions would experience in the 1940s, Latin American in the 1960s, and African and Asian in the 1970s.

Amid these difficulties, Filene continued to be supportive, but his community interests during that period were drawn more to the development of the Chamber of Commerce. He had helped create the Boston chamber, and he was a leader in the formation of the international organization. Filene hoped that local and international chambers would prompt business people to recognize the need for the economy to reward more completely the many as well as the few; to promote the benefits of increased consumption as well as the advantages of increasingly efficient production.

Filene was also drawn into a widening range of activities in World War I. Having helped Woodrow Wilson secure the presidential nomination in 1912, he was in continual contact with Washington officials throughout the following eight years. Shortly after the war broke out, Filene became convinced that the United States could not avoid some type of involvement unless the conflict could be stopped or contained. Along with other prominent business people, academics and religious leaders, he helped form the League to Enforce Peace in 1915 and contributed $25,000 to its development.[29] It was an organization that advocated the active pursuit of peace as opposed to the more common American preference for the neutral avoidance of war. Subsequently, it would help pave the way for the creation of the League of Nations and would prompt Filene to support the international peace movement at the end of World War I.

Filene was drawn further into public service when the United States entered the war, and he volunteered his services to the nation. Given all these activities and his continuing role in the operation of the family business, it is perhaps amazing that he had any time or energy left for credit union affairs. Yet, in another sense, all of these activities were related. They were part of a liberal conception that peace was vitally important and that it could be achieved only through democratic, co-operative activities, starting in local communities and culminating in effective international organizations.[30] It was a world view that would be echoed within credit union circles for decades thereafter.

When the war ended in late 1918, Filene decided to devote much of his time and personal wealth to the pursuit of peace, especially by contributing to the development of a more equitable economic order. He put aside more than $5,000,000 to support the Edward A. Filene Good Will Fund and the Twentieth Century Fund, both charged with conducting research into economic and social issues. Both funds also undertook research into co-operative solutions for a variety of social, economic and political problems. The Twentieth Century Fund was particularly important for the development of credit unions because it funded all the development work of the movement from its formation in 1920 until 1934.

When Filene learned what had been accomplished within the American credit union movement in the first decade of its existence, he was not encouraged. By 1919, acceptable credit union legislation had been passed only in Massachusetts, New York and North Carolina, with less satisfactory legislation enacted in New Hampshire, Rhode Island, Utah, South Carolina, Oregon and Nebraska. The expansion of the necessary legislative framework had stalled and, without good legislation, the movement could not prosper.

The New York movement, heavily dependent upon the support of the Russell Sage Foundation, which had sparked the passage of legislation in 1913, was essentially concentrated in urban areas. In retrospect, the legislation was particularly important because it was the first to place a limit of 12 percent interest on all loans (1 percent per month on the diminishing amount owed). It did so in an effort to quantify a "reasonable rate of interest" — the term used by the Massachusetts leadership. It was a distinguishing feature of credit unions at the time since competing lending institutions were charging up to 52 percent.[31] Subsequently, this definition would remain in force in the United States and Canada until the 1970s; it would be used throughout much of the rest of the world until the 1980s and even, in some areas, the 1990s.

The New York movement devoted much of its efforts to organizing people within ethnic communities across large geographic areas, a practice that was becoming increasingly controversial because it made creating the requisite strong bonds very difficult;[32] even the strong bonds of, for example, the Irish community would not create a cohesive credit union in a city as large as New York.

The North Carolina movement was also struggling and, in retrospect, was involved in kinds of lending that were unusual in the early American movement. It had emerged in rural areas among poor farming families through the efforts of the state Department of Agriculture and the state College of Agriculture and Engineering.[33] From the beginning, the North Carolina movement encountered difficulties, largely because of the lack of training for leaders, the weaknesses of community bonds and the seasonal, cyclical shortage of deposits. Its problems would, for a long period, inhibit the further development of credit unions in rural places. In fact, its problems continued to echo for fifty years, meaning that many American credit union leaders would doubt that rural credit unions could function effectively.

New York Municipal Credit Union in the 1910s, an example of an early large credit union. (COURTESY OF CUNA)

Despite these limited successes, Filene and others decided to bring together representatives from the existing movements, prominent business people and trade union leaders. The National Committee on People's Banks was organized as a result. Despite its name, the committee was formed to promote credit unions and to press for legislative reform at the federal as well as the state level. The committee accomplished little, but it did provide some needed publicity and, more importantly, raised the issue of how the credit union movement might be promoted more effectively at state and federal levels.[34]

Filene recognized that the struggling movement required a forceful leader able to work on legislative priorities as well as actively organize credit unions, first in Massachusetts and then in other areas. He found such a person in Roy Frederick Bergengren, a forty-year-old lawyer educated at Dartmouth and Harvard. A native of Gloucester, Massachusetts, Bergengren had practised law in Lynn, where he specialized in helping low-income clients. In 1911 he became Lynn's first commissioner of finance, a key figure in the new commission form of government he had helped bring to the city.[35] Bergengren had served in the army during the war, achieving the rank of captain in the ordnance corps by 1918. Returning home, he moved briefly to Wenham, Massachusetts, where he entered the candy business. This diverse background served him in good stead in the credit union movement in which he would spend the remainder of his life.

Like Filene, Bergengren had an instinctive commitment to the principle of public service, and that aspect of credit union work always appealed to him. Moreover, as he learned about the movement, its history, thought and possibilities, he developed a crusader's passion for its promotion.

Filene first hired Bergengren in early 1920 as acting manager of the Massachusetts Credit Union Association.

Roy F. Bergengren, first manager of the Credit Union National Extension Bureau/Credit Union National Association and promoter of credit unions in the United States and other countries. (COURTESY OF CUNA)

Bergengren's task was to expand the state movement, which he did with some success, organizing nineteen credit unions within a year. Nevertheless, the MCUA was in a difficult financial situation and was reorganized into the Massachusetts Credit Union League in July 1921. The league relied heavily upon volunteer leaders, of whom Frances Habern was particularly important: until her death in 1938, she would play a major role in building the state movement. In the process of this transformation of the movement, it appeared briefly as if Bergengren would have to find a new job outside credit unionism.

Instead, Filene, impressed by the work Bergengren had done, offered him the opportunity to lead a national campaign for credit union development. The two men had a simple agreement, a partnership: Filene would provide the money, Bergengren would do most of the work. They were an effective team even though, as Bergengren later recalled, they "differed on almost every phase of the work except that [their] job was jointly to get on with the job".[36]

Filene and Bergengren called the new organization the Credit Union National Extension Bureau. The bureau, whose office was in Boston, had four objectives: secure the passage of credit union laws in all states; assist in the organization of credit unions once appropriate legislation was in place; help organize state leagues; and work toward the formation of a national association of leagues.

From its formation until it was restructured as the Credit Union National Association (CUNA) in 1934, the bureau depended upon the dynamic and resourceful leadership of Roy Bergengren; there is no doubt that he was the person most responsible for its success. He was more than capably assisted, however, by Agnes Gartland, a native of Cambridge, Massachusetts. Gartland worked as secretary to A.L. Lowell, president of Harvard University, before joining the bureau in 1928, where she remained until 1934, moving to work with CUNA for four more years. Afterward, until 1959, she worked for the Massachusetts movement. Gartland always remained in close contact with Bergengren, a close friend and constant advisor; she was also a sympathetic voice for the development of the international movement.

Gartland was far more than a conventional secretary: she operated the office when Bergengren was away on his many trips; she organized credit unions in her own right; she managed the distribution of supplies to credit unions; and she served in a variety of capacities at the local and state levels. In the early years of the bureau, especially, she was a third if informal partner, an important figure in its operations.

Filene's involvement in the bureau before it became CUNA was most directly as a founder. Bergengren later estimated that Filene contributed over $1,000,000, a particularly large and generous sum at the time. Fortunately, perhaps, because he was not easy to work with, Filene did not participate very often on a day-to-day basis. Nor would Bergengren, who was a powerful personality with equally strong views, have been able to accept much daily intervention from anyone, even the individual paying the bills.

Agnes Gartland, secretary to Roy Bergengren, organizer of credit unions and first manager of CUNA Supply. (COURTESY OF CUNA)

Filene, however, played a continuing role through his ideas. The principles he had worked to establish in 1915 became ingrained in the American movement and helped to define the "credit union idea" — essentially the populist credit union — as it was fashioned in the 1920s and 1930s. Moreover, through his writings and speeches he continued to provide a profoundly important perspective on credit unionism.

Filene did not see credit unionism as a minor part of American life. For him it was potentially central to the dominant trends of the times. Specifically, credit unionism was a natural corollary of two of the main economic changes that he believed had transformed the American economy in his lifetime: the changes associated most often with the work of both Frederick Winslow Taylor and Henry Ford.

Taylor was the father of "scientific management", a concept that gained wide popularity in the early years of the twentieth century.[37] Born in 1856, Taylor started work at the Midvale Steel Company in 1878. In 1881 he introduced time study to the plant and began to study seriously — one of the first to do so — the nature of work; shortly thereafter, he began to publicize his findings. In 1893, as his theories became known and his views were sought by a widening range of business and public service leaders, he established himself as a consulting engineer.

Taylor showed how a careful analysis of a worker's work patterns could eliminate waste time and motion, thereby saving money. His ideas were often applied selectively by managers who chose to use only those elements that generated short-term profits, but Taylor was also interested in how routinized work in industrial places could be made more rewarding and interesting for workers. In the early years of the century Taylor, assisted by his disciples Frank Gilbreth and Henry Gantt, steadily expanded his enquiries to consider a wide range of management tools, including cost accounting, planning sessions, enhanced supervision of employees, and incentive systems.

Filene was attracted to this management approach,[38] and that is partly why he and his brother made the Filene department store a model employer for the time. It had a profit-sharing plan, an insurance programme, a retirement benefit and a health programme for its employees; it insisted on Saturday closures so that employees could have more time with their families; and it offered many educational and recreational activities for its employees. Edward Filene was also committed to turning over the store to the employees to run as a worker-owned co-operative. He believed that by pioneering in this kind of employee empowerment, he was implementing an aspect of Taylor's work that was just as important as the simple drives for greater efficiencies and profits.

Filene was equally impressed by the revolution in production associated with Henry Ford. The mass production of automobiles had ushered in a new economic age, "the era of big-machine production". In fact, for Filene the problems of production had been resolved; the problems for the future were those of consumption, in particular the financing of consumption. For those problems, the best hope was the extension of financial ownership and control into the hands of ordinary people. As Filene said in a speech in California in 1936:

> What is needed is that the American masses shall learn the art of constructive self-government in this machine age — in this age in which life is no longer organized on a small community pattern but in which all Americans are more or less dependent upon what all other Americans are doing.[39]

In fact, Filene argued, unless the democratization of capital occurred, the modern industrial societies would devolve into some kind of economic feudalism or anarchy. That was the reason credit unions were so important: they would allow the masses to have a stake in, even significant control over, the distribution of money. Unless working people could increase their purchasing power to make continued expansion possible, unless they directly benefited from economic change, the result would only be either reduced production or, worse, violence and dictatorship. That was why Filene became so committed to credit unionism and why he was able to impart such a powerful vision for the movement to all those who could glimpse the possibilities. It was a vision that would echo down through the years in the work of many credit unionists, especially those interested in the development of the international movement.

For all his apparent idealism, Filene was an intensely practical person. He had little use for charity, but he had a deep

faith in the capacity of people to improve themselves as long as they had good information and the discipline to use it effectively. He also was enamoured with the idea that credit unions could be harnessed to conventional businesses; so was Bergengren, and that is partly why so many of the early credit unions were associated with employee groups.

The early 1920s was a good period in which to encourage credit unions. The consumer revolution, so fundamental to North American society in the twentieth century, was about to undergo one of its great manifestations. The combination of mass production, generally rising wage scales, and improved transportation services created the amorphous but expanding middle class.

Credit unions would play an important role in that revolution, helping people consolidate debts and purchase cars, refrigerators and radios. They would assist families in accumulating the funds to educate their members, young and old. They would encourage people to save for their retirement and medical emergencies. They would become, for many people,

Cigarmakers' Credit Union, Boston, a typical closed-bond credit union in the 1920s. (COURTESY OF CUNA)

an important ally in gaining the benefits promised by the economic blossoming of North America.

Credit unions also provided a valuable alternative to the instalment plans introduced by many retailers and large stores as a way to encourage the purchasing of consumer goods. The new system, widely accepted, soon created extensive burdens for many families, debtloads that threatened to become permanent because of the interest rates charged. Credit unions were one way to escape that burden.

The credit union movement grew steadily during the 1920s. In addition to Bergengren, there were numerous enthusiasts scattered increasingly all across the United States. Every state had its own pioneers, its own cadre of leaders that gave the movement life and vitality. While most of the early promoters were men, a few were women. One of the first was Angela Melville, who worked for the National Extension Bureau from 1923 to 1925; she worked briefly in Jamaica organizing credit union study groups, but most of her time was devoted to trips through the American Midwest. Another was Julia Connor, who started her career in Pennsylvania and subsequently undertook, in 1934, to work for the federal government on behalf of the development of credit unions.

Whenever he could, Bergengren helped directly in the formation of credit unions during the 1920s. His main priority, however, was securing good legislation in as many states as possible. When he started his organizational work in 1921 there were 199 credit unions and only four reasonably acceptable state laws. Securing adequate legislation in the remaining states was always time-consuming, often difficult and sometimes exasperating work. It involved learning about the political situation in each state, selecting political champions to lead the cause, advising local leaders as they prepared legislation, fending off the attacks of people in the lending business, and watching to make sure that legislation was not changed at the last minute.

Some states were notoriously difficult, most often because of the lobbying of other financial institutions. It took eight years of effort, for example, to secure the passage of legislation in Washington State; Bergengren never succeeded in getting legislation in Connecticut; he found Pennsylvania and Ohio "stubborn"; he had to help lead a "thrilling campaign" in

Angela Melville, secretary of the Credit Union National Extension Bureau and enthusiastic promoter of credit unions. (COURTESY OF CUNA)

Michigan; he was frustrated in Pennsylvania when the proposed act was rendered useless by last-minute changes. In the remaining states, the task was easier but still time-consuming.[40] Nevertheless, by 1929, twenty-three states had, in Bergengren's view, acceptable credit union legislation. By 1934 the number had increased to thirty-two, and to a large extent the struggle for appropriate state legislation had been won.

In preparing legislation, training volunteers, and encouraging interested business people, Bergengren criss-crossed the United States several times. He later recalled, probably with little exaggeration, that he had slept in thousands of beds, "most of them on Pullmans".[41] His constant travelling meant that those closest to him, particularly his children, paid a high price for his involvement; his family would not be the last to contribute indirectly to the organization of credit unions.

Bergengren also played an important role in the war on loan-sharking, partly because it cast credit unions in a favourable light and partly because of his passionate hatred of usury. He participated in loan-shark investigations in several states, and he was fond of recalling some of the details, including one case where a railway employee was paying 3,400 percent per annum interest on what was originally a small loan.[42] These investigations helped lead to the enactment of a Uniform Small Loans Law in many states. The law brought licensed lenders under supervision and limited interest rates initially to 42 percent and subsequently to 30 percent; in the process, credit unions received widespread publicity as a way in which people, particularly those with limited incomes, could lend to each other at less than 12 percent per year. The fight against usury would be a primary impetus in the development of credit unions in the United States and elsewhere for many years. It would be a principal reason why various movements would cling to the 12 percent interest ceiling for so long.

Despite the growth and increasing publicity, Bergengren and Filene were dissatisfied because, in their view, not enough credit unions were being formed. They estimated that 75,000 credit unions were necessary in the United States before the full potential of the movement could be realized. By 1930 they were convinced that it was no longer reasonable to expect the leadership of the National Credit Union Extension Bureau to accept so much responsibility for the development of local credit unions; the time had come for state leagues to play a larger role. They further decided that each league should hire a managing director, meeting salary and other costs through dues levied on member credit unions.[43]

The establishment of the managing director position was a major step, in that it ultimately provided a network of experienced and capable, if sometimes rather independent, managers. It also greatly expanded the organizational capacity of the movement, leading to the employment of fieldmen (as they were then called), the encouragement of competition for the creation of new credit unions, the development of a wide range of resource materials, and the emergence of a usually healthy debate over different perceptions of the movement's future.

The credit union movement made rapid strides in the United States during the Great Depression, which started in 1929 and did not end until the outbreak of World War II a decade later. In many ways it fit perfectly into the general New Deal reform ideology that came to dominate American society during the period: it was focused on ordinary people; it encouraged self-help, self-reliance and self-responsibility; it was critical of the excesses of pure capitalism without advocating revolution; and it was a movement that could engage the hearts as well as the self-interest of its adherents.

Credit unions were also financially successful. In 1937 a Princeton University study of the ability of different kinds of thrift plans to survive the adversity of the Great Depression found that 34.5 percent of all bank deposits had been lost, as had 35.9 percent of company investment funds, 74.5 percent of employee stock purchase funds, and 32 percent of investments in building and loan societies. In contrast, only 6.7 percent of investments in credit unions had been lost.[44]

Such favourable reports, coupled with positive stories in popular magazines and newspapers, helped the rapid expansion of the movement. They also stimulated interest in other countries. During the late 1920s, both Filene and Bergengren visited Europe to inform co-operative leaders and organizations about the development of credit unions in the United States. Bergengren corresponded with people in areas influenced by Americans: Puerto Rico, other Caribbean islands and the Philippines. In late 1930, Bergengren visited Welland, near Niagara Falls in Ontario, Canada. There, with the assistance of George Keen, secretary of the Co-operative Union of Canada, he organized a credit union among employees of Plymouth Cordage,[45] a company with a history of support for credit unions in the United States. It was Bergengren's first effort at direct organization of credit unions in other countries.

The successes of the movement in the United States largely depended upon the networks through which the National Extension Bureau worked. The most important of these consisted of sympathetic company owners and managers. The appeal was successfully made to "enlightened" employers who, like Edward Filene, believed it was important for employees to improve their economic position through self-help. They were part of an important sector in North American management thinking that cautiously experimented with "welfare capitalism" as a way to improve efficiency, withstand the criticism of labour organizers, and head off the growing strength of socialism. Credit unions fit — and still fit — this mode of thought perfectly, especially since they incurred few expenses: at most, the provision of some space, and perhaps the help of a company bookkeeper.

Many credit unions in the United States, therefore, were organized on the basis of employment. In many instances they developed in companies that had a tradition of "bucket shops" — a system whereby one or more employees would loan fellow employees money between paydays. Some of these systems had become exploitive, charging high rates of interest — in some instances 100 percent per annum.[46] In such situations, employers were easily convinced of the value of credit unions as a way to avert bad feelings among their employees.

Employee-based credit unions had benefits for both employers and employees. For example, companies rarely had to worry about making employee loans, and they eliminated the need to provide pay advances. They were convenient for making deductions from salaries (for example, for medical insurance), especially if all payrolls were deposited in the credit union — a practice that also helped to stabilize the credit union. They could assist employers in dealing with requests to garnishee an employee's wages, a common problem when workers faced an unexpected financial crisis or were unable to cope with their financial obligations.

From the employees' perspective, a workplace-based credit union meant convenient, consistent access to their pay packets. It gave them the opportunity to earn interest on savings. For most, it made possible loans at less than usurious rates; for a few, it meant increased status, especially for members of the board and, perhaps more importantly, members of the loans committee. Less concretely, the credit union was often very much a social nexus, supporting educational activities, sponsoring parties and dances, operating bowling leagues, and providing scholarships for the children of members.

From the credit union perspective, the employment bond encouraged members to have a personal interest in the credit union because it was made up of workplace friends and associates. Moreover, should a member have difficulty making loan payments, there was relatively easy access to weekly or monthly wages or salaries, assuming the employer would co-operate. Perhaps most importantly, credit unions could provide immediate, convenient and efficient services to their members, particularly if the "host" company provided office space and accountancy backup, as was often the case.

Many of the employee-based credit unions were located in the manufacturing and transportation industries. Two other important groups were public servants (particularly employees of the post office, often among the first in many states to organize credit unions) and teachers. Both groups had the capacity to spread information about credit unions across state lines through professional associations. These two groups had a profound impact in the early years of the American movement, as did similar groups in the formative years of movements in several other countries. The public servants often provided valuable leadership in securing increasingly useful legislation, in developing accounting skills generally, and in providing financial stability through their reliable, if not always high, salaries. Teachers were important for the same reasons, but they also

Great Fleet Credit Union in Miami, 1940-1941, an example of a successful closed-bond credit union of the period. (COURTESY OF CUNA)

provided necessary skills and consistent support for the educational activities that helped volunteers learn their responsibilities; they also enthusiastically supported the educational programmes many credit unions undertook for the public generally and young people specifically.

Teachers, in fact, provided the network through which the first American credit union outside the continental United States was organized. In 1935, a number of school teachers from Hawaii, attending the annual convention of the National Education Association, learned about credit unions. When they returned home they organized the Big Island Credit Union; within the next six years, and with the help of an organizer from the Farm Credit Administration, they helped form a further fifty credit unions. Over the next decade the credit union movement made remarkable progress on the islands, attracting the support of more teachers and a large number of public servants as well as plantation, sugar refinery and cannery workers. They were also particularly popular among some ethnic groups, notably Filipinos.[47]

Trade unions also provided a useful network for the establishment of the movement. In some states, notably Michigan, Pennsylvania and Texas, trade unions encouraged their members to form credit unions and helped employees to convince employers of their benefits; a few trade unions directly organized credit unions among their locals and within labour temples and councils. The credit union idea conformed well with the side of the trade union movement that emphasized improving the general welfare of working people as well as struggling for the more direct benefits of higher wages, shorter hours and pension plans. The trade union connection would never be formalized or widespread, but it was significant in some areas and, perhaps most importantly, it reinforced the movement's commitment to "the little man".

Another important set of networks was within the Christian churches, particularly the Roman Catholic Church, where interest was part of a deepening concern over social and economic issues that went back to the last half of the nineteenth century. As Europe industrialized and Marxism emerged, the Roman Catholic Church (somewhat belatedly, many charged) started to respond. In 1891, Pope Leo XIII published *Rerum Novarum*, an encyclical that denounced the excesses and exploitation of conventional capitalism and called for the empowerment of working people through their own organizations, including co-operatives. In 1931 Pope Pius XI published *Quadragesimo Anno,* a call to social action that had a particularly strong appeal as the Great Depression worsened. Basing their work on these two encyclicals, a growing number of Catholic activists embraced co-operative forms of organizations, including worker, agricultural and banking co-operatives.

In North America, and ultimately in many other parts of the world, the parish credit union became commonplace. In these credit unions, priests often played crucial roles, but so did lay people, most frequently Roman Catholic women. They tended to be smaller organizations, very committed to their religious communities, reliant on volunteers for a longer time than other kinds of credit unions, and involved with social problems of the wider community. Concerned about ethical issues, they helped reinforce the idealism so common in the American movement during its formative years. They were also particularly supportive of work done to expand credit unions to Roman Catholics in other countries, particularly Latin America and parts of Asia.

A fourth network was provided by bonds of ethnicity. Jewish and Irish immigrants were important in the American movement's earliest years. Almost immediately, however, they were joined by Poles, Germans, Ukrainians and Scandinavians. In many instances, these immigrant groups were reviving experiences with co-operative banking in their native lands: they saw credit unions as continuations of what they had known, as useful examples of the mutual aid activities common in the immigration process, and as integral parts of the communities they were building in their new homeland.

A fifth network (of some importance in states like Wisconsin, California and Minnesota) was the established co-operative movement. There was some interest in credit unions within the agricultural co-operative movement, but little progress was made, partly because of the unfortunate experience in North Carolina (described earlier), but mostly because of the challenge of finding, in rural areas, a common bond as cohesive as that provided by workplace, union, ethnic and religious associations in urban areas. The more important ties were with consumer co-operatives, most frequently found among people of Scandinavian background. The Co-operative League of the United States of America (CLUSA), the national organization for consumer and other kinds of co-operatives, was strongly supportive of credit unions in the late 1920s and throughout the 1930s; it repeatedly advocated their formation in many of its educational activities.

Unfortunately, the relationship with consumer co-operatives was difficult because of partisan politics. Some of the most fervent advocates of consumer co-operatives were also supporters of the Communist Party. Their attempts to link CLUSA to that party in 1927 and 1928 precipitated a crisis in co-operative circles and alarmed the leadership of the credit union movement, particularly Edward Filene and other business leaders sympathetic to credit unions. That crisis would be long remembered, and for some years it would help make close collaboration between the consumer and credit union movements difficult, if not impossible.

The problem was exacerbated by Upton Sinclair and his co-operative activities in California during the 1930s. That

A Dane County, Wisconsin, farmer signs a loan application at his co-op credit union in 1941. (Courtesy of CUNA)

dramatic political development produced deep tensions in California society that ultimately limited the career of Jerry Voorhis, one of the most thoughtful American co-operative leaders, while it coincidentally helped make possible the career of Richard Nixon. In 1946, in one of the bitterest and dirtiest campaigns in American congressional history, Nixon unseated Voorhis, thereby making his rise to the presidency possible, and Voorhis's long — and distinguished — co-operative career necessary.

The difficult relationship with co-operatives in the United States, while not eliminating the occasional joint initiative, typified the American credit union movement until the 1980s. In fact, it influenced how many American credit unionists viewed the emergence of credit unions in other countries for many years. In parts of Canada, much of Africa and Asia and a few countries in Latin America, the ties with other co-operatives were common and natural, a tendency that considerably concerned Americans who feared left-wing political movements.

The most subtle, but in some ways most important, set of networks was within the adult education movement. In a sense, adult education had been associated with the co-operative movement from the beginning. While he placed deepest emphasis on the education of young people, Robert Owen always advocated the importance of educating and training older people as well. The Rochdale Pioneers, from 1954 forward, regularly set aside 2.5 percent of their surpluses for educational purposes, mostly aimed at adult learning. The Workers Educational Association in the United Kingdom had largely grown up within co-operative circles. In Denmark, and subsequently in other Scandinavian countries as well as Ireland and Canada, the Folk School introduced the concept of life-long learning, pioneered in methods of adult education, and sometimes directly examined co-operative issues.

Within North America, the ties between rural organizations, many of them co-operatives or supportive of co-operatives, and the Chautauqua movement at the turn of the century and in the early twentieth century, were strong. The land grant universities in the United States, and some Canadian universities concerned with agriculture, all developed extension departments in the early years of the century;

many of them offered courses and learning sessions devoted to the study of co-operatives. Nearly all of the co-operative organizations, especially the agricultural marketing and consumer sectors, developed membership and board training programmes as they emerged; some of them developed extensive public information programmes, including the sponsorship of journals, the publication of pamphlets, and the use of radio.

The goals of adult education, as it developed in the 1920s and 1930s, were diverse: for some observers it was primarily remedial — to protect society from the follies of ignorance. For others, it was simply a means of self-improvement, a way to secure necessary training. For still others, it was a means whereby people could realize their full intellectual, artistic and cultural potential. At different times, credit union leaders in both the United States and Canada emphasized all of these priorities as they sought to prepare credit union leaders as well as members for their responsibilities.

Roy Bergengren was drawn to all three of these emphases, although he was most consistently concerned with the practical training of credit unionists so that they could operate their credit unions effectively. Under his leadership the Credit Union National Extension Bureau used its scarce resources to develop training materials, particularly for directors and subsequently for secretary-treasurers. His efforts were encouraged by Filene, who deeply believed that good decisions — if not proper living — were possible only when one "had the facts". It was a theme Filene emphasized repeatedly in many of his speeches and writings, and was the reason he devoted so much of his fortune to the Twentieth Century Fund.

Bergengren found the most complete inspiration for the role of adult education in co-operative enterprise across the Canadian border in the small Nova Scotia community of Antigonish. Eastern Nova Scotia had suffered economically during the 1920s because of underproduction in its coal mines and the stagnation of its fishing and farming industries. A group of priests and lay people within the Roman Catholic Church, angry about the resulting poverty and concerned by the growth of radical politics, established an Extension Department in the town's university, St. Francis Xavier. A trio of leaders emerged, starting with two priests, Jimmy

Tompkins and Moses Coady, in the late 1920s, and A.B. Macdonald, a powerful lay organizer, in the early 1930s. With the assistance of a group of women and men, these three forged an effective and powerful movement aimed at economic and social betterment through adult education and co-operative organization.[48]

The Antigonish method was essentially a very simple one. An organizer — a field person or a professor associated with the Extension Department — would come to a community

Moses Coady, the best-known leader of the Antigonish movement, at St. Francis Xavier University from 1929 to 1959. (COURTESY OF CUNA)

and, through the church or some other networking agency, set up a meeting of local citizens. The organizer would then lead a discussion on the prevailing economic and social situation in the community, demonstrate that most problems could be analyzed intellectually, and encourage the group to consider the possibilities offered by co-operative action. If all went well, the meeting would then lead to the formation of study clubs to consider the problems more fully and explore the nature of co-operative solutions. In many instances, the clubs met weekly, usually in someone's home, for a year or more before establishing a co-operative.[49]

Bergengren first visited Antigonish in 1931 at the invitation of Jimmy Tompkins, who had been informed about the Extension Bureau by George Keen. Bergengren participated in a conference to consider problems confronting rural Nova Scotia;[50] he made a deep impression, partly because of his oratorical gifts, but mostly because of the sincerity of his message. Bergengren demonstrated that the credit union was the ideal focus for the adult education approach being developed in Antigonish. His ethical preoccupation, his general optimism about the possibilities of human personality, and his infectious enthusiasm were all welcomed by the people of Antigonish.

When Bergengren returned to the United States he prepared a draft of a credit union act for Nova Scotia; the legislation was enacted by Nova Scotia during the winter of 1931. Bergengren returned to Nova Scotia in December 1932, to resume his career as an international organizer of credit unions. The weather is not always hospitable in Nova Scotia in that month, and Bergengren, Coady and Macdonald were unable to reach Canso, the then-isolated community where Tompkins was the priest. Instead, they went to Broad Cove, where they organized a credit union at a hastily called meeting; the following night they organized another at Reserve Mines. Because of the impact of the study clubs and the local leadership of Jimmy Tompkins, almost any community in the area could have been chosen.

It is difficult to evaluate how deeply adult education techniques became intertwined with the credit union movement. Certainly, the study club idea was commonplace in the United States in the early 1930s, partly because of Antigonish, partly because other groups were pioneering the same approach.

Certainly, the Antigonish approach was instrumental in creating credit unions elsewhere in English-speaking Canada, and, equally certainly, this approach was exported to many countries around the world, from the late 1940s onward, through the international activities of St. Francis Xavier University. It would be extremely important in assisting in the development of credit unions around the world. For some ardent advocates in North America and elsewhere, credit unions were, in their essence, a form of education as much as a means of economic betterment.

By using these networks and the resources generously provided by Filene, and by creating the position of managing director within the state leagues, the credit union movement made remarkable progress: by the mid-1930s there were over 3,000 credit unions in the United States. The movement then began to consider how it should strengthen its national organizational efforts to take advantage of economies of scale. That stage was not easily achieved in the United States, nor in any of the countries in which the movement would subsequently emerge.

Creating effective regional or national organizations and building profitable service companies is never simple in any credit union or co-operatively structured system. By their very nature, credit unions are inevitably drawn to their members and communities; they do not easily surrender power or find an appropriate, accountable managerial structure for their joint initiatives. That was no less true in the United States than it would be elsewhere; it took two generations of often acrimonious debate to achieve the kind of stability for which the American credit union system would ultimately become known throughout the international movement.

The first step in the development of a national movement in the United States was the passage of the first piece of federal credit union legislation. That occurred in 1932, during the last days of the Hoover administration, when an act was passed to allow for the incorporation of credit unions in the District of Columbia. This event was important for the movement because it permitted public servants working in the capital to organize their own credit unions. Senator Morris Sheppard of Texas played a major role in the passage of the act, and he would continue to support the expansion of the movement within the American Congress until his death in 1941. The 1932 act was not initially well understood, even by the legislators who voted for it. As one radio commentator reported, a bill to create banks for working people had been passed, "but nobody seems to know anything about it".[51]

The move to create a national presence for the American movement was further encouraged by the New Deal of the Roosevelt administration. Franklin Roosevelt had been supportive of credit unions when he was governor of New York State, and some of the most prominent individuals in his Washington administration were sympathetic to them. Thus, while never a high priority for the federal government, credit unions were accorded a significant role in how the "New Dealers" sought to expand the credit-generating capacity of working people. In 1934, the government passed legislation to allow for the formation of federal credit unions and for the creation of savings and loans associations, a kind of community bank.

The possibility of federal credit unions was an important innovation, for several reasons. First, it meant that it was no longer necessary to secure legislation in all states, particularly those whose legislators were unsympathetic or hostile. Second, it made possible the implementation of the same kind of rules for credit unions serving similar types of people in more than one state. Third, it gave more power to the elected leadership (as opposed to the membership) than had been the case in state statutes: for example, it made it possible for the board of directors to appoint the supervisory (later called audit) committee rather than have it elected by the members.

The creation of savings and loans associations was also important for defining the nature of credit unions in the United States. They were given primary responsibility for mobilizing funds on a local level for the purchase of housing through mortgage loans; that, plus a strong community bank tradition in the United States, meant credit unions were limited generally to encouraging saving and to giving personal loans for (initially) specific purposes. That division of roles helped make it difficult for several years for American credit unionists to move into mortgage lending, a comparatively complex business to learn, whereas credit unions in some other countries embraced that business early in their history.

The most important national initiative, however, took place on August 11, 1934, when the Credit Union National Association (CUNA) was formed at Estes Park, Colorado, to replace the Filene-financed Credit Union National Extension Bureau. The association was the result of the belief of Bergengren and others, not least Filene himself, that it was necessary for the fledgling credit union movement to manage its own affairs; it was time to be less reliant upon the generosity of the Boston millionaire.

One of the first subjects explored by CUNA was insurance. During the Great Depression the problems confronting low-income families became even worse if their chief breadwinner died. Even a loan of $50 or $75 seemed overwhelming when a widow was not employed. Loan insurance was offered by some insurance companies, but the premiums were high, and it was difficult to find companies that served all parts of the country. Thus, during the early days of CUNA the leadership investigated the possibility of forming a company to insure loans taken out by members in local credit unions. The event that triggered this action occurred in 1935 when a power linesman was killed shortly after taking out a loan for $800. His co-

Edward Filene, Roy Bergengren and Claude Orchard, arguably the three most important leaders in the American credit union movement in the 1930s. (COURTESY OF THE BRIDGE)

workers paid off the loan, but the credit union and the national organization were concerned about this burden falling on his friends; it was time to find a better form of insurance.

In May 1935, CUNA's executive committee formed CUNA Mutual Insurance Society, incorporated under Wisconsin law but able to serve credit unions all over the United States. CUNA Mutual was initially financed by a $25,000 loan from Edward Filene; he loaned a further $10,000 as the first claims came in. From that point onward, the company never looked back — it became an instant financial success. As the 1930s went by, CUNA Mutual devised a series of disability plans that ultimately helped thousands of credit union members. In 1937 the company implemented a life insurance programme available to credit union members. In 1938 it introduced low-cost life insurance which covered credit union members to the amount they had invested in their share accounts, although the shares that were accumulated between ages fifty-five and seventy carried decreasing amounts of insurance.[52] All of these insurance programmes were offered at rates significantly lower than those available elsewhere during the 1930s and subsequently.

The importance of these insurance programmes can hardly be overemphasized. It was very difficult for low-income people to secure and maintain insurance in those days, even when they had regular work. The adversities of the 1930s, moreover, accentuated the need for insurance and encouraged many families to purchase insurance whenever they could. CUNA Mutual benefited from this situation and grew to more than $130,000,000 in insurance in force within ten years; in the same period it distributed over $4,000,000 in benefits.[53] It was one of the most remarkable success stories in the early years of American credit unionism.

At the same time as CUNA Mutual was being developed, the national leadership sought ways to acquire bookkeeping and promotional supplies for credit unions through joint purchasing. In 1934 a department was opened within CUNA to pursue this objective. The next year, CUNA, along with CUNA Mutual and the state leagues, organized a new co-operative, CUNA Supply, to carry out these tasks. Initially managed by Agnes Gartland, the new co-operative was technically independent of CUNA, but its board consisted of directors and management personnel drawn from CUNA, thereby assuring unity of purpose for at least the early years.

Amid the planning for an expanded national structure, the leaders of the American movement decided it was time to move from Boston to a city more centrally located within the United States. Madison, Wisconsin, was selected. As Filene said, Madison had "an atmosphere of democracy and research",[54] because it had been profoundly influenced by Scandinavian democratic traditions; in addition it was reasonably close to Canada[55] and had an excellent university, the University of Wisconsin. Madison also had convenient railway connections to many parts of the United States, and rail was then the customary way to travel, an advantage that would fade somewhat when air travel became more common. Moreover, Madison was close to many of the states where the movement was expanding, and it was in a state with a strong league as well as a history of supporting co-operative organizations. Finally, land prices and taxes were low. The move took place in late 1935, and CUNA took over an old mansion that was subsequently named Raiffeisen House.

The emergence of the national organizations and the development of a new national focus marked a significant transition in the American movement, a transition accompanied by a change in the faces of the American leadership. One face — Edward A. Filene — departed. Perhaps the proudest months of his life occurred in 1932 when he made a tour of credit unions in the United States. Grateful credit unionists turned out by the thousands to hear him speak; brass bands played; he was showered with gifts. On several occasions, as his biographer wrote, Filene "stood before the roaring crowds with tears running down his cheeks". Shortly thereafter, as the new national organizations took shape, his direct involvement declined. Filene died in 1937.

New faces appeared, including Tom Doig, Claude Orchard and Orrin Shipe, all of whom would profoundly influence credit unions for the succeeding two decades. Doig started to organize credit unions in the Minneapolis post office in 1923. He joined the Extension Bureau in 1930, becoming assistant managing director of CUNA in 1935. Doig at first worked very effectively with Bergengren but gradually became critical of his boss's administrative weaknesses.

Edward Filene (front, left) at Los Angeles Breakfast Club. Beside him is Lillian Schoedler, his long-time administrative assistant. Beside her is Aaron Sapiro, the great "evangelist" of the pooling movement and co-operative enterprise. (COURTESY OF CUNA)

Orchard came from the personnel department of the Armour Corporation in Omaha, Nebraska. He had helped organize credit unions in several Armour plants, making it one of the largest groups of employee-based credit unions in the American movement. Orchard moved to Washington in 1934 to become the administrator of federal credit unions, a position he would hold until his death in 1953. He worked closely with CUNA, not always easily because of changing attitudes on the part of federal regulators, and helped to promote the formation of federal credit unions through organizers employed by his department. In fact, as the years went by, most of the credit unions formed in the United States were under federal charter.

Shipe helped organize a credit union in a Buffalo insurance company in 1934, when he was twenty-one years old. He joined CUNA in 1939, serving as a field secretary in Kansas City before moving to Madison as educational director and editor of *The Bridge*. A restless and creative leader, he helped develop the bonding system for credit unions affiliated with

CUNA. Shipe would become one of the earliest proponents of an international programme.

In addition to these particularly prominent figures, there was a host of new leaders at the state and local levels. These people were inevitably reflective of their times; most particularly, they were shaped by the experiences of the Great Depression, an influence that would significantly affect the American movement for at least twenty-five years. It meant that the movement would defiantly reject other kinds of financial institutions; that it would proceed carefully with new initiatives; that it would be steeped in traditions of volunteer control; and that it would be emotionally committed to "the little man". It was a heritage of remarkable cogency — the

Thomas. W. Doig, organizer of 1,000 credit unions, managing director of CUNA, CUNA Supply and CUNA Mutual from 1935 to 1955. (COURTESY OF CUNA)

epitome of the populist credit union — but equally, it had some limiting perspectives.

The Great Depression also helped shape credit unions in other lands. Within Quebec, the onset of the Depression shook the provincial movement, because it had invested heavily in bonds whose value plummeted. The movement was forced to organize itself in a very disciplined fashion within four regional unions and a strong provincial federation. It adopted a rigorous auditing system, a considerable degree of centralization, and a unified set of promotional activities. The result was the emergence of a very stable system that grew from 180 *caisses* and $7,500,000 in assets in 1932, to 562 *caisses* and $25,000,000 in assets by 1940.[56]

Orrin Shipe, organizer of 200 credit unions, holder of many different positions in CUNA, first managing director of the World Council of Credit Unions. (COURTESY OF CUNA)

Within English Canada, the most remarkable development was the way in which the credit union movement expanded, generally within a more community-based and co-operative framework. It spread westward from Atlantic Canada and its base in the Antigonish movement; it also spread northward, particularly into the industrial heartland of Ontario, from the United States. The movement was embraced by a wide range of enthusiasts — from co-operative organizations, adult education circles and church groups, to political parties, concerned communities and ethnic associations. By the time the decade came to an end, credit unions had spread all the way to British Columbia and were poised for a remarkable period of expansion in the 1940s.

Credit unions also began to appear outside of North America, although on a much more limited basis. In the Philippines, co-operatives patterned after American models were begun as early as 1909. In 1915, the government of the Philippines passed a Rural Credit Co-operative Law, which was followed by further legislation in the 1920s. In the years after that, a widespread but poorly regulated agricultural credit movement developed. The first organized credit union, the Vigan Community Credit Union, was started in 1938 by Reverend Allen Huber, a Protestant minister[57] and the director of rural development of the Philippine Federation of Evangelical Churches. He became a close friend of Roy Bergengren, from whom he learned much about how to start credit unions. By the time the United States declared war in 1941, Huber had helped organize thirty credit unions.[58]

Elsewhere in Asia, the first co-operative banks in Thailand were created in 1916 when the government sponsored village co-operatives fashioned on the Raiffeisen model. They were organized to help farm families escape from indebtedness and the control of local moneylenders.[59] In the 1920s Mohammed Hatta, one of Indonesia's most prominent independence leaders, introduced several forms of co-operatives, including co-operative credit societies. Also in the 1920s, the co-operative banking movement began in Japan, largely among trade unionists and Christians much influenced by the leadership of Toyohiko Kagawa, the most famous Japanese co-operative leader of the period. Similarly, in mainland China, Catholic and Protestant missionaries helped form numerous co-operatives, some of which even survived the Revolution of 1949. While most of the Chinese co-operatives were worker co-operatives, a few were co-operative banks fashioned on the Raiffeisen model.

Across the world, in Jamaica, the 1930s were as dirty, if not as dry, as in the North American heartland. Jamaica also experienced severe riots and civil disobedience between 1937 and 1939, unrest that was duplicated in many other islands in the Caribbean. The result was the rapid formation of trade unions, the growth of an independence movement, and considerable consternation within the ruling British elite on many islands. In places like Kingston, the Roman Catholic Church began to consider its obligations regarding social action; this led to the formation of the first organized study clubs, loosely patterned on the Antigonish model. Memories of these clubs would linger for a generation and encourage many in the 1940s to turn to credit unions as a way to help forge better links among all classes and races of people.

Amid this growing international interest, CUNA took its first steps toward becoming an international organization. At a meeting of the national directors in Madison in May 1940, CUNA agreed to include credit union leagues from anywhere in the Western Hemisphere. Within a few years the credit union leagues in the ten Canadian provinces had joined CUNA, prompting several American leaders and many rank-and-file credit unionists to become enthusiastic about the potential for credit union development around the world. The American movement was beginning to see the possibilities of an international and not just a national focus.

As the American movement started to look outward, it generally possessed a remarkably clear view of the idea of credit unions. While it is difficult to summarize the experience of the nearly 11,000 credit unions in existence in the United States in 1941 (and the nearly 1,500 in Canada), it can be argued that the dominant credit union form was the populist mode, and that its main theme was the emancipation of ordinary people. This does not mean there were not other important defining themes: for example, the need to develop managerial capabilities and strong institutional frameworks at the local, regional and national levels. It does mean that the American movement had achieved a broad consensus on where

credit unions fit into the economy, whom they served, how they were organized, and how they should be operated. It was an approach worked out with much effort and some pain in the period between 1909 and 1941, an approach that would dominate the North American movement for at least a generation thereafter and be replicated, in some places with even greater passion, in many countries around the world.

The American model stressed the idea that credit unions were not charitable institutions. They were institutions that offered people who were generally ignored or abused by the existing banking industries the opportunity to create their own financial system. They were self-help organizations that operated in the marketplace under appropriate legislation. The American approach placed great emphasis on legislative background: it preferred distinctive, separate legislation rather than regulations absorbed within either a financial act or an omnibus co-operative act, and it supported an effective inspection system — by both governments and credit union officials. It struggled, therefore, to create legislation that assured the uniqueness of credit union structures, that encouraged training programmes for directors and secretary-treasurers, and that favoured lending for "productive and providential" purposes.

The most powerful of many symbols used to represent the people whom those credit unions served in this period was "the little man under the umbrella", a symbol widely used by the early 1940s. It featured a happy man with a beaming smile walking confidently under a credit union umbrella that protected him from a downpour of "hard times, sickness, and financial distress". It was a perfect rendering of the view, honed in the Great Depression, of the capacity of credit unions to help those whom Charlie Chaplin successfully captured in his films about "the little tramp"; it reflected the New Deal's apparent preoccupation with the "ordinary American"; and it was the central symbol of the populist credit union in both the United States and other countries.

A necessary corollary of this emphasis on "the little man" was a commitment of service to members. Early in the 1930s Elmer Bloom, a credit union officer in Missouri, allegedly coined a slogan for credit unions: "Not for profit, not for charity, but for service".[60] It was a slogan that would be widely used for decades, and it touched a particular chord among many credit union supporters. For directors it suggested similarities to a service club in which individuals and groups voluntarily donated many hours of time to the service of the members. It also meant that credit unions were constantly measured on how well they were meeting member needs, and it suggested that ultimately the most important reward might not be a financial return on deposits.

Put another way, the credit union, in its formative years, had a vision of emancipating ordinary people from the burdens of poverty. It also had a commitment to emancipating people through education — narrowly in the sense of helping them understand and operate a financial institution, more broadly by informing them about the operation of the economy, if not society. That emphasis came partly from the subtle association

"The Little Man Under the Umbrella", the credit union symbol for many years in many countries of the world. (COURTESY OF CUNA)

with the adult education movement, but it was implicit in the co-operative heritage from which credit unions had sprung.

The American movement also possessed a deep commitment to the inherent values of the closed-bond system, particularly the bonds created by workplace relationships. The remarkably successful application of that approach in the United States justified the commitment, because it meant that members who knew each other were best situated to make good lending decisions and to ensure faithful repayment. They could also effectively encourage their fellow members to follow the practice of thrift and borrowing for providential purposes.

The other elements of the structure of the American credit union, shaped through many adaptations of numerous state acts, were clear and consistent. The members were in charge through annual meetings and, in the early days, even monthly membership meetings. The democratic process was further ensured through the annual election and accountability practices governing executive, credit and supervisory committees. In many credit unions, too, there were educational committees that undertook an extensive range of activities among members and the general public. All told, therefore, there could be as many as thirty people playing meaningful roles in the functioning of any given credit union. It was inevitable that the business of the credit union would be widely known among a significant group within the membership.

The American movement also devised a convenient and easily understood management system. It formulated a simple profit-sharing system that allocated 20 percent of any surplus to a reserve fund and then returned the remainder to members. It charged a flat rate of 1 percent per month on the diminishing balance of any loan, a convenient and competitive way to calculate loan charges and balances. Moreover, the insistence on loans for only providential or productive purposes, such as medical or educational expenses, taxes or home repairs, automobiles or farm equipment, made good sense and encouraged members to remain loyal to an institution that helped them meet their vital needs.

This system, of course, relied greatly upon volunteer leaders, and they would dominate the American movement until well into the 1950s, as they would the Canadian movement. Secretary-treasurers, as the managers were called, were, for the most part, really paid volunteers who were recognized in a minimal way through modest honoraria for their exceptional efforts; in most credit unions they served on a part-time basis unless the membership was over 100. And even when the secretary-treasurers became full-time employees, they were closely controlled by the elected leadership, at least until the emergence of the second stage of credit unionism in the 1940s, when managerial influence started to become ascendant; by the 1960s it would be dominant.

The basic structure of the state and national credit union system was in place by 1941. Local credit unions were associated in chapters, really mutual-help associations of credit unions grouped by geography or category (religious, company or ethnic). In the formative period, the chapters were particularly important vehicles for the education of directors, the training of secretary-treasurers, and the promotion of new credit unions. It was through the chapter that credit union supporters were turned into convinced advocates, even credit union missionaries.

The chapters were supported by state and provincial leagues which increasingly became, as the 1930s ended, the main vehicle for the expansion of the movement. Leagues had a primary educational function, particularly for the education of directors. They were also the lobbying organization for relations with governments and publicizing the movement's activities. Their conferences and conventions were highlights in the annual cycle of credit union activities, and their leaders participated in the deliberations of CUNA's annual meetings. It was a logical and dynamic system which, when operated effectively, was vitally important for a large number of devoted credit union enthusiasts.

The subsidiary organizations, notably CUNA Mutual, were also an integral part of the American system, even by the early 1940s. The loan and life insurance services were stable economic initiatives that served the movement well. They were important structural additions that did much to define the national interests of the movement, and they clearly demonstrated that the American movement was growing into the second stage of credit union development, the stage typified by a strong and well-supported national point of view.

Thus, when Bergengren and his associates began to consider expanding the credit union movement globally in 1941, they did so with confidence, buoyed by a remarkable record of success, particularly in the United States. While influenced by broad co-operative perspectives, they were imbued with a deep commitment to the American idea of credit unionism.

In the context of World War II, they also unconsciously adopted a kind of missionary perspective that could assume a sense of superiority not unlike that found in the Christian missionary experience of preceding centuries. It would not be an easy attitude to transcend, even by more secular proponents of credit unionism generations later. It was also an attitude of resolute conviction of the rightness, the appropriateness, of the credit union cause. Roy Bergengren and Tom Doig captured elements of that vision in a book they wrote shortly after the movement began its growth outside of the continental United States and in the midst of World War II:

> We, of the credit unions, have been privileged to see a great light. We have discovered that our salvation comes from within; that we hold the solutions to baffling problems which have caused great inequalities in our economic life. We are, without knowing it, in the van of a new and better day which will be possible of attainment when the threat to democracy has been completely eradicated from the face of the earth.[61]

The story of Credit Unions

F. W. Raiffeisen organized the first credit unions in Germany in 1848 to help poverty-stricken peasants. His "people's banks" spread all over rural Europe.

At about the same time, Herman Schulze-Delitsch began organizing another type of credit union to serve small business men and craftsmen in German cities.

Alphonse Desjardins, Canadian newspaperman, brought the credit union idea to Quebec in 1900. A credit union, he said, is an association of men, not of dollars.

Edward A. Filene, Boston merchant, believed so much in credit unions that he underwrote the Credit Union National Extension Bureau, now the National Association.

Roy F. Bergengren, manager of the Bureau, secured the passage of many state credit union laws and a national law. He organized credit unions in a number of states.

As credit unions spread over the country, it was discovered that the average man is honest! Consumer loans began to be considered "safe" and interest rates were pushed down.

The big difference between credit unions in the United States and in Europe is that here most have been organized for groups of industrial employees.

The first credit union in the U.S. was organized in 1909; now there are 10,000 in the country, with 4,000,000 members. Assets now amount to $400,000,000. Truly "people's banks"!

Today the credit union, with its philosophy of service to members and self-help, with membership open to all, stands as a great symbol of the democracy we're fighting for.

How credit union history looked to the American movement in the midst of World War II. (COURTESY OF *THE BRIDGE*)

CHAPTER THREE

THE AMERICAN MODEL
1941-1954

We are the only organization in the world which has the know-how and the resources to help people build for themselves a better economic life, which becomes possible when usury is abolished and savings are accumulated. To this opportunity attaches an inevitable responsibility.

Roy F. Bergengren

The credit union movement has reached maturity and has a big job to do in a troubled world. It should co-operate with every force now fighting to restrain communism to prove the superior worth of democracy.

Roy F. Bergengren

UNDERSTANDABLY, BUT NOT TOO WISELY, THE United States and Canada chose mostly to ignore the rest of the world for the twenty years after World War I. During the 1920s and 1930s the two countries drifted into different kinds of isolationism, for the most part disregarding the ominous rise of totalitarianism in Europe and Asia. Isolated by the Pacific and Atlantic oceans, they generally avoided the thought of a coming war, devoting themselves as much as possible to the pleasures of consumerism in the 1920s and then contending with the adversities of the Great Depression in the 1930s.

The awakening came a little earlier in Canada, which declared war on Germany and Italy soon after the summer of 1939. For most Americans the war initially meant little more than the welcome return of a vibrant economy; reality set in on December 7, 1941, when the Japanese attacked Pearl Harbor. For nearly four years, both countries were swept up in terrible conflict. Moreover, in the years that followed, neither country was able to return to isolationism, or to escape for long the often brutal realities the century had produced: the horrors of total war, genocide, and atomic warfare, the impacts of a series of communications revolutions, the dangers of uncontrolled population growth, and the threat of environmental suicide. They would help shape the broad perspectives within which credit unions would be understood.

World War II dramatically changed American and Canadian societies in many ways: it engaged nearly all the resources of both countries; it enlisted most of the youth of one generation; it altered workplace relationships; and it completely dominated the economy until 1945. By its end, the war left the two North American countries in an enviable position of global dominance.

The credit union movements in the two countries were profoundly affected by all these changes. The most immediate impact was the way in which the concentration of financial resources behind the war effort restricted the growth of credit unions. In the United States, one of the first actions of the federal government when war broke out was to regulate the financial system so that the savings of individuals and families were utilized for the waging of war. Intensive campaigns for the sale of war bonds, strict controls on the production of many consumer goods, restrictions on the construction of homes, and limitations on the expansion of businesses meant that, even though more people found work, they had only limited ways in which they could spend their money. This meant that credit unions, like other financial institutions, had to change their strategies, especially since the movement resoundingly supported the war effort.

It was not easy to reverse direction and assume this different approach. During the last years of the 1930s and through to 1941, American credit unions had tended to move away from an emphasis on thrift and to encourage members to borrow, to make up for the decade of denial associated with the Great Depression. The national credit union organizations had also developed their institutions on the assumption of growth, in the belief that more resources would become available as more credit unions were established and more people joined the movement.

Suddenly, because of the war effort and government restrictions, credit unions had to once again preach the virtues of saving and thrift to their members, as they had done in the 1920s. They had to adjust to slowed growth, even decline. Those changes had considerable impact on the operations of many local credit unions and, particularly, on the economic health of their national organizations. The income of CUNA Mutual and CUNA Supply, for example, declined significantly as total assets and the numbers of credit unions dropped; the result was four difficult financial years for the management and boards of the two organizations.

For some American credit unionists, the downturn in credit union development, whether measured in numbers of credit unions or numbers of members, was alarming. Between 1941 and 1945, the number of credit unions in the United States dropped from 9,891 to 8,680; the number of members decreased from 3,316,574 to 2,842,989.[62] In part, this decline was the result of the enlistment in the armed forces of many of the more youthful and effective leaders from both the federal and the state levels: it seemed inevitable that the best of the organizers — perhaps because they were instinctive volunteers

— were among the first to enlist. In part, the slowed growth was the result of the fact that Bergengren, now over sixty years old, no longer had the energy or, given the national scope of his work, the time to concentrate sufficiently on specific areas to foster the organization of new credit unions.

As the negative trend developed, segments of the boards of CUNA and CUNA Mutual became increasingly vocal in their criticism of Roy Bergengren's management record. Some of them, in fact, had been critical since the late 1930s. The criticisms had some validity, because Bergengren, while a magnificent organizer when he had the time, and a successful lobbyist whenever it was necessary, was not a particularly gifted administrator. They also found a receptive audience in some circles of the movement.

Tom Doig, the assistant manager, was an ambitious and capable man whose work brought him in contact with the new leadership within the state leagues, and over the years a growing number of state leaders, who had come to believe he should be the managing director, lobbied on his behalf. In some ways, Doig's rise marked the beginning, on a national level, of the emergence of the managerial credit union. The resultant tensions forced Bergengren to resign in 1945 following a long and bitter battle that deeply divided the movement. He was replaced by Doig, who would serve as managing director of the Credit Union National Association for ten dynamic and often difficult years. One of the most ardent advocates of the rapid expansion of credit unions, he achieved the remarkable record of leading in the formation of over 1,000 credit unions throughout the United States.[63]

As for Bergengren, he soon took up the post of managing director of the Vermont League, a position he held until his death a decade later. It was, in effect, a demotion and, rather sadly, his last active years, while productive, were somewhat embittered. Like many other charismatic leaders in the early history of credit union movements, Bergengren found himself pushed aside as the movement he had largely started gained stability under the leadership of others: people who have the talents to build movements do not necessarily possess the right skills to lead once the movement is well established. Or, perhaps just as often, they achieve one of the best tests of good management by creating their own successors — but in this case, just a little sooner than he had hoped. Credit union organizations in which populist cultures are transformed into managerial cultures typically endure considerable pain.

In contrast to the slowdown in the United States, the Canadian movement sprang to life during the war, especially in the latter years. In Quebec and in French-speaking areas of the other provinces, the *caisse populaire* movement gathered momentum as the economy flourished. The movement in Quebec was noteworthy for its continuing capacity to create an integrated provincial structure based on regional federations and a strong provincial central organization. In 1944 the Desjardins movement established its own general insurance company, La société d'assurances des caisses populaires, followed by a life insurance company, L'assurance-vie Desjardins, in 1948.

The Desjardins movement was unlike the movements in the United States and English Canada in that its local organizations, the *caisses*, tended to remain small and uniform. Many were originally organized within parish networks and continued to be based on those networks for many years. The role of the Roman Catholic Church started to decline during the 1950s, however, to be replaced by an increasingly pervasive nationalism; it was an emotional commitment that would grow as the years passed.

In short, the Quebec movement, even by 1940, had developed a particularly well-integrated approach. While aware of the co-operative heritage, it had fashioned a strong ideology based largely upon the needs and aspirations of the province's Francophone majority. That ideology involved a sense of history, of exploitation, of cohesion; it was based on strong community associations, for the most part originally through parish bonds. The *caisses*, somewhat controversially on the local level, had developed managerial capacities early in their history, and that capacity increased dramatically as the organization grew. The movement developed strong ties to the provincial government, and by the late 1930s, its leaders had important connections with the province's political elite. In general terms, the movement had established the strongest, most integrated provincial network in Canada.

The most remarkable expansion, however, took place in the West, especially in the Prairie region, where an extensive co-operative movement fostered the rapid growth of credit unionism. The movement prospered particularly in the countryside, most obviously in Saskatchewan and Alberta, where it successfully met the needs of farm families, especially those living on smaller farms. The movement in the two provinces also built upon the pent-up anger and regional dissatisfaction that resulted from the Great Depression. The two provinces had suffered greatly during the "Dirty Thirties", and not even the preoccupations of the war would erase the anger that the period had created; that hostility would contribute significantly to the growth of credit unions during the 1940s and 1950s.

Somewhat slower but still significant growth took place in Ontario and British Columbia, although the expansion in those provinces, particularly Ontario, occurred largely in urban centres. The growth of the urban (for the most part) employee-based credit unions was unique in the Canadian experience; in the other provinces, including Atlantic Canada, credit unions were more commonly based on geographic associations or community ties. This preference for community credit unions emerged in most of Canada for three main reasons. First, there were no community-based banks, as there were in the United States. Second, the larger chartered banks did not serve the needs of low-income people, meaning that there were important needs for community credit unions to meet. Third, the English-Canadian movement outside of industrial Ontario grew up within the traditions of the larger co-operative movement, especially the co-operative stores, but to some extent the agricultural marketing co-operatives as well.

These co-operative traditions were inclusive, both in the variety of people they involved and in the range of activities they undertook. They embraced all kinds of co-operative organizations, and a significant percentage of the co-operative leadership at that time envisioned the creation of an economy in which co-operatives dominated, if they did not completely control: they envisioned the creation of a kind of co-operative commonwealth. For most prominent English-Canadian activists, the credit union was just the "financial arm" of the co-operative movement, and, in fact, could fulfil its central objective only by playing that role.

The Canadian emphasis on community-based credit unions was not just a minor variation on the American model. Community-based credit unions have different kinds of challenges and other opportunities. The standard challenge they face is that they do not normally have strong, natural bonds of membership. To some extent, this was less true in smaller rural communities with populations in the hundreds where survival had often meant uniting in formal and informal co-operative enterprises: the kinds of places common, for example, in the western grain belt or the rural parishes of Quebec.

In the larger towns and cities, the problems were more complex. Specifically, the almost inevitably loose bonds of association typical of urban community credit unions meant that evaluating the character of borrowers was more difficult, chasing down delinquent borrowers was harder, and building enthusiasm among the membership was more complex. American leaders, therefore, looked with suspicion on the Canadian innovations, and their suspicions, counteracted by considerable Canadian pride, contributed to more than thirty years of sometimes testy relationships. Those tensions would colour the way in which credit unionists from the two countries would tend to view the expansion of credit unions overseas.

The English-Canadian idea of credit unions brought a deeper co-operative perspective to the fore than either the American or Quebec models. In most regions of English Canada, it was also committed early to the possibilities of community credit unions. It had to struggle, therefore, with the problems inherent in larger memberships and geographic notions of bonds of loyalty rather than the more binding attitudes based on places of work, religion and ethnicity. It was very much a "bottom-up" movement steeped in the early years, in the values of populist credit union organizations. Scattered across more than 3,000 miles, regulated by provincial statutes, differentiated by regional loyalties, the English-Canadian movement would be slow to develop a national consciousness and even slower to develop effective national organizations.

Despite the somewhat different paths they followed, the American and Canadian credit union movements started a long period of steady expansion at the end of World War II. In the United States the expansion continued to be built upon the growth of closed-bond credit unions, most notably those associated with employee groups. By war's end, workers, who had unionized at an unprecedented rate, were militantly searching for ways to improve their position; establishing credit unions in their plants and factories was one inexpensive way in which they could do so. At the same time, employers, now widely influenced by "modern", "enlightened" management practice, were more willing to provide benefits such as credit unions. It was relatively easy, therefore, to preach the gospel of mainstream American credit unionism. It was also understandable that many Americans would prefer the closed-bond credit union.

At the same time, the end of the war ushered in a long period of North American dominance within both the global economy and world politics. Despite the rhetoric of the Cold War, the United States was clearly the world's predominant military and economic power, its influence evident in all parts of the world. The expansion of the American military, after a brief decline at the end of the war, was renewed as the arms race with the Soviet Union and then China gathered momentum and the Korean War broke out. For more than two generations, American expenditures on armaments would fuel the economy, almost as if the country were continually waging war. For both the United States and its close ally, Canada, it would be a period of unprecedented economic growth and material achievement, a time of growing consumer confidence for the widening middle class.

The American and Canadian peoples embraced the consumerism of the modern age with virtually unquestioning enthusiasm. The accumulated savings of the war years made possible the proliferation of suburbs, while the expanded industrial capacity created by the war was transferred to the production of consumer goods. It was the beginning of thirty years of almost uninterrupted prosperity and confidence which would not be shaken until the economic uncertainties associated with the oil crisis of the 1970s appeared. It was an era in which everyone, it seemed, believed — with some justification — that they belonged to the middle class, a time when the need for inexpensive, accessible credit became nearly universal.

Credit unions were part of the rise of the broadly defined North American middle class. They rose with the rising salaries of blue-collar workers, many of whom earned significant incomes in manufacturing industries; they attracted large numbers of people in government, education and the service industries. The resultant growth was substantial: by 1954, there were 15,000 credit unions in the United States, with more than 7,200,000 members and $2,200,000,000 in assets; Canada had 3,8000 credit unions with 1,500,000 members and nearly $600,000,000 in asssets.[64]

The expansion of the two movements in these years is best explained by their capacity to meet the needs of people poorly served by the larger financial institutions, particularly through the provision of consumer and, in the case of Canada, mortgage loans. In both countries credit unions pioneered in providing flexible services, operating offices in factories or small neighbourhoods, and in being open at convenient times. Through CUNA Mutual they provided a measure of financial stability in times of bereavement, a benefit widely appreciated by those who remembered the 1930s. Moreover, through their advisory services they helped individuals and families burdened with the large debtloads encouraged by instalment purchasing plans and easy credit terms. As so many credit union leaders of the time commented, credit unions permitted many North Americans, who would otherwise have been left "outside the gates", to participate in the "American dream" — and its Canadian variant.

Much of the movement's growth during this period in the United States and Canada came in the form of thousands of small credit unions. They were created as the movement was extensively promoted through radio programmes, newspaper articles, pamphlets, songs, and even plays. CUNA prospered as these new credit unions were organized and began to need services; in 1946 it opened offices in Washington to lobby government and in Hamilton to serve the Canadian credit unions. In 1950 CUNA opened Filene House, the new national headquarters in Madison, Wisconsin. The cornerstone was laid by Harry Truman, president of the United States, attesting to the importance the American movement had achieved and to its adroit handling of relations with government.

As the rapid growth took place, few credit union leaders — like those in many other countries in later years — stopped to wonder if there was an optimum size for credit unions or whether an increase in the numbers was the best way to grow. Rather, they competed among themselves to see who could create the most credit unions, to see who would earn "the founders pin", given to individuals who directly helped in the formation of one or more credit unions. They were following the methods of growth preferred by credit unions motivated by a populist culture.

The rapid and, in retrospect, easy growth of credit unions in the period 1945-1954 created a kind of assertive optimism that blended easily with the general North American confidence of the period. It is not surprising, therefore, that the North American promoters of credit unionism in the 1940s and 1950s — as well as later — could be inordinately confident of what they represented. They were the natural products of a society in ascendancy, the "New Romans" aware more of what they could impart than what they could learn. It would

Marking the opening of Filene House in Madison, Wisconsin, in May 1950. (COURTESY OF *THE BRIDGE*)

take a series of difficulties to shake that rather naive and simplistic world view, and it would not happen before some serious mistakes were made.

Looked at from another perspective, the decade after the war, while it marked the beginnings of the managerial credit union, also witnessed the flowering of the populist credit union in the American and Canadian movements. It was an era in which the most demanding problem seemed to be the training of enough directors and secretary-treasurers to meet the apparently unending demand. The commitment to "the little man", to the possibilities of helping more people control their own destinies, was important, perhaps the most obvious message the movement had to impart. It was a message that would be easily and appropriately transferred to the promotion of credit unions in other lands. In fact, within a few years, as the American and Canadian credit union movements started to change, it became increasingly important for many of its leaders to see elsewhere why their movements had been started in the first place.

Some credit unions started to take on "managerial" as opposed to "populist" cultures, even in the early 1940s: e.g., this Chicago-area credit union in 1942. (COURTESY OF CUNA)

The populist credit union also meant the virtually complete control of credit unions by the volunteer leadership. "Emancipation", a common theme in the populist perspective, meant helping people escape the bonds of grinding poverty and encouraging them to help themselves through co-operative effort. The preferred credit union was small and catered to limited and specific needs — it meant extensive education programmes, informal lending practices, frequent social activities, and collegial decision-making among people who knew each other well. It often worked best among groups of employees who understood each other's needs and frailties so well that they could build effective organizations based on that knowledge.

Structurally, the original populist culture favoured regional and national organizations geared to creating credit unions, providing an appropriate legislative framework, and concentrating upon educational and lobbying activities. It encouraged leaders who were flamboyant and dedicated, men and women who were not necessarily informed technically but who could move people to action and create enthusiasm among diverse groups.

Above all, the strong populist perspective of the 1940s and 1950s played a major role in how Americans and Canadians initially defined the credit union mission around the world. Indeed, it was a perspective that would be replicated in nearly all parts of the globe, and, as in the United States and Canada, it would last for a generation, if not two or three. It was the culture that long shaped American and Canadian views on how credit unions should be developed in other lands, and, in fact, would do so even after much of the American and Canadian movements had gone on into the next culture, a culture typified by increasing management domination.

As the two movements began looking outward, they also shared a powerful sense of mission shaped by the ideological commitments of World War II and its immediate aftermath. The war had heightened awareness of the democratic cause, as difficult and diffused as that cause was to define. For many credit unionists in the two countries, their movement, through its promotion of economic democracy, was an integral part of the struggle for a more democratic world; for many of them, that campaign was at least as important as the enhancement of political democracy which had supposedly been the central issue of World Wars I and II.

The dropping of the atomic bombs on Hiroshima and Nagasaki in 1945 particularly alarmed many thoughtful credit unionists and confirmed the need to press for greater economic democracy both at home and overseas in the decade that followed. Art Danforth, a long-time co-operative lawyer, writer and intellectual, caught the mood well in an article that appeared in *The Bridge* for February 1946. In it he appealed for no less than an international crusade on behalf of the credit union and wider co-operative movement. For him, as for many idealistic credit union leaders, "political action without economic action [is] futile and rootless".[65]

Danforth's and similar appeals found receptive ears among committed co-operative people in the most powerful region on earth. Both the United States and Canada were in remarkably privileged positions at the war's end: their international stature was at unparalleled heights, their financial systems were by far the strongest in the world despite accumulated war debts, and their cultures, particularly the American cultural industries, were widely supported and imitated. They were the most privileged victors of World War II. For the co-operative idealists, however, that victory would be justified only if the equitable distribution of economic power around the world was achieved through the widespread application of the co-operative model of enterprise.

The emphasis on the challenges confronting democracy took on particular and poignant meaning as the relief needs of hundreds of thousands of refugees in Europe became evident. Near the end of the war in 1944, the Co-operative League of the United States organized the International Co-operative Reconstruction Conference in Washington. Its purpose was to study the role co-operatives might play in assisting European refugees and in helping rebuild Europe. As a result of this conference, various American co-operatives, including the credit union movement, raised some $93,000 in just a few months for relief programmes in Europe.

The success of this project encouraged co-operative leaders and others to organize the Co-operative for American Remittances to Europe, or CARE, in 1945. Encouraged by several government officials as well as church organizations

and trade unions, CARE's objective was to provide relief, usually in the form of $15 packages of food and clothing paid for by individuals or groups. Many of these packages were initially distributed in Europe through the surviving consumer co-operative movements in the United Kingdom, France, Norway, Finland and Poland. Between 1945 and 1960, the value of the packages distributed through the European co-operatives exceeded $50,000,000.[66]

CARE soon expanded its activities into development projects in several countries. A wide range of American and Canadian co-operative organizations — the National Rural Electric Cooperative Association, the Co-operative League, the Co-operative Union of Canada, Cooperative Food Distributors Association Nationwide, as well as CUNA — contributed to the support of self-help activities in Europe, Malta and Southeast Asia by providing ploughs and farm tools through these programmes. Participating in CARE became an important learning experience for many people who later supported the development of credit unions overseas; indeed, it was in working for CARE that they first started to think about international development issues.[67]

At the same time, several European and North American governments turned to co-operative forms of enterprise in order to promote the economic growth of developing countries and to meet humanitarian obligations. Some embraced credit unions — along with other forms of co-operative organizations — as a way to help withstand the rise of communism. In the United Kingdom, for example, the Fabian Society, much influenced by the co-operative theorists Beatrice and Sidney Webb earlier in the century, encouraged the Labour government of the day to promote co-operatives in the colonies, especially those, such as India and Kenya, on the road to independence.

Many of the new national leaders in the colonies, having studied at European universities and been influenced by European political thought, absorbed the various European perspectives on co-operative development. As they came to power, therefore, many of them included co-operatives as key parts of their programmes. In countries like India, Sri Lanka, Ghana, Uganda, Kenya, Belize, Barbados, Jamaica and other West Indies islands, for example, the emerging national leaders were usually supportive, in some instances enthusiastic, about using co-operatives to help achieve economic independence.

At first, the emerging nations tended to prefer the extension of forms of financial co-operatives already in place, forms generally known as "thrift and credit co-operatives". These kinds of financial co-operatives, although similar to credit unions, were different in four main ways. First, they were typically governed by co-operative statutes, which meant that standards of care and government inspection might be inadequate for financial institutions. Second, they could be intertwined with government programmes for rural or fishing loans, meaning that governments might play an intrusive role in the day-to-day operations of the societies. Third, thrift and credit societies would typically lend a member no more than the amount he or she had on deposit unless the loan was backed by someone else, or the government; this obviously, could be a severely limiting factor, and it encouraged government involvement.[68] Finally, they were often associated with the financing of co-operatives and might have elected directors who were involved with other kinds of co-operatives, a relationship that could lead to bad lending practices unless it was carefully controlled.

Credit unions could find a place amid such enthusiasms, although sometimes with difficulty. The challenges were to ensure that appropriate legislation was passed; that democratic systems were genuinely followed; that lending was made on reasonable business premises; and that government regulation was supportive and regulatory, not intrusive and unduly restrictive. These challenges would be particularly obvious in regimes where co-operative departments tended to be paternalistic or the economy so fragile that governments could not afford, in the short term, to leave any financial institution alone.

Within the United Nations a growing interest in co-operatives became evident among bureaucrats and national representatives. Almost from the beginning, the UN emphasized co-operatives in its housing, planning and building programmes. Many of the individuals involved in the United Nations Relief and Rehabilitation Association (UNRRA), for example, had a history of involvement in co-operatives. The Washington employees of UNRRA organized their own credit union in 1945; it assisted new employees of the association, many of whom were themselves refugees.[69] Its success helped in the development of CARE and led to the formation of a large credit union among employees of the UN in New York and later in Paris. All of these activities probably played a role in encouraging the UN to support the development of co-operative institutions generally; it certainly was an example used by UNRRA employees when they went to developing areas of the world in the later 1940s.[70]

The growing international interest in credit unions and other forms of co-operative credit soon had an impact on CUNA. As the war came to an end, the number of enquiries about how to form credit unions increased substantially. Letters arrived from Europe, Asia and Africa; a steady stream of visitors came to CUNA's offices in Madison; articles on overseas possibilities appeared regularly in *The Bridge* and its successor, *The Credit Union Magazine*. Moreover, by the early 1950s, American and Canadian credit unionists became more aware of the movements in other countries, as inexpensive airfares and favourable exchange rates encouraged them to travel more widely. Places that were merely wishful thinking for an earlier generation now became holiday destinations for the middle class; parts of the world that were once exotic and known largely through travel literature became readily accessible.

The most successful early efforts in expanding outside continental North America, however, lay relatively close to home — in the Caribbean. The Caribbean movement had officially begun in September 1941, when a Jesuit priest from Boston, Father John Peter Sullivan, started the first successful credit union in Kingston, Jamaica. Sullivan brought information on the American credit union movement to Jamaica; he was also much influenced by the Antigonish experience. The credit unions he helped start in Jamaica became a model for much of the credit union movement that emerged in the Caribbean during the next decade.

Sullivan, who had arrived in Jamaica amid the political turmoil of the late 1930s, saw credit unions as a form of "practical Christianity". He became a tireless promoter of them, travelling all over Jamaica to encourage their formation, using a bicycle when war-time restrictions limited the amount of gasoline available for his automobile.[71] He was particularly effective in gathering around him a group of young people, many of them from St. George's College, a prominent high school founded by American Jesuits on the island. A.A. "Paddy" Bailey and Lorrell Bruce, part of this group, played major roles in the Jamaican, West Indian and international movements. During the early 1940s Sullivan and his protégés scattered throughout the island, organizing study clubs and credit unions of all kinds, Catholic and Protestant, rural and urban, African, native and European.

It is easy in retrospect to pass quickly over, or even to ignore, the "nerve" it must have required to undertake these activities. Most of the organizers were young. Many of them were of African descent in a society that was not always tolerant, and they were advocating that the poor carry out economic activities many believed were beyond their understanding. It was within that context that the "human potential" message of the Antigonish movement and Catholic social action philosophy was so important.[72] As Paddy Bailey often put it in later years, the most important thing was "to be courageous, to be willing to stand up, and to understand the limitlessness of the potential of human beings".[73] It is a

Lorrell Bruce, who played a major role as a leader of the Jamaican credit union movement and as a conciliator within the international movement.
(COURTESY OF CUNA)

perspective that applied in other parts of the world as well. It took some nerve to come from "outside" and promote credit unions; it could take even more nerve to stand up and be counted among your own family and friends and within your own community.

Sullivan and his associates built upon the adult education movement that had been started in the 1930s by two co-operative enthusiasts associated with the Jamaica Welfare Limited. They took advantage, too, of a growing interest in co-operatives encouraged by British administrators and colonial public servants. They found it advantageous to work through the agricultural societies and the existing thrift and credit societies as well as other co-operative entities.[74]

By 1948, the group had organized 178 study clubs. These clubs, using materials from Antigonish, would study lessons, usually once a month, for as long as a year, before they organized their credit unions. It was a system that had been widely used in Canada, and it would be used extensively in many other parts of the world over the succeeding decades. The early credit unions in Jamaica were supported by public servants, teachers, Roman Catholic parishes, and small communities; such patterns of association would subsequently be duplicated in many other countries.

Almost from the beginning, the Jamaican credit union leaders were anxious to become part of the international movement. As early as 1942 the Jamaican credit unions (four in number) had formed a league; the Jamaica Credit Union League became active — although not registered with the government or CUNA — in 1943. In 1946, the league began to consider joining CUNA, but this did not take place until 1950, three years after it had finally become a registered society. Sullivan served as the first president from 1943 to 1947 and as its managing director from 1947 to 1957. He was also directly involved in the beginnings of the credit union movement in Belize, Guyana, Curacao, Antigua and Barbuda, Colombia, the Dominican Republic, Haiti, the Bahamas, and Trinidad and Tobago.

In Trinidad and Tobago the movement began in 1942. Its most important founder was Malcolm Milne, a San Fernando solicitor, the commissioner of income tax, and a prominent lay member of the Roman Catholic Church. Having read about the Antigonish credit unions in *The Catholic Digest* and having corresponded with Father Sullivan in Jamaica, Milne gathered a group of supporters, including Father J.P. Long, George Lera, Charles Piontkowski and Edgar Baker. The group enthusiastically began to promote credit unions throughout the islands. Like most credit union organizers of the time they relied upon study groups to reach large numbers of people. Over the following three years they gained a receptive audience and, in 1945, succeeded in securing a government ordinance under which credit unions could be formed.

Milne and his associates encountered many people with desperate needs, especially within the black working class, people who had no access to existing financial institutions. During the long period of slavery, the African Trinidadians had developed a wide range of ad hoc co-operative institutions and strategies to help them improve their circumstances.[75] They had relied upon the traditional *sou sou* for emergency funds in the past; they had also adapted the structures of the English "friendly societies" to meet their social and economic needs.

Tom Doig with Mother Mary Adele and Mother Mary Alicia of the Roseau Credit Union, one of the earliest credit unions in the Dominican Republic.
(COURTESY OF CUNA)

These institutions, however, were increasingly insufficient in a society that was becoming more reliant upon cash and easy access to credit.

Even before the legislation in 1945, some twenty credit unions had been formed among the black working class. Within a decade another 200 were formed, most of them also among African Trinidadians.[76] A growing number of the credit unions — in fact, soon the majority — were organized outside the Catholic church, among employee groups and within communities. As the number of credit unions grew, the government established a co-operative department to oversee, guide and assist their development.

As in other parts of the world, the early credit unions in Trinidad and Tobago were simple organizations — in some instances, deposits were literally kept in suitcases under the bed of the secretary-treasurer. Many of them remained associated with the Roman Catholic Church and were led by Roman Catholic clergy and laity. Among the prominent supporters within the clergy was Father Delahunt, who was also much influenced by the thought and organizational methods of the Antigonish movement. Some of the credit unions were organized on a parish basis and admitted only Catholics; however, over time, most of the Catholic credit unions would change their common bond and admit non-Catholics.

The movement in Puerto Rico started in 1943. Its early supporters were university employees and, especially, farm people. It, too, was much influenced by the Antigonish model, particularly in the decade following World War II.[77]

In British Honduras (now Belize) the movement also began in 1943 with the establishment of St. Peter-Claver Credit Union in the Toledo District. Father Marion M. Ganey, a Jesuit, and Father Sutti, a lay priest, were the most prominent of a number of priests, nuns and Catholic lay people who dominated the early history of the movement.[78] Ganey would go on to become one of the most famous, resolute and commanding figures in the early history of the international movement. A native of Gillespie, Illinois, he frequently corresponded with Roy Bergengren, who, despite his departure from CUNA, remained an influential figure in international credit union circles. Moreover, Ganey, like Sullivan, regularly attended the annual meetings of CUNA and CUNA Mutual. Invariably, at these meetings, both of them would make eloquent appeals for the expansion of the international movement.

In 1953, Ganey moved to Fiji where he helped in the beginnings of that country's credit unions. The interest in Fiji was part of reawakened general interest in co-operative banking that began to emerge as the Pacific/Asian region recovered from the disruptions of World War II. Some of the region's co-operative movements had suffered greatly during periods of Japanese occupation, in some areas stretching back to the 1930s.

In the Philippines, most of the credit unions were forced to go underground or close their doors within months of the Japanese occupation. Two of them — Batae Christian Credit Union and Pias National Credit Union — were able to stay active until the last part of the war, but even they were forced to close down in the final days of the occupation.[79]

During their often brutal occupation, the Japanese forced the development of some 5,000 agricultural and food co-operatives upon the Philippine people, largely to facilitate the movement of food supplies. Consequently, when liberation occurred, there was a period during which co-operatives, including credit unions, were not widely supported. It would take more than a decade before credit unions, as well as other kinds of co-operatives, could stage a comeback, but the drive to begin that renewal was evident by the early 1950s.[80]

Indeed, the growing interest in credit unions could be seen in many parts of Asia by the 1950s. The most obvious networks that encouraged credit unions were within the Roman Catholic Church. Following the war, many Roman Catholics in the Pacific/Asian region embraced adult education, community development and co-operative action for a wide diversity of reasons. Some, fearing the rise of "atheistic" communism, saw this three-pronged approach as a way to combat it. In contrast, others saw ways in which Christians could address the social justice and economic disparity issues raised by Marxism — in short, to demonstrate that Christianity and Marxism were not completely antithetical. Most were primarily motivated by the immense social and economic needs they saw around them, particularly in the rural villages where farm people were struggling to enter into

market economies, and in the many southern cities where mushrooming slums were creating immense social and economic needs. This Catholic activism, in its Asian form, became evident in the late 1940s and 1950s; it would bear bountiful fruit in the 1960s.

The Australian movement also showed considerable promise. It was begun in the late 1940s largely by Kevin Yates, who had been stationed in western Canada during the war. While in Canada, and on trips to the United States, Yates had visited a number of credit unions, before returning home full of enthusiasm for the possibilities of credit unionism. In Sydney he joined others to form the Universal Credit Union Co-operative. The movement grew steadily, the earliest successful credit unions being of the closed-bond type, particularly among government employees and industrial workers. Most of the credit unions were situated in New South Wales, the state in which Sydney is located. By the later 1950s, though, the movement was beginning to emerge in the state of Victoria as an extension of an already strong co-operative movement. Somewhat later, it started to spread to other states as well.

The opening of the Universal Credit Union Co-operative, Australia's first credit union, in Sydney in 1946. (COURTESY OF CREDIT UNION SERVICES CORPORATION)

The opportunities for expansion overseas, therefore, were plentiful as the world recovered from the war, and the 1950s wore on. Those opportunities, however, would have to be seized by a relatively few people; most American and Canadian credit unionists were preoccupied by the internal problems of their own movements. At first glance, those problems, which began in the early 1940s during the controversies of Bergengren's last years as managing director of CUNA, were the result of a clash of personalities and the struggles of competing groups.

This was partly true, and that is largely how the circumstances were understood at the time. Basically, though, they were symptomatic of more fundamental changes, changes that were similar to those that would confront credit union movements in many other countries in the succeeding decades. While the changes were most fundamentally associated with the broad transition within credit union circles from populist to managerial cultures, they manifested themselves most obviously in debates over structure.

The struggle over structures within the United States was caused by the emergence of CUNA Mutual as a powerful organization in its own right, but also by the development of strong state leagues. Significant growth within credit unions almost inevitably forces some institutional changes, and that was the underlying reason for the management problems that surfaced within CUNA during the early 1940s and lasted for a generation.

The growth pressures were primarily related to the expansion of CUNA Mutual, whose origins ironically owed much to the work of Bergengren in the mid-1930s. CUNA Mutual had grown faster than anyone had thought possible when it was formed. It provided services that were appreciated generally by the memberships of credit unions all across the United States. It had a sales network through the credit unions that could be mobilized readily and profitably, and it was operating a kind of business that, while not easily learned, was almost invariably profitable once effective management personnel was in place.

Moreover, CUNA Mutual generated significant income and thus could create the kinds of reserves and surpluses unknown for many years in any other credit union organization. Unlike CUNA, for example, it did not have to rely on the precarious practice of having to earn annual dues; it had the luxury of generating surpluses and using them as it saw fit. In short, CUNA Mutual was more like a conventional business and, for that reason, tended to attract directors and managers who had little time for the inevitable uncertainties and preoccupation with process issues that characterized life at CUNA and, most particularly, populist credit unions. The result was that the two organizations developed distinctly different cultures that could not be brought together easily, especially if they had to collaborate on a daily basis.

The underlying structural issue was how to harmonize the governing and management systems of CUNA Mutual and CUNA, the organization that had given it birth. Originally, CUNA Mutual was to be the servant of CUNA; that is why Bergengren remained technically in charge of both organizations. As CUNA Mutual prospered, however, and pursued its own course under the leadership of an increasingly specialized management group, the relationship was strained to the limit. Tom Doig tried to follow Bergengren's approach and retain control of both organizations, but he achieved only limited success in the beginning. Nevertheless, the difficult marriage lasted until the mid-1950s before breaking apart; even in separate but linked houses, the relationship remained uneasy until the 1970s. Like many other national movements that came later, the American credit union movement had to find its own arduous, and sometimes acrimonious, way to an appropriate national structure.

CUNA was also confronting the difficult problem of how to accommodate the addition of movements from other countries. When the Canadian leagues were admitted, starting in 1940, many American credit unionists tended to see them as just more leagues, thereby underestimating the Canadians' national commitments. As the 1950s unfolded, a growing number of Canadian credit unionists (but not an overwhelming majority) became more concerned about achieving Canadian priorities: building a strong national credit union structure; developing Canadian insurance programmes; taking an independent approach to international development; and working closely with other Canadian co-operative organizations. In 1945, some of the credit unionists organized the Canadian Confederation of Credit Unions as a way to meet these goals. The confederation never achieved the kind of momentum some Canadian leaders hoped for, creating a persistent uneasiness that would present problems in the coming decades.

The emerging credit union movements in other countries showed little of this uneasiness until the later 1950s. Their ambitions initially were just to be admitted to CUNA and to have a representative on CUNA's board (at that time, all leagues had at least one representative on the board). Usually, they achieved these goals without much difficulty. By 1953, there were representatives from Puerto Rico, Jamaica and the Dominican Republic on the board, in the early years most frequently priests who had helped start the movements in those countries.

The American movement was also in the process of adjusting to the emergence of strong state leagues and leaders. The movement had started in a highly centralized way through the work of Filene and Bergengren. As appropriate legislation was created in various states, however, it was inevitable and necessary that local leaders become responsible for the formation of credit unions, the education of directors, and the beginnings of centralized banking services. For the most part, they did so through their leagues and chapters.

By the early 1940s leagues had their own managing directors, most of them dynamic figures in their own right who were   unwilling to accept direction from Madison or to purchase without question the services that CUNA had to offer; some of them even questioned the services provided by CUNA Mutual. The result was that Bergengren and then Doig found it increasingly difficult to retain the support of some of the managing directors.

In March 1942, the managing directors of the state leagues attending the St. Louis convention decided to organize themselves into the National Association of Managing Directors.[81] The purposes of the association were these: to provide a forum for the exchange of ideas and information; to promote professional development; to make recommendations to national organizations; and to supply resources for the national organizations. It was immediately an important organization because its members were among the most influential in the movement.

In 1946 the national association came up with the following principles:

> Open membership within the common bond;
> Democratic control: one member, one vote;
> Beneficial credit for members only;
> Promotion of thrift;
> Non-profit service;
> Equitable opportunity for all members.[82]

It is significant that this group took upon itself the task of defining the "credit union" idea for the times. It shows not only their commitment to that idea, as they fashioned it, but also their innate and natural desire to shape the movement according to their own lights. They would become even more desirous of doing so as the years passed.

State and provincial leagues also grew, because as credit unions expanded, they naturally felt the need for central financial institutions to help them carry out new functions. They needed to move funds easily from one credit union to another; to accumulate necessary reserves and invest them prudently; and to join together for the purchase of supplies and services not provided through CUNA or CUNA Mutual. These needs first became obvious in the United States, especially in Michigan, but they were felt most deeply in the 1950s in Canada where the growth of community credit unions so intensified demands for loans that they easily outstripped initial member deposits. The needs were even felt in the comparatively smaller movement in Trinidad and Tobago, where agitation for the creation of a credit union "bank" started in the mid-1940s, when the movement was just beginning.

The creation of regional entities, first departments of leagues and then central credit unions, complicated the structures of the American and Canadian movements. Increasingly, there were strong state, provincial or regional groupings that could question the ambitions of the national leaders, and even thwart them if they felt disposed to do so. In Canada, where there was never a strong national focus for credit union activities, that was particularly true and would remain so until at least the 1990s. Moreover, the stronger leagues and centrals soon possessed groups of trained professionals whose experience and qualifications could surpass those of the national organizations.

The American movement was also starting a long period of adjustment as the management of credit unions began to change. From its inception, the American movement had been run by volunteers. Within local credit unions, most of the work was done by volunteers serving on boards of directors and supervisory committees. The most important official, the secretary-treasurer, was normally a volunteer as well, although many of them received modest honoraria; by the later 1940s a few of them were even receiving modest salaries.

In nearly all cases, however, secretary-treasurers were playing a greater role. In the larger credit unions, they were facing the challenges of employing staff, operating multiple premises, making different types of loans, and finding ways to manage relatively large asset bases. For many of them, the only way to respond to these challenges was to absorb the essential practices of other financial institutions — to become more like small banks. The problem was this: could one imitate the stronger, almost pervasive competitor and yet remain distinctive? It was a difficult question that would be asked many times in the decades that lay ahead.

At the same time, growing numbers of directors were struggling to acquire the information and skills necessary to carry out their work effectively. Their educational needs were enormous and drained much of the financial and human resources of CUNA and the local leagues. What had started out as very simple businesses were becoming complex entities. There were limits to what volunteering could provide the movement. The question was where those limits should be.

Although it was barely evident as the 1950s began, a major debate was also starting within yet another sphere: the ways in which credit unions related to their members. In some of the larger organizations the challenges came because growing memberships could not easily be closely connected to their credit unions. As staffs grew, the bonds between employees and members became less personal, and the roles of volunteers changed; in most instances they diminished. Membership meetings were held less frequently and were less well attended; finding members to serve on boards and supervisory committees became increasingly difficult. Advertising and marketing programmes aimed at diversified and larger memberships began to replace personal contact among a small group of people. The ultimate issue was how the credit unions would retain the bonds of membership as they grew larger and more professional. Debate around this issue was not intense in the 1940s and early 1950s — in fact, it would not become general until the 1960s — but it existed, and it worried the more thoughtful of credit union leaders of the time. It would emerge countless times around the world as the national movements in many countries went through much the same process.

The credit union and the American family — the protection and self-help themes in the 1950s. (COURTESY OF THE BRIDGE)

All of these debates, which went to the heart of credit unionism, were starting to escalate as the Americans and Canadians began to think about exporting credit unionism to other parts of the world. Generally, the strongest advocates for the overseas programmes came from two viewpoints of significant strength within the American movement. One included leaders who were deeply committed to the values and programmes of populist credit unions, to the possibilities of empowering people in a variety of ways. What they saw overseas reminded them of what they had known and believed in; for some, it was a relief to get away from what they saw starting to happen to the movement in their own country.

A more sharply defined perspective came from those concerned about the rise of communism and the deepening Cold War. In 1952 the national directors of CUNA had gone on record as being opposed to the spread of communism in the United States and around the world. At the February 1953 joint meetings of CUNA, CUNA Mutual and CUNA Supply, the delegates reviewed with considerable enthusiasm the need for encouraging the growth of the international credit union movement. The debate was triggered in part by a visit from American Secretary of State John Foster Dulles. Dulles stressed the need for Americans to assist in the struggle against communism by helping build economies overseas that would show people the benefits of a free-enterprise model. His call was quickly answered by CUNA President Marion Gregory, like Dulles a passionate anti-communist; Gregory vigorously promoted the credit union idea as "an instrument that can save the underprivileged people from Communism".[83]

In May 1953, the CUNA directors adopted a resolution calling upon CUNA to undertake a concerted effort to work with American aid programmes, CARE and the United Nations Economic, Social and Cultural Organization (UNESCO) to encourage the development of credit unions around the world.[84] In November 1953, the directors considered a report from the planning committee as to how they might carry out international programmes. The report was cautiously but positively received. Over the following few months CUNA representatives met with government officials to ascertain what kind of programme might be the most effective. At the same time, people sympathetic to the cause promoted the idea among American credit unionists; among them, Roy Bergengren was the most prominent and perhaps the most determined.

Bergengren had always been proud of what he had accomplished in advising people in other countries when he had managed CUNA. He was particularly proud, and justifiably so, of the role he had played in the development of the Canadian movement. Bergengren also shared the common concern about the rise of the communist states. He believed they could not be trusted, that they were intent upon world domination, and that they had to be resisted. Echoing a common American perspective of the times, he believed communism flourished wherever there were "landless, tenant farmers and city workers, crowded into slums, living in poverty and always hungry". Furthermore, he believed such poverty was caused largely by loan sharks, whose high interest rates restricted economic growth and robbed workers of the "fair fruits of their toil".[85] He believed credit unions and other forms of co-operative credit could be effective agents in undermining this influence and allowing more to enjoy the benefits of economic growth. They could be vital instruments in preventing the spread of communism.

Bergengren's views were greatly influenced by the writings of Eleanor Roosevelt and Justice William O. Douglas, both of whom, following trips to Asia in the early 1950s,[86] wrote books in which they blamed usury as a major reason for the rise of communism. Bergengren agreed, and saw an opportunity for the last great crusade of his career: the formation of an international development programme for the credit union movement:[87] "Usury is right down our alley. By fighting communism through credit union organization we will not only do a great service but put the credit union on the map".[88]

Late in 1953, Bergengren proposed a plan whereby the Overseas Department of CUNA would embark on a systematic programme to encourage credit unions outside of North America. He suggested the appointment of a full-time "man" under the managing director to promote overseas programmes. He advocated bringing one person from each of four countries (he suggested India, Pakistan, Malaya and the Philippines) to Madison for special training; these four would become the CUNA Overseas Field Force. He believed their work had to be accompanied by supporting materials in the appropriate languages and that they should be financed entirely by the organized movement in North America.[89]

Bergengren advocated the use of funds currently being spent on radio programmes that were not well received in all parts of the North American movement. He believed CUNA could work with several private and government funding agencies to foster credit unions as part of a wider programme to create modern economies in less developed countries.

Although Roy Bergengren's health was in decline as he started his campaign, he pursued, with something of a desperate passion, the expansion of the international movement. Much of the correspondence of the last eighteen months of his life was devoted to lobbying friends and associates within CUNA to support the development of an international programme. He envisioned recreating on an international level what he and Filene had accomplished within the United States:

> We will then do what Filene did — prime the pump
> wherever the credit union exists (as in the USA originally) but

there are not enough credit unions for self sustaining national associations which will eventually affiliate with CUNA. By this method we project CUNA into the battle against communism by doing something practical to assist the forces of democracy.[90]

Bergengren's motivation was simple. He was finishing the work he had started in the United States and Canada, completing his own "Crusade" (the repeated title of several of his books). His approach was steeped in the assumptions of the Allied side in World War II; it was clearly directed against the spread of communism, particularly in Asia. In fact, Bergengren saw credit unionism as a natural element in the kind of democratic society that he believed was fundamental to American life and crucial for the world's future. To the end, he believed in the primacy of the individual, albeit best manifested in co-operative relationships with others; he insisted on the value of democratic practices for the co-operative way of doing business; and he was adamantly opposed to any kind of government domination. It was a powerful vision, one that would stir the hearts of many in the generation that had taken power in the movement as he grew older. It was fundamental to the American model of credit unionism.

CHAPTER FOUR

THE POSSIBILITIES ARE EXPLORED
1954-1961

I am a missionary here in Mexico. The people in the field where I work are poor and in desperate need of a credit union. They are at the mercy of loan sharks for any money which they might need. The loans which they obtain have an interest rate of between 5 percent and 10 percent monthly. At this rate they are in debt perpetually and using all of their meagre crops to pay interest.

Letter quoted by Carlos M. Matos

Credit is a tool without which a man cannot better himself economically. If we educate people to a sense of their human rights, develop their latent talents, arouse their energy and their hopes, and then deny them the tool — money or credit — they need to achieve these ends, we have prepared them for communism.

Father Dan McLellan

I T HAD BEEN A LONG DAY. THE LAST DEBATE AT THE meeting of CUNA's national board had gone on longer than expected. Relieved that the vote had finally been called, Father McIver pulled out his watch:[91] it was 10:10 in the evening, May 15, 1954. A few minutes later the motion was passed unanimously.[92] CUNA now had an international programme, called the World Extension Department (WED), with its own organizational structure and an initial annual budget of $50,000.

Roy Bergengren, seriously ill but present at the meeting, had won his last crusade. In his stirring address on the motion, he said:

I have come to this meeting with my heart set on this one final accomplishment — and now I say to you that in this troubled world, our organization of Catholics, Protestants and Jews and men and women of every political persuasion and black men and brown men, our organization which so typifies the capacity of the human race to work as a unit and try to prove that the brotherhood of man really means something — this step — will make this meeting one of the most memorable meetings in the history of the credit union movement — from the bottom of my heart I thank you not only personally, but on behalf of the great man with whom it was my humble privilege to be associated in this great business of creating the credit union movement in the United States and Canada.[93]

A few months later, on November 11, 1954, Bergengren died, an unrelenting advocate to the end of his life for the expansion of credit unionism.

In a sense, Bergengren had personalized his role in creating the World Extension Department and, in keeping with his penchant for thinking himself involved in "crusades", had exaggerated his own role. In another way, though, his involvement had deep symbolic significance. He contributed substantially to the notion that it was a "movement" priority to expand overseas. He helped, intentionally or not, to establish both his own and Filene's position as heroic founders — the kind of figure any movement requires in order to have a popular appeal and to motivate later generations. His final victory would become an impressive monument.

At the 1954 meeting, the department was given a relatively clear but open-ended and demanding mandate. It would respond to enquiries from countries outside the United States and Canada about the formation and development of credit unions. It would work with training facilities, colleges and universities, particularly in North America, to train people from other countries who would then return home to build credit union movements. It would attack usury, "one of the greatest abuses in less developed countries",[94] thereby providing a simple, effective yet potent weapon to improve people's economic situation. In the process, it was believed, the department would help solve "the unequal distribution of wealth by enabling man to permanently help himself improve his condition".[95] Finally, amid the optimism of the formative period, the department would encourage the increased practice of democracy, initially within the common bond of the credit unions, but ultimately in the wider society as well.

The World Extension Department was formally established on October 18, 1954. On the recommendation of Roy Bergengren, CUNA appointed Hans Thunell, a former employee of CARE, as director. Thunell stayed only a few months before returning to CARE, to be replaced by Olaf H. Spetland, a recent immigrant from Norway who would remain director until 1963. A resistance fighter during World War II, Spetland was a transparently honest individual who had the important quality of being easily accepted by a wide range of people around the world. Under his leadership the department made steady, if unspectacular, progress.

Regardless of Spetland's efforts, however, the management of the department was watched keenly by the managing director of CUNA: until 1955, it would be Tom Doig; in 1956 and 1957, H.B. Yates; from 1957 to 1961, Vance Austin. The WED director (at various times also called the chief) reported directly to the managing director who was responsible to the board of CUNA for the department's oper-

ations. Although a relatively small initiative in terms of the resources allocated to it, the department had a high profile because it was important to many people, and it was regularly discussed at CUNA meetings.

During its first seven years, the department developed slowly; its mandate — to take credit unions to the world — was very broad and had yet to be thought through. Just as importantly, it did not have adequate funds. The bulk of its income came from 10 percent of the dues that leagues paid annually to CUNA. During the first few years this meant an assured income of only $50,000 to $60,000, barely enough to employ two or three people and to run an office; by 1960, the dues income had risen to $80,000, better but still not enough. From the beginning, therefore, the department had to seek funds through special contributions from individuals and member organizations, as well as through grants from foundations or government agencies sponsoring international development. Some states and provinces — Illinois, Michigan, Saskatchewan and Manitoba, for example — initially responded generously to the appeals for funding. All together, it was enough — with some small grants from foundations — to start a programme, but it was not enough to do as much as its supporters wanted.

The response to these limited early efforts, however, was more than encouraging. Building upon the work of the previous decade, WED corresponded with people in forty countries during its first year; within twelve months that number had increased to eighty-two, in forty of which the department advised in the establishment of credit unions;[96] by the end of the decade it was over one hundred. By 1960, too, the department was responding to more than 1,200 letters of enquiry each year. In order to do so, it published a growing volume of materials in Spanish as well as more limited quantities in other languages, including French, Portuguese, German, Japanese and Korean. The department also began to prepare slide presentations and film strips, the start of what would become a significant use of various media.

The department welcomed a growing number of international visitors to Madison each year; some were financed by credit union leagues, such as Illinois, Missouri and Michigan, others by the American government and a number of private organizations, such as the Ford Foundation. The visitors came from countries as diverse as Ireland, Vietnam, Italy, Iran, Trinidad and Tobago, Fiji, Australia, Germany, Ghana, Malaya, India, Turkey and the Netherlands Antilles. After seeing the offices and the complex being developed for CUNA, CUNA Mutual and CUNA Supply, they were sent to the centre for co-operative studies at the University of Wisconsin. At both places visitors were usually involved in seminars from which they went out for visits and perhaps work sessions in local credit unions or in league offices, mostly in nearby states.

WED also established a working relationship with the Foreign Operations Association in the State Department in Washington. Through that connection, the department shipped hundreds of information packages annually to interested people throughout the world. This activity clearly assisted in the formation of many credit unions; it also helped to demonstrate to the American government the growing interest in credit unions around the world. It was the begin-

In the 1960s an increasing number of visitors arrived in Madison. J. Orrin Shipe meets with Rev. Gregory B. Semba (Tanganyika), Rev. Andrew P. Salawanje (Nyasaland) and Rev. Henry Agogo Makakale (Basutoland).
(COURTESY OF CUNA)

ning of what would become a long-standing relationship with successive Washington administrations in their various overseas activities.

The department also worked with CUNA's public relations section to compile statistics on the growing number of credit union movements around the world.[97] This was important work, often made frustrating because of the varying degrees of accuracy in how records were kept. In some countries, exaggerating the successes was common, because doing so helped to attract funding, at least for a while; in others, there were simply not the resources to maintain good record-keeping. It was nevertheless vitally important for the department to be at least approximately correct and consistent. Statistical records were necessary to make effective applications for grants and, perhaps most significantly, to measure the progress that had been achieved.

WED also began to create, offer and sponsor conferences and training sessions outside Madison, both in the United States and in other countries. Beginning in 1956 with a conference in Kingston, Jamaica, it sponsored training sessions in Central and South America: San José, Costa Rica (1958); Santiago, Chile (1959); and Caracas, Venezuela (1960). It also sponsored an extensive series of workshops in a steadily growing number of other countries in Africa and Asia, as staff visited an increasing number of countries around the world. In fact, wherever staff travelled, they were expected to offer workshops and training sessions to people in the field. They were also expected to help in the development of credit union legislation, their perspectives on this topic having been shaped largely by the evolution of credit unions in the United States.

During the mid- and late 1950s, the World Extension Department began to recruit individuals in other countries. A.A. "Paddy" Bailey, among the first to be employed outside the United States, was hired in the summer of 1957 to work in the Caribbean. Bailey had been active within the Jamaican credit union movement as a volunteer working with Father Sullivan from 1939 until 1949, when he joined the Jamaican Ministry of Co-operatives as an inspector of credit unions. A committed enthusiast for credit unionism as well as a devout Catholic who moved easily among the remarkably diverse people of Jamaica, Bailey soon started to visit nearby islands to encourage the formation of credit unions; it was the beginning of the kind of work he would do for over thirty years.

Bailey would have a long and distinguished career with the department and within the international movement. A man of quiet dignity, with a commanding presence, a strong, clear voice and a subtle understanding of institutional politics, he would play a role within the international movement similar to Bergengren's in the early years of the American movement. Like Bergengren, Bailey became particularly well known for his understanding and passionate statements about credit union and co-operative philosophy. Like Bergengren, too, he could work with a wide range of people and stir their enthusiasm and commitment.

A.A. "Paddy" Bailey, an international ambassador for the credit union movement from the 1950s until the early 1990s. (COURTESY OF CUNA)

In the same period, José Arroyo Riesta was hired in Mexico to assist a promising movement that had started through church auspices but was having difficulty achieving stability. He stayed in Mexico only briefly, however, because the national federation was weak and unable to support the costs of his work. Building the Mexican movement would be a gradual process, not a matter of sudden growth and easy organization.

Toward the end of the 1950s the department started recruiting in the Far East. The results would be evident in the 1970s. This willingness to hire people outside the United States reflected a remarkable commitment, not always easy for North Americans to appreciate and implement, to hire local people whenever possible to ensure local control and accountability. It was not necessarily the easiest way to start national movements, but it was the best way to ensure their long-term success.

WED's activities must be seen in the context of burgeoning interests in international development during the post-war period. By the early 1950s there was a growing recognition around the world that economic disparity was a threat to peace and continuing prosperity, as well as (arguably) a violation of human rights. Experiences with refugees after the war had shown how joint international efforts could build stronger economies; they had demonstrated some of the ways in which production could be increased and, just as importantly, how consumption could be expanded. For many in a generation that understood how underconsumption had caused the Great Depression, the continuing prosperity of the world — as well as its future security — depended upon spreading economic growth into regions still suffering from the impact of war or only partly included within international marketing systems.

Much of the early enthusiasm for international development programmes came from the United Nations and its associated organizations. In 1954 the United Nations published a report entitled *Rural Progress through Cooperatives* which strongly endorsed the international co-operative movement. The report was widely distributed and read; even more than twenty years later, it continued to attract support for the international movement.[98] This was followed in 1957 by *Economic Development of Under-Developed Countries, Co-operatives*, which in turn was followed by other UN documents during the next three years on the role co-operatives could play in community development, providing low-cost housing, promoting modern economic growth, expanding agricultural production and organizing fishing communities.

Within the United Nations network, the United Nations Education, Scientific and Cultural Organization (UNESCO), the International Labour Office (ILO) and the Food and Agriculture Organization (FAO) all promoted co-operatives as effective tools for economic and social development. The ILO was particularly important because it had a long history of involvement with co-operatives, including co-operative banking, going back to its formation in 1920. The support of these organizations contributed significantly to a resurgence of co-operatives in many parts of the world. In particular, it helped the work of the department because it legitimized the co-operative approach to economic and social change and encouraged governments to support it. In some parts of the world, too, the department worked closely with some of these organizations, most commonly in Africa where it would be frequently associated with the ILO in encouraging better management of credit unions and in promoting credit unions within the trade union movement.

The United Nations further assisted the development of the co-operative movement when it declared the 1960s the "Decade of Development". That declaration encouraged many countries, especially the Scandinavian nations but also Canada and the United States, to devote considerable sums to development projects around the world. As they did so, they became increasingly impressed by the effectiveness of co-operatives in fostering economic and social development. This emphasis, in turn, provided remarkable opportunities for credit union enthusiasts; specifically, it helped attract increasing support for the work of the World Extension Department.

Many of the co-operative organizations in developed countries were attracted to the possibilities of foreign assistance programmes, for both idealistic and business reasons. As European co-operative organizations regained their economic health in the late 1940s and early 1950s, they became involved in development programmes, especially in Africa and Asia. The International Co-operative Alliance, which had been preoccupied with European co-operative movements since its formation in 1895, began to explore the possibilities of development programmes, particularly in India and Africa. The Raiffeisen movement in Germany and the Netherlands embarked upon international activities, particularly in Africa and Latin America.

The World Extension Department had to struggle to find its role within both the international development and the international co-operative communities. That was not easy, because it had to insist upon retaining its own unique capacity to contribute; it had to advocate both a distinctive kind of development and a specific form of co-operative organization. At the same time, the department had to associate with other forms of co-operatives around the world. That, in turn, necessitated a changed attitude within some credit union circles in North America, particularly in the United States. Remaining aloof from other co-operative organizations and kinds of co-operative endeavour, as was the norm in the United States, was not possible overseas. Put another way, the American and Canadian movements were forced to return to their nineteenth-century roots; they had to overcome the North American tendency to forget how much had been borrowed and to appreciate the debt owed to others.

The department also had to find its place among the many private initiatives on behalf of development assistance that were emerging within the United States and Canada. In the United States alone, over fifty organizations became involved in relief, education and development programmes in the years after World War II. These included such organizations as Experiments in International Living, International Volunteer Services, and the Brethren Service Committee. Cumulatively, the activities of these organizations helped increase understanding of the nature of poverty in other lands and the issues involved in trying to introduce global economic change. The work of CUNA can be seen as part of this more general awakening in the United States and Canada to the need for addressing poverty in many areas of the world; it was part of a widening commitment among many to combat poverty, overseas as well as at home.

By the early 1950s there were many co-operators in both the United States and Canada who were drawn to the issues of international development. Within the Co-operative League of the United States, in which many credit union enthusiasts were active, Executive Director Jerry Voorhis led a vigorous campaign to encourage co-operatives and co-operative supporters to become involved in developmental programmes overseas. In Canada, the Desjardins movement and the Co-operative Union of Canada assisted many overseas co-operators, including people interested in credit unions, to come to Canada to study co-operative organizations. Many of them came to the formal educational programmes at Levis and Antigonish; others came (until the formation of Western Co-operative College in 1964) for informal study tours of co-operatives in western Canada.

From the viewpoint of the World Extension Department in the 1950s and early 1960s, the most important Canadian training programme was at Antigonish. The remarkable burst of co-operative enthusiasm around Antigonish during the 1930s embraced the cause of international co-operative development, especially credit union development, in that period. In part, this was possible because of the publicity given Antigonish by Roman Catholic networks around the world, even though the programme was open to non-Catholics, many of whom attended. In part, the message became known because of the notable group of talented men and women in the small Nova Scotia community. By the 1950s, Moses Coady had taken on some of the attributes of a saint: magisterial, passionately committed, philosophical and yet approachable, he became arguably one of Canada's best-known citizens internationally, just as Antigonish became one of the country's best-known places. Coady was always in demand as a speaker, and he travelled widely in North America — from the United Nations in New York to a fishing co-operative in Prince Rupert on Canada's west coast — to promote "the co-operative way".

A steady trickle of visitors and students came to Antigonish after World War II. By the later 1950s the trickle had grown into an annual stream of co-operative and community activists. In 1959, a few months after Coady's death, the university opened a new building to house the Coady International Institute, an organization devoted to training people from outside Canada in the essence of "the Antigonish

approach". For a number of years, staff of the World Extension Department lectured in the courses at the institute; afterward, they would typically welcome graduating students to Madison for further training.

Between 1959 and 1964 the Coady Institute trained over 2,000 people in how to use adult education to build communities, primarily through co-operatives and, especially, credit unions. The impact of these trained leaders within African, Asian and Latin American credit union movements was considerable, in some national movements even pervasive, especially in the 1960s. Many of them made remarkable contributions at the national level in countries where the department undertook its work.

The Antigonish influence was strong because it offered an effective kind of community development through adult education. Its emphasis on study groups, as careful preparation for its brand of adult education, had a very broad appeal in international co-operative circles during the late 1950s and 1960s. Many European movements, but especially those in Scandinavia, built or expanded co-operative colleges during that period; they assisted overseas countries, notably in Africa, to build similar institutions. Many of the educational activities undertaken by the department were centred in these colleges, even though there were some fundamental differences between the Scandinavian and the mainstream North American credit union approaches to co-operative development.

The burst of co-operative educational activities helped create an extensive range of new support materials — books, pamphlets, film strips, slides, films and workshop handouts prepared in considerable numbers. People trained in the methods of adult education, armed with the new media (whenever possible), Gestetners (a kind of duplication machine) and flip charts, became commonplace in the co-operative and credit union movements in the developed world; almost simultaneously they became evident in the new programmes in the developing world. The department would become one of the most effective proponents of the new educational approaches, largely because the training of leaders was so fundamentally important to the success of local credit unions and because the adult education traditions of the 1930s had become so ingrained.

The international development programmes that emerged in the 1950s tended to emphasize community development. That meant programmes with broad social as well as economic objectives; for some people involved in aid programmes, it also meant political objectives aimed at the total restructuring of economically underdeveloped societies. That broad, diffused approach — as opposed to a narrower approach emphasizing the building of strong economic institutions — became an issue of growing importance and considerable debate as the 1950s came to an end.

As in the building of the movements in the United States and Canada, the expansion of the international movement from 1954 onward required the assistance of a strong, supportive network. One developing network consisted of individuals who contacted the World Extension Department or who visited Madison or state leagues because they had heard of credit unions and wondered if they might be useful in their own societies. The department kept careful records of these visitors and successfully enlisted their support when it came time to start work overseas, especially in the Caribbean and Africa.[99] While immensely valuable, by itself that network could grow only slowly and haphazardly, and by its nature was too gradual and accidental to be the central network for growth.

Another network consisted of public servants, from New South Wales in Australia to the Philippines to Puerto Rico to Ghana, who wondered if credit unions might be useful tools for development. This network, which could be very useful and would become more so in the 1970s, nevertheless had its problems. Many public servants already had responsibilities for existing co-operative endeavours; naturally enough, they would often carefully protect these activities from any new form of co-operative enterprise, especially one that argued strongly against a powerful role for governments in co-operative affairs.

Ultimately, the most important network of all was within the American and Canadian movements and included volunteers and employees who were interested in expanding the international movement overseas. The most interested and powerful of these individuals were involved in the World Extension Development Committee, a group that regularly reviewed the department's activities and sought assistance from within the movement. In addition, there were individuals scattered across the two national movements — in states like Michigan, Illinois, Texas, Minnesota and California, and in provinces like British Columbia, Ontario and Saskatchewan — who supported the department's programmes. This group, however, was not large in the beginning and required careful attention before it achieved the size and influence that the department required.

The Roman Catholic Church provided the network of greatest immediate importance during the department's early years. The church's interest was the natural continuation of its deepening concern about social justice issues evident since the late nineteenth century. It was also stimulated by the work of Pope John XXIII, who had grown up on a poor Italian farm and had written passionately about the plight of the rural poor, especially in a 1961 encyclical, *Mater et Magister*; in it, and in some of his other pronouncements, Pope John urged support for self-help organizations and argued for permissive legislation for co-operative institutions. His work encouraged a generation of priests and nuns angry at the poverty they saw around them in parishes all over the world.

It seems impossible to find an emerging movement in the 1950s and 1960s that did not have powerful leaders from the Roman Catholic Church. Rarely does one find a picture of a significant credit union meeting in those years in which priests or nuns were not present. There were few educational programmes that did not owe something to a Roman Catholic institution — the venue, the publications, the educator, sometimes all three. Nowhere was the role of the church more evident than in the Caribbean where the movement made significant headway during the 1950s. In British Honduras (now Belize), which was associated more with the islands than with its mainland neighbours because of the British imperial connection, the key early momentum came from the church, Anglican as well as Roman Catholic.[100]

THE CARIBBEAN

In Dominica, the movement was started in 1951 through the efforts of a Roman Catholic nun from Belgium, Sister Alicia De Tremmerie; by the end of the decade it had grown to twenty societies with 7,500 members.[101] Another key figure in the Dominican movement's early history was Harvey "Pablo" Steele. Born in eastern Nova Scotia, Steele had been a student and participant in the Antigonish movement during its halcyon days in the Great Depression. He joined the Scarboro Fathers, based in Toronto, and went to China in late 1938. There, he barely escaped imprisonment by the occupying Japanese and escaped to India, where he became a chaplain in the Allied forces under General Stilwell. In 1946, he became a missionary in the Dominican Republic, where he devoted much of his time to the formation of credit unions and other co-operatives.

In his work Steele sought to replicate what he had known in Antigonish. He was also much influenced by what he had observed of an Indian co-operative movement located in and around the region of Chota-Nagpur, 300 miles from Calcutta; it had been started by a Belgian priest, Constant Lievens, at the turn of the century.[102] Steele helped train a number of people in

Credit unions became well known in the Caribbean region through meetings of co-operative organizations, such as this meeting of the Caribbean Co-operative Confederation in Puerto Rico in 1959. Father John P. Sullivan is in the front row; immediately behind him is Olaf Spetland. (COURTESY OF CUNA)

the Dominican Republic in both general co-operative as well as credit union work; by 1954 he and his associates had started a flourishing co-operative movement before it was harshly limited by the government of General Rafael Trujillo in 1959. During the following seven years, the country was traumatized by a civil war and the fall of no less than six governments. Amid the turmoil, much of the general co-operative movement disappeared, but the credit union movement survived and gained new momentum in the 1970s. Steele returned to Canada in 1961, and two years later moved to Panama to start a co-operative training centre, the Inter-American Co-operative Institute. In Panama he and the institute would work with the World Extension Department to some extent, educating volunteers about the philosophy of the credit union/co-operative movement and training people for management.

Intellectually, Steele was an example of what was called at the time "the radical centre". In other words, he was repelled by aspects of both capitalism and Marxism. He thought the underlying materialism found in both camps was wrong, and he believed passionately in the capacity of people to build a more equitable world. Steele was opposed to violent revolution but he believed in the necessity and desirability of radical political and economic change. A striking figure with piercing eyes and a mane of white hair, he was a splendid orator who disturbed people intentionally; he was a useful ally but also a man who sparked considerable controversy most of his life. At a local level, there would be many like him in the 1970s.

The movement in the Caribbean during the early years consisted of small credit unions scattered over some twelve islands. By the end of 1962 there were 406 credit unions in the region, 117 of them in Jamaica, 208 in Trinidad and Tobago; in each of the remaining ten islands there were between one and nineteen. Many of the credit unions were small, typically with a few score members and only $2,000 to $3,000 in assets. All told, the Caribbean credit unions served about 62,000 members and had about $6,000,000 in assets. As they grew in numbers and sophistication, they developed their own leaders and became less reliant upon church support and leadership. They also became increasingly associated with the civil servants responsible for their supervision; indeed, one of their challenges was not to become too close and too dependent.

Despite the preponderance of small credit unions, and the inevitable limits on surplus funds that this meant, in 1956 the credit unions on the islands decided, with the support of the World Extension Department, to form a confederation. Called the West Indian Confederation of Credit Unions, it was established by credit union groups in the former British Caribbean colonies. The Jamaican movement was the most prominent force in the confederation, being the first movement outside of North America to affiliate with CUNA International and taking a leadership role in assisting credit union development on several other islands. The movement in Trinidad and Tobago also played an important role from the beginning.

The confederation's office was originally located in Kingston, and Paddy Bailey's main task as an extension department employee when he came on staff in the summer of 1957 was to help with its development. He and the confederation had a challenging constituency to serve. It included islands with populations as low as 13,000 and areas as small as 50 square miles, others with populations of 150,000 and areas of 4,400 square miles.[103] The confederation was

A.A. "Paddy" Bailey in conversation with Father John P. Sullivan, his mentor from Jamaica. (COURTESY OF CUNA)

confronted, therefore, by dramatically different situations in numerous communities scattered over considerable distances and populated by people of significantly different backgrounds and circumstances.

In addition to these geographical, cultural and economic differences, the West Indian confederation was also hindered by the failure of the former British colonies to form a political union in the 1960s. That union might have facilitated the formation of a stronger central organization. On the other hand, this failure encouraged the confederation to reach out beyond the limitations of the old British imperial system to embrace credit unions on islands not formerly controlled by Britain. The future would nevertheless be complex as the confederation struggled to find the resources to serve a growing number of credit unions, most of which had little left over to support initiatives beyond their own communities and most obvious needs.

LATIN AMERICA

Aside from the Caribbean, the region receiving the most attention from the mid-1950s and through the 1960s was Latin America. Although there had been efforts as early as the late 1930s, the movement really began in South America in 1955, when Father Daniel McLellan, a Maryknoll missionary from Denver, Colorado, went to the Peruvian village of Puno on the shore of Lake Titicaca in the Andes. At first ignored by the people of the community, McLellan gained their attention by using skills he had learned as a boxer to fight a bull,[104] an episode that was subsequently vividly described in articles published in *The Reader's Digest* and *The Saturday Evening Post*. The articles had an unanticipated result: they helped significantly in gathering support from American and Canadian credit unionists for overseas programmes, particularly in Latin America.

McLellan initiated a series of study sessions on credit unions, using materials from the World Extension Department as well as from St. Francis Xavier University. The credit union he helped form rapidly became a remarkable success, financing taxicabs for members, building a large co-operative housing project, and sponsoring an extensive educational programme.

In 1957 and 1958 WED provided McLellan with an assistant who prepared educational materials, operated training sessions and advised on appropriate legislation. Within five years the Puno credit union had amassed assets of some $325,000, a remarkable sum, given that the average annual income of the community — and most of its members — was $200 per year. More importantly, McLellan, his CUNA assistant and a growing number of experienced and resourceful Peruvian leaders built upon this successful beginning to create a national movement that within five years boasted 240 credit unions and a membership of 40,000.[105]

Father Daniel McLellan, promoter of Peruvian credit unions, whose bull-fighting prowess made him well known in the United States and Canada.
(Courtesy of CUNA)

As the 1950s came to an end, the Peruvian movement was widely publicized as a successful example of what credit unions could do in a developing country. Started as a reaction to abject poverty, the movement attracted support because of growing resentment among the Peruvian people, in part because of a land system that restricted ownership and institutionalized pauperism. More significantly, and somewhat ambivalently, credit unions were associated with the tensions inevitable in an economy that was being modernized at a rapid rate. In some ways, they were reactions to the harshness of some of the changes but, by amassing the capital that made changes possible, they were also contributing to the transformation of the communities in which they existed. Credit unions must look forward as well as backward: if they fail to do either, their success — in the fullest sense — will be less than it ought to be.

In 1958, with donations from the United States and local credit unions, the Peruvian movement established a training centre at San Marcos University in Lima. It was both an educational institution that helped elected people and secretary-treasurers learn how to manage their credit unions and a human development centre concerned with the empowerment of ordinary people. The centre soon attracted a dynamic group of Peruvian enthusiasts who became missionaries for the credit union message. By 1963, with the help of their foreign benefactors, they had developed a movement with over 300 credit unions and some 96,000 members.[106]

The experiment in Peru was instrumental in galvanizing support for Latin American programmes in the United States and Canada. Reports of its progress were features of the annual meetings of CUNA in the 1950s, and several leagues, through the department or through independent initiatives, contributed to its growth. In 1961, American Vice-President Hubert Humphrey, after attending the first Inter-American Congress of Co-operatives in Bogota, went on to Peru, where he visited Puno. Deeply impressed by what he saw, he came home determined to promote credit unions and other kinds of co-operatives within the American international assistance programme. He would soon find an opportunity to do so.

The Colombian movement also had its beginnings in the 1950s. Many of the early leaders were priests, notably the

Jesuit Francisco Xavier Mejia, who visited Madison, as did Carlos Julio Nino, another key early leader. The Colombian movement was one of the first in the region to attempt the creation of a national federation. In 1959, following tours by Spetland and Matos and another by Alfonzo Verduzco, then manager of a WED office in Mexico, the leaders of the Colombian movement laid plans for the establishment of a federation, the Colombia Credit Union League (UCONAL).

The Mexican credit union movement owed much of its early success to the efforts of well-meaning clergy and several charitable organizations. In fact, the charitable dimensions were so emphasized that the movement did not develop an effective management cadre for some time, suffering from a lack of stability, too great a reliance on inadequately prepared volunteers, and an unengaged membership.[107] Nevertheless, by 1960 there were over 275 credit unions in Mexico with a membership of 30,000.[108] Unfortunately, they lacked a sound legislative framework within which to function, and they were unable to move easily to the next stage of national co-ordination.

Credit union development began in Brazil and Venezuela in 1959, when the World Extension Department started to work with government officials in the training of volunteer leaders. The situation in Brazil was complex. In part the Brazilian movement reflected indigenous co-operative traditions, but it was also based on the co-operative experience of Portugal and some Mediterranean countries. Those European traditions encouraged a broad community focus, a deep commitment to the principle of mutuality and a strong belief in charity. Brazil also had a strong co-operative movement that carefully protected its autonomy and did not readily welcome foreign initiatives, at least at that time.

Given the differences and complexities, it was inevitable that the leaders of the various Latin American movements would want to create their own confederation. They started to do so in the 1950s, and an early association was formed in 1959. Even more than the Caribbean confederation, it served a remarkably diverse group of credit unions that reflected differing cultural backgrounds, varying economic situations and competing political associations. It was even more ambitious than the Caribbean initiative and suffered from the same basic problem: the grassroots credit unions were hard pressed to find the funds to support the confederation's expenses.

AFRICA

By the 1950s Africa was becoming increasingly important as an independent voice in the global community. The hold of the European imperial powers was in decline: the German empire was already gone, and the British, French and Dutch empires were being shaken by independence movements. Within a few years they too would finally disappear. As the independence movements flourished they found themselves drawn into the Cold War struggles; indeed, many of the new African leaders became particularly adept at playing one side off against the other, especially when it came to securing aid.

The emergence of credit unions in Africa was inevitably affected by the rise of African nationalism and particularly African socialism. There was no single generally accepted definition of African socialism at the time, nor can one be identified with the passage of the years. It included people who were influenced by Marxism, those who were committed supporters of an extensive welfare state, those who sought a particularly "African" way to synthesize the great European ideologies of the nineteenth century, and those who sought to resolve contemporary problems through a revival of ancient communal traditions. African socialism included such diverse people as Jomo Kenyatta, Julius Nyerere, Tom Mboya and Kwame Nkrumah; it sought to suit people as different as the Bantu, Ashanti and Ibo.

Ironically, credit unions were also extensions of the imperial experience into the present. Most of the powers in Africa since the turn of the century had encouraged some type of co-operative banking, generally in connection with efforts to develop marketing co-operatives. For the most part, they preferred the introduction of savings and thrift societies under fairly rigid, centralized government influence; apparently without exception, they did not insist that these societies be based upon strong member control.

The main development of savings and thrift co-operatives, however, occurred after World War II, when imperial powers, development agencies and incipient nationalist organizations turned their attention, in different ways, to the issue of how to cope with poverty and population problems in the "Third World". Deciding that one of the important keys to resolving these issues was credit, they gave increased emphasis to savings and thrift societies.

In Nigeria, a locally based co-operative banking system was created in the years 1951 to 1953. By the early 1960s, it had a reported 1,300 societies under the general supervision of the national government. In Uganda, co-operative savings and thrift societies started to appear in 1946, primarily, it would appear, to serve non-Africans;[109] they numbered in the hundreds by the 1950s. Similarly, in Tanganyika there was at least one financial co-operative serving settlers prior to 1954.[110] The numbers of thrift and credit societies would grow even faster as these countries escaped from European control.

The first continuing credit union in Africa was probably formed at Jirapa in northwestern Ghana in September 1955, founded by Father J. McNulty, a White Father from Scotland. Over the next fifteen years more than eighteen other credit unions were formed in Ghana, largely through the networks associated with the Roman Catholic Church. Shortly thereafter missionaries helped start credit unions in Nigeria and Sierra Leone. By the early 1950s there was also considerable interest in Tanganyika, Kenya, the Belgian Congo and Uganda. These beginnings would lead to extensive work in Africa by the World Extension Department in the 1950s and subsequent decades.

THE PACIFIC

Meanwhile, missionaries were also actively promoting credit unions in the Pacific during the 1950s. In January 1954, the indefatigable Father Marion Ganey arrived in Fiji at the invitation of the governor, Sir Ronald Garvey, who had moved to the island from British Honduras. Garvey's interest in credit unions had been sparked by the concerns of Ratu Sir Lala Sukuna, the most influential "Chief of the Land", who held the government post of Secretary of Fijian Affairs. Sukuna had told Garvey that the lack of savings was one of the most important obstacles to the development of a modern economy in Fiji.[111] In traditional Fijian society, for example, people lived in family groups bound together in clans headed by powerful patriarchs. They possessed little in the way of private property, and wealth was calculated in terms of yams, mats and tapa. Thus, as the market economy began to develop, conventional "western" saving was initially regarded as a kind of hoarding and of limited importance to life's chief events — birth, marriage and death. If a modern market economy was to be established, this attitude toward saving and lending would have to change.

The change began in the sugar industry. The development of that industry, which was fundamental to the nation's economy, meant that local farmers had to have access to credit at reasonable costs. Consequently, in 1947 a Co-operative Act was passed to enable the formation of thrift and credit co-operatives. The first society, formed in 1954 at Votualevu, Nadi, soon became a model adopted by people in some 150 other communities. Most of the new societies were restricted to the sugar-producing region, and the government wanted to see the development of credit unions in other areas. It showed its good faith by providing a grant of £5,000 and passing a separate Credit Union Ordinance.

Within a few months of Ganey's 1954 arrival in Fiji, he had sparked the formation of the first credit union, as distinguished from a savings and loan society. Located in the village of Kalokollevu near Suva, it was called the Bergengren Credit Union. From the beginning, its activities helped train a number of Fijian leaders for the national movement, particularly Ioane (Jone) Naisara. Using the connections of the Roman Catholic Church, these leaders created an extensive grassroots movement that spread quickly through the Fijian village system. In fact, it was arguably embraced with too much enthusiasm, because it led to the formation of a great number of credit unions, many of which would soon prove to be too small to be reasonably efficient. To meet the demand for education, a league was formed with Marion Ganey as its first managing director. By 1957, 231 credit unions had been formed, with over 24,000 members and assets of £139,000.

Word of the success of the Fijian movement soon spread to nearby islands. In 1957 Ganey travelled to Samoa, where he helped organize nine credit unions in six months.

Building a stable movement in Samoa was difficult because of the shortage of trained people, typically the most common problem credit union movements confront in their formative years.

AUSTRALIA

To the south, the movement in Australia, now a decade into its development, was beginning to show some of the characteristics of the older North American movements. In 1956 the credit unions in New South Wales had formed a Savings and Loan Co-operative Association to provide loan syndication and support activities. By 1962 there were 126 credit unions in New South Wales and 36 in Victoria. The Australian movement made concerted efforts to establish close ties with North America during the 1950s. Representatives from Australia regularly attended CUNA gatherings, some at their own expense, others with the assistance of the Australian movement. During their visits, they typically spent time with several state and provincial credit unions. In 1957, Olaf Spetland visited Australia; the next year, two Australians, Clarence Murphy and Keith Young, spent several months in Madison and then went on to visit credit unions in several other states and Canadian provinces.[112] Despite the distances involved, the Australian movement was closely tied to North America from its earliest years. A particularly strong connection was forged between credit unions in Victoria and credit union leaders in British Columbia.

ASIA

As the 1950s came to an end, interest in credit unions gathered momentum in Asia. A series of visits by Olaf Spetland, Carlos Matos and some of the elected leaders helped spark interest in the late 1950s and early 1960s, particularly a tour organized by Matos in 1957. There was also a growing volume of communications between the Madison office and Asian enthusiasts, particularly in Korea, Thailand and Malaya.

In 1953, Father Charles J. Young, after training in Canada, started a credit union in what would become Bangladesh. Two years later, the Christian Credit Union was established in Dhaka and it helped credit unions in nearby communities.[113] That same year saw the formation of the first credit union in the Philippines since the end of the war; within two years another 159 had been created.[114]

In the latter part of 1957 the Korean Committee on Voluntary Agencies met in New York City to discuss what could be done for the 25,000,000 refugees in South Korea. Participants discussed the possibilities of encouraging credit unions and other kinds of co-operatives. Following the meeting, Sister Mary Gabriella Mulherin, a Maryknoll nun from Scranton, Pennsylvania, who had worked in Korea and seen the poverty that had resulted from the war, went to Antigonish to study its extension programme. Returning to Korea, she recruited a group of Korean leaders, including Kang Jyung Tyul (Augustine Kang), Lee Sang Ho and Park Hee Sup Ho to start the movement. In 1960 they created the Holy Family Credit Union in Pusan. It was the beginning of what would become one of the most remarkable national movements in credit union history.

Indonesia had perhaps the most complex beginnings of any Asian movement. During the Japanese occupation, what had been a strong co-operative movement was obliterated. When Indonesia gained independence from all foreign control in 1949, the left-leaning government envisioned resuscitation of the national economy, with considerable emphasis on co-operative endeavours. The government was particularly concerned about the plight of the native Melanesians, who were less well off than their Chinese, Indian and Dutch compatriots;[115] for that reason, they became particularly important in the movement as it emerged. During the early 1950s the credit union idea received wide publicity in Indonesia and would lead to considerable growth in the 1960s.

Given all this interest throughout the region, the World Extension Department and CUNA saw the need to do more, even though resources were limited. In May 1958, CUNA passed a resolution that accepted credit unions from anywhere in the Eastern Hemisphere; the movement had become genuinely worldwide in scope. In 1961, the department organized its first Asian seminar in Bagio City, the Philippines; it was the beginning of what would be important efforts by the department in Asia during the 1960s and especially the 1970s.

IRELAND

At the same time as all the activity was beginning in Latin America, Africa and Asia, the department turned its attention to Europe. Most importantly, it was in contact with people in Ireland, where the 1950s were not proving to be kind. A depression lasted for most of the decade, meaning that unemployment soared while most of yet another generation emigrated to other countries. Poor people had virtually no access to credit, except from family and illegal moneylenders. At the same time, those with some income were learning that the "hire purchase" and credit card systems could be a curse. In large part, the credit union movement was a reaction to such economic and social problems.

The credit union system was also a child of Irish nationalism and pride. As Ireland (or at least the southern twenty-six counties) severed its last ties with the United Kingdom in 1948, many Irish leaders became concerned that freedom from Britain would lead to just another kind of domination: the British would be replaced by either the increased control of foreign corporations or the emergence of a communist state. They sought a different alternative, one that emphasized co-operative ownership. Their views echoed a long history of involvement with co-operatives that went back to the later nineteenth century, when Horace Plunkett and George W. Russell fashioned a powerful co-operative movement in the Irish countryside. Russell, better known as "A.E.", joined Plunkett's Irish Agricultural Organization Society in 1896 and spent much of the next eighteen years promoting the development of village banks organized on the model of the Raiffeisen system, particularly in western Ireland.[116]

Russell's work, along with that of R.A. Anderson and Plunkett himself, produced a vibrant co-operative banking sector in Ireland in the years before World War I. By 1908, 268 co-operative banks had been formed throughout Ireland, with over 17,000 members and loans outstanding of £53,000. Unfortunately, in the economic and political uncertainties after World War I the movement collapsed; only 138 banks survived, leaving a co-operative banking movement with a bad reputation, one that persisted even into the 1950s. These historic problems inhibited the development of credit unions for more than a decade.

As in so many other countries, much of the initial promotion of co-operatives, especially credit unions, in Ireland came from men and women involved in adult education and influenced by the social teachings of the Roman Catholic Church. In 1948 the Board of Extra Mural Studies at University College, Dublin, started its first programme in adult education; it led to a Diploma in Social and Economic Studies. Most of the students were sponsored by the trade union movement, and within a year some of the courses were exploring the possibilities of the co-operative movement. Three particularly important individuals attended the 1948 programme and continued their studies for more than five years: Nora Herlihy, Seamus MacEoin and Sean Forde: in time, these three would be recognized as the founders of the Irish credit union movement.

Nora Herlihy, a Dublin teacher, grew up in the community of Ballydesmond in County Cork, where she had witnessed widespread unemployment in her youth and seen the necessary emigration of most of the people in her generation. The plight of

Pioneers of the Irish credit union movement. Sean Forde is seated second from left; Seamus MacEoin is immediately behind him; Nora Herlihy is seated on the far right. (COURTESY OF CUNA)

that community became an important impetus for her credit union work. Like many of her associates, Herlihy always maintained a strong commitment to the importance of "community", by which she meant not just a physical place but also "a sense of belonging, of caring, of supporting all [that] brings a sense of hope to the residents".[117] That kind of commitment, along with a passionate belief in the possibilities of democracy, became the most important features of the Irish movement; they made Irish credit unions the most determined and effective proponents of the value of the populist credit union.

The credit union movement emerged in Ireland in the wake of a partly successful attempt to form a co-operative store and a worker co-operative in Dublin in 1954. Intrigued by the challenge of finding capital for co-operative and other community-based enterprises, Herlihy explored the possibilities of forming a credit union. She secured information from the CUNA offices in Madison and started to study the philosophy and structures of credit unions. In 1955, when she learned that Joseph Collerain, the founder-treasurer of the Humble Oil Company Employees Credit Union in Texas, was visiting Ireland, she arranged for him to speak to the Irish National Co-operative Council. Collerain spoke with great passion about the accomplishments of his credit union, concluding with the proclamation that one of the objectives of credit unions was "to make the market-place a fit place for Christ to walk in".[118]

As an enthusiast for adult education, Herlihy was irresistibly drawn to the thought and practices of the Nova Scotian movement; she obtained some of the writings of Moses Coady and other Antigonish leaders. Indeed, the Irish movement became perhaps the truest continuing crusaders in the northern parts of the world for the tradition started among Scottish- and Irish-Canadians in Atlantic Canada during the 1930s.

In 1957, the Irish credit union enthusiasts who were associated with the National Co-operative Council organized the Credit Union Extension Service. One year later Cumann Muintir Dun Oir (Donore Credit Union) and Comhar Creidmheasa Dun Laoghaire (Dun Loaghaire Credit Union) were formed,[119] and in 1960 the Irish movement formed the Irish Credit Union League (changed in 1972 to the Irish League of Credit Unions). By 1970 there were 366 credit unions with over 222,000 members and over IR£12,000,000 in assets.[120] One of the credit union world's most distinctive movements had been formed; it would soon make itself heard.

NORTH AMERICA

Meanwhile, back in the United States and Canada, the movement was undergoing remarkable change, the most obvious being growth. In the United States between 1954 and 1961, the number of credit unions increased from 15,000 to 20,600, the number of members from 15,000,000 to 20,600,000, and the assets from $2,270,000,000US to nearly $6,400,000,000US.[121] In Canada during the same years, the number of credit unions increased from 4,000 to 4,600; the number of members went from 1,700,000 to 2,700,000 while assets grew from $600,000,000US to $1,500,000,000US.[122] The growth included credit unions of all types, but the division between American and Canadian credit unions, generally

St. Louis Parish Credit Union, Waterloo, Ontario, Canada, 1954. As in many credit unions during the early years, in North America and elsewhere, much of the daily work was done by women. (COURTESY OF CUNA)

between closed-bond and community credit unions, widened. Beneath that division, however, was a remarkable similarity in entrepreneurial spirit and restless pursuit of growth. In the case of some leaders and organizations, it seemed to be growth for its own sake and not for some deeper purpose.

As the two movements grew, all five of the spheres within which credit unions function were disturbed: the way they related to members was transformed; the ways in which they thought about community were simultaneously less clear and broader; the ways in which they related to the state became more complex; the national structures experienced considerable pressure for reform; and management systems were altered as new technologies were added and expertise changed. Growth brought its own demands, making reform necessary and disturbing old relationships. Most importantly, and as always, growth was exacting its own price.

Changes in relationships with members and in management styles and techniques were most obvious in the larger credit unions. As they grew, the qualifications necessary for managers began to change. Accountants, who had once been rare in credit unions, had become commonplace in all except the small ones. Managers, who were once largely "home grown", increasingly were professional bankers trained in other kinds of financial institutions. Members, who were once known personally to employees and managers, were now becoming increasingly anonymous. Where informal word of mouth had once been the normal way to attract members, marketing and advertising became the norm. Whereas volunteers, perhaps meeting as often as weekly, had once provided most of the labour, paid and (quite often) unionized staff had now become crucially important.

Many larger credit unions also became different places. Some of them moved out of workplaces and downtown back streets to main streets. Their architecture tended to mimic that of other financial institutions. New technologies, especially bookkeeping machines, transformed interiors, creating "teller" lines and segregated offices. The professional training of staff increased the likelihood of reliable service but could devalue informal contacts. In short, considerable segments of the American and Canadian movements were changing from populist to managerial credit unions.

In the 1950s "teller" lines became commonplace in many American and Canadian credit unions, such as in this Teamsters' Credit Union. (COURTESY OF CUNA)

The managerial phase can be thought of as a period when more bureaucratic and professional leaders assume dominance within credit unions. It is a phase in which professional leaders, accountants, lenders and machine operators become more important. It requires leaders who are technically sophisticated but not necessarily committed to the hurly-burly of organizational activities; they will typically be more comfortable with balance sheets than member meetings. It means careful attention to bookkeeping, rigorous lending policies and careful management of assets.

Moving from the populist to managerial cultures within the large American and Canadian credit unions was not so much a revolution as a slow and sometimes painful evolution, affecting different credit unions in different ways and at different rates. For the most committed credit unionists, moreover, the challenge was not whether to choose one culture over the other: it was how to put the "old wine" of the formative years into the "new bottles" of the emerging managerial systems. Or, stated a little differently, it was facing the perennial challenge of all co-operative organizations: how to retain social purpose and yet run effective business organizations, especially as the stakes grew larger. It was not an easy task, but it attracted the best minds and the most committed credit unionists in the 1940s and 1950s — and afterward.

One manifestation of the change was that the role of the secretary-treasurer evolved. Significantly, in larger credit unions the manager was replaced by a general manager and would soon give way to a chief executive officer; these titles themselves suggest a changing relationship. Some of the larger credit union managers and boards, convinced that they had unique problems, began to meet, especially in the United States. Similarly, the managing directors of the leagues, building upon the organizational work done with their group in the 1940s, became more independent and vocal. The organizational dynamics of an expanding credit union movement and growing credit unions undermined whatever uniformity remained from the time when nearly all credit unions were similar in size and motivated by shared ideals.

The most difficult and obvious problems, however, lay in the way in which the credit unions of the United States and Canada sought to work together. Nationalism was a factor. There was a strong feeling of Canadian nationalism after the war and more than a little anti-Americanism, making it difficult to forge the truly integrated American-Canadian movement that many Americans thought desirable and natural. Moreover, the Canadian movement, reflecting the country's traditional regional and national divisions, had great difficulty achieving a consensus on how the national credit union movement should be organized. All told, Canadians were not the easiest credit unionists with whom to work.

On the other hand, from 1955 to the early 1970s, the American movement was deeply, sometimes it seemed hopelessly, divided. In the winter of 1955-1956 Tom Doig was forced to retire as managing director of CUNA, CUNA Mutual and CUNA Supply because of ill health. Through careful diplomacy and the sheer weight of his personality, he had held together the two different groups in control of the main organizations, CUNA and CUNA Mutual. After Doig's retirement, his carefully controlled balancing of forces disintegrated. The CUNA board preferred one of its former presidents, H.B. Yates, as a replacement. The CUNA Mutual board wanted Charles Eikel, Doig's assistant managing director. Despite painful attempts at compromise, neither board would give in, and the management of the two companies was completely separated. Eikel remained in charge of CUNA Mutual until his retirement in 1973. Yates gave way in 1957 to Vance Austin, who would manage CUNA until Orrin J. Shipe took over in 1961; Shipe, in turn, would hold the office for a decade.

The turmoil created by this power struggle within the American national structures permeated all levels of the two national movements. It meant that the annual elections, especially for the CUNA board, were fiercely contested, in keeping with some of the best — and some of the worst — traditions of American politics: slates were prepared; votes were sought vigorously; speeches were crucially important; partisanship became commonplace; and personal attacks frequent. Canadians and others often held the balance of power and sometimes abused that position. It was a colourful but not always edifying period in credit union history. For recently arrived outsiders from the Caribbean, Latin America and Asia, it must have seemed mysterious, even incomprehensible.

Despite the hurly-burly, the two movements prospered. Surprisingly, too, the national organizations went from strength to strength and dealt with the problems of growth in a generally efficient and effective manner. Even more remarkably, as the turmoil worsened, the World Extension Department was able for the most part to stay above the storm. It managed in those years to help increase the number of credit unions outside the United States and Canada from 700 to over 3,000, membership from 165,000 to 700,000 and assets from $46,000,000US to $55,000,000US.[123]

The department was also essentially in good shape. It had developed a small but efficient staff in Madison, had begun to hire people in other lands, was helping to operate two institutes in Peru and Fiji, had gained the respect of other co-operative organizations, and had developed good relations with the American government. All told, and especially considering the funds at its disposal, it had made a better than commendable beginning. The possibilities had been explored and, in general, they had been explored well.

CHAPTER FIVE

ENTERING THE WORLD OF INTERNATIONAL DEVELOPMENT
1962-1970

... never before have we been blessed with such material wealth, yet never have we been so dependent upon others. This is a time of opportunity and challenge for the cooperative movement. The scene has been set, as it was in Flammersfeld in 1849. The people have been cast, the setting remains basically the same — the pockets of poverty and usury throughout society — a time of opportunity, a time to serve. Will the challenge be met?

Kenneth J. Marin

THE INTERNATIONAL WORK OF THE AMERICAN AND Canadian credit union movements expanded significantly between 1962 and 1970. In the years before 1954, the work had been carried out almost entirely by a few highly committed American and Canadian volunteers; after 1954 only a small coterie of employees was involved, although their contributions remained crucially important. So too was the involvement of volunteers in other lands, mostly people associated with the Roman Catholic Church. Many of the most influential leaders in the emerging national movements were priests, nuns and Roman Catholic lay people, in the beginning most often from the United States, Canada and Ireland. Rather quickly, though, and not always without acrimony, the church leaders were replaced by people drawn from the local community and from both within

and outside the church. That process would accelerate in the 1970s as the movement spread beyond its original networks around the world and as more people took responsibility for the movements in their countries.

Considered another way, most of the leaders in the international movement through to the 1960s were amateurs, in the best meaning of the word. Typically, they were individuals strongly committed to credit union philosophy and influenced by ideals of social justice and stewardship drawn from Christianity and other religions, and from various ideologies. Those commitments, along with the small measure of status sometimes involved, explain why they were willing to donate so much time and effort to the "cause".

This dependence upon amateurs also explains why the emergence of credit unions around the world was initially a matter of chance: until the early 1960s, the creation of credit unions in "overseas" countries depended upon who had met whom, what networks were active and which individuals had influence. Nevertheless, those early experiences established the framework within which the international movement would develop, even after the amateurs were gradually replaced by more professionally trained people.

For example, the movement identified in its earliest years the three main kinds of problems it could help address in the developing parts of the world. First, it would assist people in areas where credit was generally unavailable or could be obtained only on terms that would doom families to generations of indebtedness. Second, it would provide convenient savings facilities readily available to a wide range of people, something that was especially important in parts of the world where a monetized or international market economy was in the process of developing or expanding. Third, it would help counteract a general lack of confidence in any savings institution except the traditional, informal organizations like the *tontine* and *esusu*. In short, the movement would undertake, but on an even more obvious level, the same kinds of tasks it had carried out in the United States and Canada a generation or so earlier.

Although credit unions were at least partial answers to all three problems, it did not mean that developing them would be easy. There would always be, for example, a considerable amount of distrust to overcome, principally for three reasons. First, no matter how dedicated and transparently honest they were, people from the United States, Canada, and indeed all other northern countries, would always be outsiders in southern countries. Given the long history of political, military and economic imperialism from the North against the South, that quality of "outsiderness" was understandable. Second, even the most sensitively developed programmes would always be intrusions. They would invariably create change in a society, if for no other reason than that their success would create economic differences among people. Even the most apolitical organizers were establishing institutions that would always be of interest to government bureaucrats and politicians. Third, and perhaps most difficult of all, no matter how hard they tried to assimilate, in many countries the outside organizers would always appear to be incredibly wealthy and privileged. The complexity of what was being attempted was far greater than anyone appreciated in the early years; it would be incomparably more difficult than the challenges met during the formative period in the United States and Canada.

Yet the rewards could be most satisfying. Removing families from the control of moneylenders created a kind of freedom unprecedented in the experience of many southern peoples in recent generations. In Lima, Manila and Mexico City it meant the opportunity to own a taxicab or to operate a small store. In the agricultural villages of Kenya, the valleys of the Philippines and the hills of Ecuador, it could mean expanding crop production or owning enough livestock to make a decent living. For women almost everywhere, it could mean achieving a kind of economic security they had never known, perhaps through the purchase of a sewing machine or a washing machine. For many younger people, accumulating family financial resources allowed them to find new kinds of work or to pursue educational opportunities that otherwise would have been unattainable. For entire villages, credit unions could lead to employment for a generation in danger of never finding work or of being forced to move to the burgeoning slums on the edges of overcrowded cities.

In its early work overseas, the World Extension Department, naturally enough, projected outward what had been learned about starting a movement in North America, particularly in the United States. That meant, for example, attempting to secure legislation similar to what had been found useful in the 1930s and 1940s: in other words, legislation that suited the idea of credit unionism typical of the formative period. Such legislation would establish the appropriate structure for credit unions by providing for the election of executive, supervisory and educational committees at annual meetings; by requiring regular inspection while assuring independence from government; and by enabling credit unions to own central organizations to meet their educational, stabilizing and support requirements.

Securing such legislation in foreign lands was frequently difficult. In some countries the existing regulations were embedded within co-operative or co-operative and thrift statutes that tried to meet a wide range of purposes. The legislation could be inadequate in its requirement of the diligent management of financial institutions, and could insist upon extensive government control. Some of the incorporating legislation was also very old, going back to the 1920s and even earlier. The laws nevertheless met the needs of many co-operative groups adequately, even very well; changing them would require careful diplomacy so as not to antagonize co-operative groups that should be natural allies of credit union advocates. Lobbying for appropriate legislation was often at least as difficult as it had been when Bergengren was helping to create the legislative framework in the United States and, to a lesser extent, in Canada.

In some countries, particularly in Latin America and Africa, the department found itself at odds with other co-operative development agencies, such as the International Raiffeisen Union, the Scandinavian movements and, to some extent, the Canadian movement. In the case of the Raiffeisen movement, the difference was sometimes over legislation. The Raiffeisen people did not see the need for distinctive statutes; they had been able to develop their domestic system within general banking legislation and saw no need to operate differently overseas. The Scandinavian movement was committed to multi-purpose co-operative entities and did not object to government playing a strong role. The Canadians were generally more sympathetic than the Americans to close collaboration between credit unions and other co-operatives. The department, in fact, could find itself in competitive situations with other co-operative organizations around the world, not the happiest situation.[124]

The department also possessed a strong commitment to creating national and continental federations to serve local credit unions. In part, it was simply carrying forward the preference for federated structures that had been developed over a century of experimentation within the international co-operative movement, including the co-operative banking experience in Germany. Co-operative people had come to favour federated forms because they allowed for, even encouraged, regional and local diversity, a necessity if organizations were to have significant degrees of local control.

In part, WED was reflecting its own experience. The American movement, in particular, had been served well by the federated system. Despite all the tensions, CUNA was more than merely an effective organization; it had been led by capable management and was always able, albeit sometimes painfully, to overcome any of the problems caused by regionalism and the varying sizes of credit unions. It was deceptively difficult, however, to create and foster strong federated systems elsewhere, especially in countries or regions where there were no strong emotional or economic factors drawing people together.

The challenge had first become evident in Canada, where an effective federated system had not been easily achieved, for several reasons: there was no national legislation; there was a clear separation between the English- and French-Canadian movements; there was no national benefactor, like Edward Filene in the United States; efforts to create national unity in the 1940s had failed; and credit unions were drawn together — to the extent that it occurred — through provincial organizations. To CUNA, this meant it had been difficult to absorb the Canadians.

The problem was that despite the weak national focus, many Canadian credit union leaders did not want their leagues to join CUNA on the same basis as their American counterparts, as some American leaders preferred. Most of the Canadian leaders wanted the chance to shape their own national system and, within the limits of regional loyalties and reasonable business efficiency, to create their own national structures. In 1958, in fact, the English-Canadian movement had created the National Association of Canadian Credit Unions (NACCU), an association of leagues affiliated with CUNA. NACCU's chief role was to provide a structure that would encourage a common Canadian perspective within CUNA; it would also undertake common projects such as moving financial resources from one region to another, undertaking joint government lobbying activities, and exploring business or service possibilities.

The creation of NACCU seemed to mean that the affiliated Canadian movement was working toward a solution for the dilemma of how a small national movement could be a part of an international organization overwhelmingly dominated by the much larger American movement. It was natural to try to apply this emerging Canadian model to larger countries and regional groupings elsewhere. In a way, therefore, the drive to create federated structures in other parts of the world in the 1950s, 1960s and 1970s — in the Caribbean, Latin America, Africa and Asia — was a natural extension of what had started in the United States in the 1930s and in Canada during the late 1950s. Natural or not, though, it was an approach that would have its costs and arguably would truncate other, perhaps more appropriate, ways of developing.

During the formative period, the World Extension Department had also started to learn how hard it was to select partners — both at home and in other lands — for its overseas programmes. Despite their many good points, positive contributions and excellent people, development assistance programmes can attract opportunists and incompetents. Choosing good partners was always a difficult challenge, frequently involving the evaluation of people from strikingly different cultures, philosophies and religions.

Moreover, WED was challenged initially by the complexities of comparatively large-scale international assistance programmes: the kind of support they increasingly received from the American and then the Canadian and Australian governments. Knowing how to manage significant human and financial resources over long distances and across national boundaries required considerable skill, much of it learned from experience. In retrospect, given the potential problems, the department steered through the early learning phase virtually untouched, in itself a remarkable accomplishment.

Designing programmes was also a challenge, especially as WED tried to avoid the trap common in many international assistance programmes of the day: allowing the recipients to become too dependent upon aid. All too often in the development assistance programmes of the 1960s, there was a tendency to create organizations or networks of people surviving largely through grantsmanship and not because of the permanent contributions they were making to their peoples and their countries. It was a trap that could be particularly dangerous in financial co-operatives; it was a trap the international credit union movement would not entirely avoid.

All the efforts to create credit union movements in the three main areas of concentration in the 1960s — the Caribbean, Latin America and Africa — were confronted by such difficulties. Typically, they became evident whenever movements went beyond the first, often heady experience of the formative period and started to struggle to achieve stability and permanence. The same pattern would appear in Asia when WED became deeply involved in that region during the 1970s.

The department's initial response to such problems, in keeping with American and Canadian experience, was to concentrate upon the training and education of directors and secretary-treasurers. The department allocated a good part of its limited resources, therefore, to the preparation of educational materials, the sponsorship of conferences and seminars, and the training of secretary-treasurers and directors. Behind

this effort was the belief, which may seem naive in retrospect but was invariably true in practice, that successful credit unions in developing countries were mostly dependent upon appropriately trained leaders and the limited expectations of the members.

Bringing educational and training materials to the people required having trainers and supportive programmes. It meant having expertise readily available whenever credit unions encountered difficulties. That is why WED emphasized national or regional support organizations, usually in the form of leagues. The inevitable problem was that the situations in the two North American countries were significantly different from those in some other parts of the world, most obviously in varying literacy rates, general familiarity with standard business practice and, above all, different cultural traditions. The world would prove to be much more complicated than it had first appeared in the 1950s and early 1960s.

Although the underlying assumptions had been established by the early 1960s, the way credit unions would be encouraged overseas was altered dramatically between 1962 and 1970. The main reason for the change was the significant funding rather suddenly made available by the American and Canadian governments through aid programmes. Managing that funding required a kind of professionalism not necessary before: it attracted people trained in development issues; it meant that the credit union movement would supervise projects like those conducted by other established aid agencies; and it necessitated enhanced standards of accountability. It also meant that the involvement of "amateurs" could only be on a highly selective basis — still important, but less central than they had been.

When John F. Kennedy won the American presidential election in November 1960, it signified an increased interest in Latin America and in international assistance by the United States. Four months after his election, Kennedy proposed an agreement with South American countries called the Alliance for Progress. Signed in August 1961 at Punta del Este, Uruguay, the agreement called for an initial contribution of $500,000,000 from the United States and a total of $20,000,000,000 over the next decade. The money was to be spent on improving conditions of rural life and land use, on housing and community facilities, and on education and public health. The Kennedy administration also helped form and fund the Inter-American Bank, which was intended as the chief instrument for the economic development of the Caribbean and South American regions. Both of these initiatives seemed to invite an increased role for co-operatives; as a result, for the next several years, American aid workers would be engaged in co-operative endeavours throughout Latin America, including many efforts to create credit unions. Most of those efforts would be assisted, if not managed, by the department.

Within the Kennedy administration, Vice-President Hubert Humphrey was the most important proponent of credit unions and co-operatives. A native of Minnesota, Humphrey had political, intellectual and emotional roots in the farmer-labour movement of that state, a movement long associated with co-operative endeavours. Throughout his Washington career, therefore, Humphrey was a continuous supporter of co-operatives, in his characteristically optimistic and enthusiastic way.

Humphrey was also one of the strongest early advocates of the idea of sending young Americans overseas to work for two years in the developing countries, an idea that led to the establishment of the Peace Corps in March 1961. The corps had 1,000 people in the field by year-end; it had another 2,000 abroad by June of 1962. Many members of the corps would work with or for co-operatives. Many would help organize credit unions in Latin America, Africa and Asia.

Humphrey's greatest contribution to the credit union and co-operative movement, however, came when he used his influence to have the Foreign Assistance Act amended in 1961 to "encourage the development and use of co-operatives, credit unions and savings and loans associations" in economically developing countries.[125] This amendment was particularly important as the Kennedy administration placed increased emphasis on aid activities. Specifically, it reconstituted aid programmes previously under the International Cooperative Administration and expanded assistance expenditures under a new agency, the United States Agency for International Development (USAID), within the Department of State. USAID's administrator reported directly to the secretary of state and the president, an indication of its significance within the Kennedy, and later the Johnson, administrations.

Vice-President Hubert Humphrey (centre) meeting with leaders of CUNA International at a dinner marking his contribution to the movement. From left to right: J. Orrin Shipe, James W. Grant, Rod Glen (president of CUNA International), Irwin Rubbalki, Robert Morgan and Elmer Johnson. (COURTESY OF CUNA)

USAID financed and oversaw economic and technical assistance overseas aimed at helping less-developed countries become economically more self-sufficient. It was drawn to credit unions and other forms of co-operatives for its overseas projects, for several reasons: it understood the important role co-operatives had played in the economic and social development of the United States; it was specifically required, by the Humphrey amendment, to encourage co-operative/credit union work; it recognized the economic soundness of many co-operative organizations overseas; it believed that co-operatives could "reach down" into all segments of society; it saw the value of co-operation in overcoming apathy and creating jobs; and it understood their capacity to encourage problem-solving on a local level.[126]

In 1961 USAID organized a Special Advisory Committee on Cooperatives consisting of representatives from the American co-operative sector, including credit unions. The committee became very important to the American co-operative/credit union movement. It was a useful forum through which to gain extensive funds for overseas development projects and to encourage closer working relationships among all kinds of American co-operative organizations. It represented an excellent opportunity to take the credit union movement to the world.

On an emotional and intellectual level, both the American and, indirectly, the Canadian movements were much influenced by the rhetoric and idealism associated with John F. Kennedy. Kennedy spoke frequently on international development, and many of his speeches were widely quoted within credit union and co-operative circles. The most commonly quoted of his challenging comments, however, was the following:

> To those people in the huts and villages across the globe struggling to break the bonds of mass misery, we pledge our best efforts to help them help themselves for whatever period is required — not because the Communists may be doing it, not because we seek their votes, but because it is right. If a free society cannot help the many who are poor, it cannot save the few who are rich.[127]

It was a call for global action that many Americans (and not a few Canadians and Australians) embraced with enthusiasm and passion.

As support for international development grew in the early 1960s, the leadership of CUNA, particularly the president, R.C. Morgan, and Olaf Spetland, sought every opportunity to expand the movement around the world. In the spring of 1961, WED prepared a report on how it envisioned expanding the movement overseas, emphasizing the need to train leaders, to obtain legal recognition for credit unions, to assist directly in the formation of credit unions, to aid in the development of central organizations and to create integrated national movements.

The report recommended the expansion of advisory services through the mail, which by that time were being carried out with people in eighty-five countries. It argued for the increased production of visual aids of various types, especially film strips and films in several languages; the department's first film, "The People of Kolevu", examining the history of the Fijian credit unions, had just been released and was well

received, and it would be followed by several other films. Above all, the report favoured more development of leaders through seminars, on-the-job training, international educational conferences and training at headquarters. It also recommended attracting increasing numbers of people to the United States and Canada annually to receive training.[128] Such visitors had become common by the early 1960s, and they would do much to encourage personal relationships within the international movement over succeeding decades. The report ended by suggesting the expansion of the limited work already underway in Mexico, Panama, the Philippines and Colombia.

The problem was that despite the generosity of some leagues, there were few resources available to do much more. It was even doubtful whether there were sufficient funds to complete what was being undertaken. That is why the possibility of attracting funds from government aid programmes became so important. In 1962 CUNA opened an office in Washington, staffed by Clarence Murphy from the California League. Its general purpose was to monitor the American aid programmes and prepare applications for funding. Murphy, who would remain in charge of the office until 1966, reported directly to the managing director of CUNA; he and his successors did not report to Spetland and his successors in the Madison office.

The primary initial task of the Washington office was to help formulate a plan for the development of credit unions around the world, with a special emphasis on Latin America.[129] Murphy and Spetland worked on the plan through the summer of 1961 and took it to the first Inter-American Congress of Cooperatives, held in Bogota in November, where it was well received by USAID representatives as well as by experts from other development organizations. The plan focused on the creation of self-sufficient movements. It argued that the movements in the West Indies, Peru, Fiji and the Netherlands Antilles were already self-sufficient and that the movements in Brazil, Colombia, Venezuela, Panama, Bolivia, the Philippines, Guatemala and "possibly" Nigeria and Tanganyika soon could be. It advocated strengthening the struggling movements in Chile and Mexico but did not propose undertaking significant work in Asia in the immediate future.

All told, the plan called for the formation of some 5,000 credit unions around the world, with 1,250,000 new members in some 25 countries by 1966. This was a very optimistic plan, based on the work done in the preceding seven years by the department when some 3,000 credit unions had been organized outside the United States and Canada.

In 1962, Jack Dublin from the Michigan League, with funding from USAID, helped develop a more specific plan for Latin America. Following a trip to the region, he proposed the sponsorship of one credit union technical assistant from either the United States or Canada in each of twelve countries. These assistants would work with local leaders — from three to fifteen in each country — teaching them how to organize and develop credit unions.[130] After about seven years the technical

The signing of contracts with USAID. J. Orrin Shipe (left) and N.P. Skow, of USAID, are signing the documents while Olaf Spetland and Robert Bonham, of USAID, look on. (COURTESY OF CUNA)

assistants would turn over all of their responsibilities to the local leaders, an objective predicated on the expectation that significant growth would be secured from the American government and that the Peace Corps would be used to assist in the promotion of credit unions in several countries. The plan was enthusiastically embraced by WED and by the board of CUNA; with a few minor modifications, it was also accepted by USAID.

In implementing the plan, WED successfully applied for assistance from USAID to help establish a more permanent presence in Washington. This was necessary because the office, called the Global Projects Office, needed significantly more resources to liaise effectively with USAID on a regular basis, to make proposals for overseas activities, and to monitor projects as they were developed. The decision to turn the Washington office into an important and continuing operation, while reasonable, also opened up the possibility that the department would be divided between it and the Madison office, although both of them would be under the administration of the managing director of CUNA.

LATIN AMERICA

From 1961 to 1969, the department's first priority was its programme with USAID in Latin America, partly because the American government was expanding on an already declared interest in the region, most obviously in Mexico. The Mexican movement was started in 1950 in Mexico City by Roman Catholic priests. Although no legislative framework was secured and the banks were antagonistic from the beginning, the movement spread to several states through the energies of the Secretario Social Mexicano, a Catholic agency. The resultant credit unions were loosely organized in regional committees called CREVS that tried, with limited success, to provide effective leadership for the movement.

In March 1955, the president of CUNA, Marion Gregory, visited Mexico City, where he met leaders from the *cajas populaires*, as the credit unions were called.[131] Back in the United States Gregory promoted expansion of CUNA to Mexico and other Latin American countries. Later that year, Spetland and Carlos Matos, then a CUNA director from Puerto Rico, visited Mexico as part of a tour of several Latin American countries. Two years later a succession of WED staff started to work in Mexico.

The tour by Spetland and Matos was the beginning of what would be a remarkable burst of credit union activity in Latin America. It had its most immediate impact in Peru, where the two men helped credit union enthusiasts prepare national legislation. The tour also encouraged the formation of study groups in several Central American countries as well as Brazil. The latter effort was financed by the Illinois League, always a strong supporter of international projects. Given this series of successful developments, WED decided, shortly after Spetland and Matos returned, to appoint José Arroyo Riesta of Puerto Rico as its Latin American representative.

The appointment of a Puerto Rican was not accidental. The Puerto Rican movement became one of the most dynamic movements in the Caribbean during the 1950s and the early 1960s. It owed much of its rapid growth to the government, which assigned a number of public servants to the task of starting credit unions on the island. By 1963, they had helped organize over 300 credit unions, 200 of them associated together in the Puerto Rican league. One of the most successful credit unions was started among teachers in 1948; by 1963 it had over 16,000 members and assets of $6,000,000. Virtually all government offices had their own credit unions, and there were many credit unions serving small communities, as well as credit unions in private firms and among church groups. A few specifically served the needs of low-income people, and all were open to people on lower incomes: people ignored by the existing banking system. The Puerto Rican credit unions had a strong social commitment, and they provided members with a wide range of advice on economic and sometimes social issues, in addition to extensive educational programmes.[132]

Initially, Arroyo spent much of his time working with the Mexican movement. Mostly because of the enthusiasm of credit union advocates associated with the Roman Catholic Church, the Mexican movement was growing steadily, despite the absence of national legislation. By 1963, there were 560 credit unions with 38,000 members and savings of 21,000,000

pesos.[133] It was a movement made up of small credit unions almost totally dependent upon volunteer workers and serving the needs of the very poor.

Unfortunately, credit unions in Mexico were poorly integrated, reflecting the varied problems to be found in many Mexican states: bad roads and geographic separation, a weak national banking system, and a population with limited formal education. Moreover, the credit unions had grown too fast and with such diverse leadership that it was very difficult to create unity — a situation at least as challenging as it had been in Canada and the United States. There were immense problems in training the people necessary to guide credit unions into the management phase that typically followed the formative period. The problems were compounded by the continuing failure to extract appropriate legislation from the Mexican government. The only alternative open to WED was to assist in the formation of a national federation, a dubious enterprise given the lack of a national focus and the prevalence of small credit unions with limited financial resources. The problems

J. Orrin Shipe, in conversation with Robert Bonham of USAID, points to Mexico and Central America, site of some of the early USAID-funded initiatives. (COURTESY OF CUNA)

would reaffirm the lesson from the American experience about the importance of starting within the halls of legislatures.[134]

During the 1960s, the Colombian movement made significant progress. By 1964 it had eight employees and a remarkable record of success in organizing credit unions. In 1963, it led the 70 leagues then affiliated with CUNA in the formation of credit unions; by 1964 there were 303 credit unions with 55,000 members and nearly $2,000,000 in assets.[135] The growth had started to move outside the Roman Catholic Church through collaboration with the Labourers Union of Colombia, the Colombian Housing Cooperative and the National Agrarian Federation.[136] Much of the funding for this notable effort came from the American government and CUNA, which also provided some of the expertise, especially in 1962 when WED's Latin American office was located in Medellin.

It was within this context that CUNA signed its first contract — on May 12, 1962 — with USAID to carry out work in Latin America. This was quickly followed by a global contract that over the years would focus on other parts of the world, although it too would include some Task Orders for Latin American projects as well. These contracts ambitiously envisioned attracting 10 percent of the population in selected countries within a ten-year period. That goal suggests the confidence credit union leaders in both the United States and the Latin American countries had in the capacity of organizers to create effective credit unions quickly. Their optimism would prove to be somewhat misplaced, underestimating the complexities in moving organized credit unions into stable, well-managed and continuing organizations.

From the beginning, it was WED's plan that the management of the Latin American projects would be carried out from within Latin America, employing people from the region as much as possible. The department ran its Latin American operations briefly through the office opened in Mexico by Arroyo and managed by Alfonzo Verduzco; it then moved the office to Colombia in 1962 so that it could assist the growing Colombian movement and be closer to the projects financed by USAID. In 1963 the office was moved permanently to Panama City and renamed the Latin America Regional Office. The office grew to include eight technical experts, a publica-

tions department and a supporting staff of variable size to assist with training programmes, one of its main activities.

From early in its history, the office was extensively supervised, in the first instance by both the Madison and Washington offices and in the second by a committee made up of the president and managing director of CUNA as well as the presidents from the Latin American federations accepted as members of CUNA. Between Washington and Panama, CUNA/WED hired an extensive and changing staff to deal specifically with the USAID-financed projects in Latin America. Notable among the early employees were Angel Castro, a co-operative and worker activist from Phoenix, Arizona, Henry Cruz, a Spanish-speaker who had worked briefly in a credit union in Saginaw, Michigan, and Percy Avram, a former co-operative manager from Saskatchewan. These three men would play long and valuable roles in the work in Latin America.

As in the United States and Canada, there were at least three stages through which credit unions seemed to have to go within the developing countries. During the first stage, credit unions had to rely upon the support of a patron, a donor country or the support of their own governments. This was not new; it had been the situation with American and Canadian credit unions in their early years. The more difficult challenge lay in ensuring that dependency did not become ingrained, especially among peoples with very few funds and very limited business experience. There was the added danger that the kinds of well-intentioned people drawn to development work themselves tended to be paternalistic, especially in the early years, when religious and ideological feelings ran high. At times, too, aid programmes, no matter how well monitored, could invite corruption simply because of the amounts of funding involved and the problems of auditing. Fortunately, as in the United States and Canada, the instances of fraud were rare and generally restricted to a few secretary-treasurers and organizers taking out loans or advances beyond their capabilities to repay.

The second stage occurred as credit union movements organized national institutions. That stage had not been easily achieved in the United States and certainly not in Canada. In fact, throughout the 1950s and 1960s both the American and

Canadian movements continued to be embroiled in a series of confrontations over the national structuring of their movements. Similar difficulties were experienced in the Latin American countries, as they would be in Africa. The problem was probably more acute in the overseas movements, however, because so much emphasis had to be placed on national structures at a time when there was little economic power or stability at the base.

The third stage was the creation of continental and international institutions, an issue no less important and difficult for the Americans and Canadians. It, too, was a stage that required considerable thought, some debate, and usually a little turmoil. The problem was that, looking at the international movement as it had evolved, there was one particularly large movement in the United States, two smaller but powerful movements in Canada (only one of which was affiliated), a significantly smaller but ambitious movement in the Caribbean, and emerging movements in many other regions of the world. How did one find an economic formula and a governing structure to reflect this diversity in size, perspective and wealth? How did one create an international governing body that could meet regularly, fund itself and provide effective direction? Such issues became immediately obvious as soon as the department began its serious work in Latin America.

When the department opened its Latin America Regional Office in Panama, it appointed Herbert Wegner as director, a position he would hold until 1970. Wegner came by his credit union background naturally enough: his mother managed a large credit union for California public servants.[137] Between 1959 and 1962 he served as an international relations officer for USAID in Quito, Ecuador, advising on the privatization of government-owned companies. Wegner had then become a special projects officer for the U.S. Peace Corps from 1962 to 1964,[138] during which time he began to have close relationships with the credit union organizers working in Latin America. Under his leadership, the Latin America Regional Office grew quickly and was soon administering nearly $5,000,000US, almost all of it from USAID for projects in Latin America.[139] As the Latin American programme developed, CUNA/USAID gradually handed over more

responsibility for the emerging movements to nationals they had trained in Peru, Colombia, Venezuela, Costa Rica, Ecuador, Panama, Brazil, Nicaragua, Guatemala and Honduras. All told, during the 1960s some 3,000 credit unions were organized in Latin America, with estimated assets by the end of the decade of $180,000,000US.[140]

The training centre established in Lima, Peru, in 1962 played a key role in the early years of CUNA/USAID co-operation. As well as training a generation of Peruvian leaders, the centre brought trainees from several countries to Lima, including people from Ecuador, Colombia, Venezuela, Brazil, Bolivia, Argentina and Uruguay. These trainees then returned to their home communities where they worked with other national leaders and, in many instances, with Peace Corps volunteers to build credit unions.

The association with the Peace Corps began in 1962, with a contract to send thirty volunteers to the Dominican Republic. That project fell through, however, when the government of the Dominican Republic changed its priorities; most of the volunteers trained under this contract were subsequently sent to Peru and Chile.[141] Another contract was signed shortly thereafter to send twenty-six volunteers to Ecuador. They were trained in Madison and then in Puerto Rico where they learned the rudiments of Spanish along with some credit union and general business theory and operating practices. These volunteers were sent to Ecuador — the first "overseas" contingent — in January 1963.

ECUADOR

Ecuador was chosen because credit unions, which had started within the Roman Catholic Church in the 1950s, were on the verge of expansion. USAID representatives had invited Father Dan McLellan to Ecuador in 1961. His visit sparked considerable interest, and USAID opened a credit union promotion office with the assistance of the Catholic Relief Office and the Coady Institute in Nova Scotia. USAID also asked CUNA for help, and it sent Henry Cruz, who worked with Guillermo Freile of USAID, to assist Ecuadorean credit unionists and Peace Corps volunteers to expand the number of credit unions. Together, they built the credit union movement from four in 1961 with 200 members, to 180 in 1966 with 21,000 members.[142]

Most of the earliest credit unions were associated with the church but a growing, and ultimately much larger, number were established in rural areas.[143] The main catalyst for the growth in rural areas was Percy Avram who was sent by CUNA International to Ecuador in 1965. He introduced the concept of the Directed Agricultural Production Programme (DAPP), a programme that linked enhanced credit for farm families with improved crop and livestock production. Avram and the local credit union leaders worked with government agricultural agents to improve production through education about agricultural practice; specifically, these methods advocated scientific soil analyses and the greater use of fertilizers and herbicides. The first credit union using this approach was located in Julio Andrade, and the number of credit unions involved with the programme expanded steadily, reaching 37 by 1968. In 1967, Avram and the Ecuadorean movement sponsored a seminar that attracted credit union leaders from several Latin American countries. Thereafter, the DAPP spread rapidly throughout the Latin American movement, especially through the continuing work of Avram, who was transferred to Panama in 1967, where he remained for three years before moving to Southeast Asia to again introduce the DAPP concept.[144]

The first contingent of Peace Corps volunteers that arrived in Ecuador in 1963 was generally typical of the period. Most of them were trained in the humanities or social science disciplines, although more of them had credit union or business experience than was the case with some of the later contingents. As a group, they tended to be generalists sensitive to local circumstances, aware of the importance of cultural differences and patient in waiting for sustained growth. Those qualities were invaluable in assisting movements during the formative years.

The Peace Corps members were embarking upon a particularly interesting period of their lives. They were entering the exciting world of developmental assistance or foreign aid, then (as now) alive with remarkable complexities, maddening frustrations, impressive accomplishments and occasional corruption. They were drawn to it by the full range of human emotions and ambitions. Generally, they exhibited a high degree of enthusiasm as well as generous amounts of idealism. They brought the usual human frailties along with a varying mix of political commitment and religious conviction. Perhaps above all, they brought youth and vitality: in the words of Jack Vaughan, the regional Peace Corps director and later head of USAID, they were "high thyroid young people who weren't yet draft dodgers who cared and who had a lot of talent".[145] They could be troublesome for administrators, both credit union and government, but they were soon generally appreciated both back home and in the field.

In common with many others involved in the development business during the period, the Peace Corps volunteers did not fully appreciate the complexities involved in introducing outside concepts into other societies around the world. Rarely did they immediately grasp how much of their own attitudes and understanding were deeply grounded in the assumptions of their own societies. Like nearly everyone else, they little comprehended, when they left home, that they would likely end up learning more than the people they were trying to help and teach. They would also have to answer some basic questions largely through experience. For example, was the development of credit unionism in other countries intended to improve communities? Was it intended to develop them? If it was merely to improve, then credit unions would have more limited goals, usually restricted to economic activities. If it was to develop, then it could mean introducing a fairly broad economic and social revolution based upon empowering the masses in all aspects of their lives — economic, social and political. Co-operatives could easily be oriented toward these broader goals and in some places they were: for example, in Nicaragua, Honduras and Peru. It was an approach that was obviously fraught with peril because it could easily lead to a massive intrusion into the political and social life of the society.

The idea that co-operatives, including credit unions, should be focused specifically on improving communities through raising the standard of living of their members was the more common approach. It also carried fewer political risks, both among supporters back at home and particularly within the volatile politics of Latin America. During the 1960s the region was engaged in difficult, divisive and sometimes deadly ideological wars. The rise of Fidel Castro in Cuba and the kind of Marxism he represented alarmed the dominant American interest in the region as well as the more conservative elements of many Latin American nations. At the same time, the region was facing almost insolvable problems: a rapidly expanding population, inequitable land systems, some government corruption, overly powerful armed forces in some countries, restless student bodies and disaffected intelligentsia. Amid all the resultant tensions, anti-Americanism was common, meaning that the Peace Corps volunteers had to work carefully to be successful in their work. Considering the problems they might have encountered, it is somewhat amazing that they, and the credit union movements they helped to start, avoided serious political problems in nearly all countries.

One reason most Peace Corps volunteers generally avoided serious political entanglements was that, like other credit union advocates working in Latin America at the time, they found themselves immersed in small urban neighbourhoods or small rural communities. The earliest volunteers, particularly those who went to Ecuador, worked largely in the cities because of the obvious needs. Latin America was experiencing the beginnings of the rapid urbanization typical of the developing world in the last half of the twentieth century. People, particularly the young, were flooding into the cities looking for work and the excitements of urban life. The results were the expansion of poorer neighbourhoods, an unending need for more employment, and a desperate search for funds for all kinds of purposes; it was not unlike the situation that had spawned co-operatives a century earlier.

Usually working at first through the Roman Catholic Church, the volunteers concentrated upon helping in the organization of new credit unions or in the improvement of existing credit unions. They spent much of their time assisting managers and directors to learn necessary skills, promoting the use of the credit unions, and holding workshops for interested groups. None of these was an easy task; each meant learning a new culture, gaining a better understanding of one's own limitations and, frequently, realizing that what had been automatically accepted in North America made less sense in other parts of the world.

In the rural areas, Peace Corps volunteers spent their time working with *campesinos*, usually in community credit unions. Typically, a rural credit union had only a few score members, even after considerable effort; usually, it measured assets in the hundreds or at most thousands of dollars.[146] Size, however, is always relative, and those credit unions were at least as important to their members as were credit unions of tens or hundreds of millions of dollars in assets to their members in the United States or Canada. Working in rural communities created several challenges for people from North America. Agriculture and its technology were very different from what existed at home. Many of the volunteers, in any event, came from urban areas and knew little about the countryside. Latin American marketing systems were less monetized than in northern industrialized societies, and they were often difficult for outsiders to understand. The roles of moneylenders and middlemen were more obviously exploitive and difficult to dislodge.[147] Moreover, the volunteers stayed in the communities for only two years; the most they could hope to accomplish was to introduce the concept of democratic control and to help leaders learn the rudiments of business practice — in many instances not long after they had learned them themselves. After the promising beginnings, significant development in rural areas would require more permanent and more technical assistance.

In the course of the 1960s over 110 Peace Corps volunteers worked directly with the department in Latin America and the Caribbean. In the middle of the decade, volunteers were also sent to Africa, followed by Asia shortly thereafter. Some of the volunteers stayed involved in development work after their terms ended, perhaps working for USAID where they would become knowledgeable about, and sympathetic to, credit union projects. Others, such as Gordon Hurd, Angel Castro, Chet Aeschliman and Tony Schumacher, to mention just a few, "graduated" from the Peace Corps to work with the department or, as it was subsequently called, CUNA International and the World Council of Credit Unions. These workers would leave a decidedly Peace Corps stamp on the organization. There would always be an emphasis on service, a recognition of the complexity of development programmes, and a wisp of the idealism common within the Peace Corps, especially in its earliest days.

Normally, Peace Corps volunteers were organized into teams that worked in a given country for seven or eight years, although each volunteer normally had no more than a two-year term. After the seven or eight years, support would be withdrawn and the people in the countries involved were expected to be able to carry on with organizational and stabilization work. It was an ambitious approach, placing a premium on organizing new credit unions and creating a critical mass of credit unions quickly.

The association with USAID and the Peace Corps reinforced a natural focus within WED on nationally structured approaches. In common with most governments involved in aid programmes at the time, the American administrations believed in state-to-state assistance programmes. Such programmes showed politicians in a good light, encouraged closer ties among governments and empowered bureaucracies. Unfortunately, they did not always achieve the hoped-for results.[148] Everything depended upon the care with which projects were developed, the integrity of the people involved and the appropriateness of the methods used. Nevertheless, as the lead organization in the American aid programme, USAID was normally required to work with and through governments; its contracts tended to have national objectives, and its results were measured usually through national statistics. That inevitably encouraged a national focus within the credit union movements USAID helped foster.

Moreover, as in the early days of American and Canadian credit unionism, most overseas programmes emphasized the rapid organization and development of credit unions as opposed to gradual, relatively slow growth. The most obvious way to achieve this, indeed the way that had worked so well in the United States, was to create a national team of organizers. Thus, from the beginning, the programme in Latin America, as in other areas where USAID and the Peace Corps connection was strong, emphasized the creation of national credit union support systems. That approach was also in keeping with the "train the trainer" concept very popular at the time in both community development and management training circles. Finally, it conformed with how such organizations as the International Labour Office and the International Co-operative Alliance fostered co-operative development.

Unfortunately, the emphasis on creating credit unions through extensive national programmes left the arguably more difficult issues of stability and viability to be dealt with afterward. Some recognized the potential problems at the time but most did not. As in the mainstream movements in the United States and Canada, especially the latter, a common assumption was that growth, by creating more assets, would resolve many problems. It was an attitude that would subsequently contribute to problems when the era of easy expansionism ended in North America as well as elsewhere.

In 1964, with funding from USAID and using some of its own resources, the department produced a film, "The Small Miracle of Santa Cruz", about a family in an unspecified Latin American village. Faced with an unexpected medical bill for the ailing mother, the family, already in debt to an unsavoury moneylender, faces disaster. Then the father of the family, along with neighbours, hears about credit unions from a CUNA representative. Impressed, the father helps organize a credit union; the family secures a loan at fair interest rates; the community prospers; and the moneylender is banished. It was a movie that jaded 1990s North American audiences might find rather sentimental and propagandist, in the worst sense of the word, but it also had some basis in what actually did happen to families in need in Latin America at the time. Moreover, when the film was shown in other countries, despite the differences in cultures, it was understood and appreciated: while the plot was simple and the characters stark and stereotypical, the story was universal in the developing world at that time — and subsequently. Indeed, it was not without its parallels in some northern industrialized societies if one looked beneath the gloss of consumerism and apparent sophistication.

All told, the Latin American movement expanded remarkably during the period. By 1970 there were fifteen leagues in the region: 950,000 members in 2,949 credit unions with a reported $120,000,000 in assets.[149] They had developed a diverse and capable group of leaders, and there is no doubt that credit unions had "taken hold" in several countries. In 1970, in fact, the movement was showing significant growth, with a 16 percent annual increase in savings.

On the other hand, there was some doubt whether the overall master plan for the region, developed during the period of immense optimism in the early 1960s, was realistic or suffi-ciently sensitive to the outlook of Latin American peoples. By the mid-1960s credit unions in some of the Latin American movements were not paying their dues to their regional orga-nization, partly because they were not strong financially, partly because they saw it essentially as an outpost of the North American (and particularly the American) movements. They knew that most of the outside money came from USAID, not from donations from the North American movements, and that most of the key staff were North Americans.[150] It would take some time, much longer than the enthusiasts early in the decade had expected, before Latin American credit unionists would take control of their own movements.

AFRICA

Interest in creating credit unions in Africa also grew signifi-cantly during the 1960s. Indeed, virtually all sub-Saharan African countries saw the beginnings or the expansion of the movement during the 1960s. The first co-operative savings and thrift society, for example, was formed in Mauritius in 1960; in Lesotho, 1961; Malawi, 1962; Cameroon, 1963; Kenya, 1964, Liberia, 1966; Sierra Leone, 1967 (although there had been some organizational activities prior to 1945); Togo, Zambia and Botswana, 1967; Swaziland and Ethiopia, 1968.[151] The growth rates in these countries differed, but by the later 1960s there were substantial movements on the continent. Nigeria reputedly had some 2,500 societies, although (since they were not well integrated or inspected) that number was probably inflated. There were over 200 in Tanzania, over 60 in Kenya, more than 30 in Lesotho and another 30 in Cameroon.[152]

The overall growth achieved during the 1960s was encour-aging. By 1970 the continent officially had nearly 3,400 credit unions with a membership of 193,000 and assets of $248,000,000US.[153] There were twelve countries with credit union federations and thirteen others with promotion commit-tees. Most of the credit unions were small, both in membership and assets, but they represented considerable potential if the resources and appropriate development strategy could be found. Moreover, during the late 1960s,

expansion spread beyond "Anglophone" Africa into "Francophone" Africa, usually with the assistance of people from the Quebec league and the Desjardins movement.

Inevitably, these emerging movements were caught up in the struggles for independence that swept most parts of Africa in the 1960s. Those confrontations were often violent and bitter, although in some instances the colonizing powers gave way gracefully to what was an inevitable development. In no country, however, was the changeover from imperial masters to national leadership easy; the inherited political and economic frameworks would not permit it. The borders of many new countries, for example, had largely been shaped by the vagaries of imperial politics; they rarely conformed with underlying economic, racial or pre-conquest history. As a result, the political structures were often manufactured and inappropriate. The result was a series of countries ultimately ill-situated to confront easily the demands of a modern indus-trial, let alone post-industrial, world. Many of them would also be difficult countries within which to start and, particularly, to sustain credit union movements.

Many of those in charge as the African nations escaped their European masters were strong advocates of co-operatives. This might — or might not — be helpful when people started to form credit unions. Several of the new leaders were influenced by the writings of Marx, a few had studied in Moscow; they had absorbed, therefore, the co-operative — or, more accu-rately, quasi-co-operative — structures of the Soviet Union, notably in agricultural production and consumer stores. That tradition would rarely be supportive of credit unions or other forms of co-operative banking, especially if they were commu-nity-based and insistent upon independence from the state.

More of the national leaders were influenced by democratic forms of socialism, such as moderate French socialism or the Fabian ideals of the British Labour Party. The Fabian tradition, in particular, with its strong commitment to co-operative forms of development, deeply influenced individuals like Julius Nyerere of Tanzania and Kwame Nkrumah of Ghana. It is not surprising, therefore, that support for co-operatives became a central feature of their forms of African socialism, at least in the formative periods of the new nation states. That tradition, however, also tended to favour savings and thrift societies that could be closely identified with government objectives: for example, extending government-backed loans to farm families. Leaders from that tradition did not always welcome the more independent approach associated with the North American credit union movement.

The issue was not just a matter of ideology. The governments of the new African countries were facing immense challenges. Their resources were limited, while human and communications infrastructures were stretched to their limits. Many national economies were largely dependent upon staples whose prices could fluctuate wildly in international markets, while the education systems were too limited in size and scope to sustain rapid modernization. Looked at from that perspective, it is understandable why governments wanted to have control over savings mobilization programmes within their borders, which meant that they did not favour independent credit union movements.

Whatever their roles within the emerging national entities, the African credit union movements soon produced their own leadership groups. By the end of the decade, in fact, there were strong national leaders within nearly all African movements. The problem was that they had to survive on inadequate incomes. All of the movements were severely limited in the resources they could afford for national and certainly regional organizations. For that reason, the leaders and their movements were dependent upon government assistance and, even more, upon contributions from overseas.

The Roman Catholic Church, therefore, remained instrumental in the movement's early development in Africa. In addition to individual priests, there were several bishops, such as Dalieh in Liberia and Dery in Ghana, who supported the expansion of the movement. Dery, who had studied credit unions at Antigonish, was particularly sympathetic, and his impact spread beyond his own diocese. The Catholic orders involved in spreading credit unionism in Africa included the White Fathers from Canada and the Maryknolls — both nuns and priests — from the United States. Among the Catholic universities, as in other parts of the world, St. Francis Xavier University in Nova Scotia played a remarkable role in training clergy as well as lay people, both Catholic and Protestant.

There were also two Roman Catholic charitable organizations that were particularly important in Africa. The Catholic Relief Services (CRS) contributed funds to several projects and became the department's "chief co-operating agency in Africa".[154] CRS also supported the work of Father Joseph Van den Vries, a Dutch priest who worked out of Nairobi. Van den Vries would long support the development of credit unions on the continent, notably in East Africa. In particular, he was a great ally of the World Extension Department.

MISEREOR, the charitable organization created by German Catholics in 1958, supported trade schools for technicians, agricultural co-operatives, basic health services, child health clinics, and self-help groups. It focused largely on rural communities and was very helpful in assisting the African credit unions to meet the needs of farm families.[155] Like the Catholic Relief Services, MISEREOR provided a series of small grants for the development of credit unions in some countries; this was particularly important in helping the credit union movement in Ghana during its early stages.

During the 1960s the Roman Catholic Church and several Protestant churches were able to increase interest in the African movement among North American credit unionists. Through their missionary programmes they publicized the

Father Joseph Van den Vries with Ethiopian people at a meeting about credit unions. (COURTESY OF CUNA)

economic and social difficulties confronting African peoples and helped sponsor a steady stream of visitors from Africa to Madison. They also contributed to the education of many African credit union enthusiasts in programmes offered by the department, the University of Wisconsin and St. Francis Xavier University, and assisted the credit union trainers, educators and Peace Corps volunteers who went to Africa during the 1960s and later.

Several Canadian and American leagues displayed a keen interest in helping the development of African credit unions. In most instances, this interest emerged from personal contacts during visits by African leaders, connections through church affiliations, and the interest of government officials. In 1961 the Saskatchewan Co-operative Credit Union League, through the encouragement of its manager, Al Charbonneau, decided to celebrate its twenty-fifth anniversary by sponsoring a co-operative savings and credit development project in Tanganyika. For Charbonneau, it was the beginning of a lifetime interest in the international movement. Some of the money initially raised in Saskatchewan ($16,000 in 1962 and $10,000 in 1964[156]) was combined with funds from MISEREOR to fund the work of Gary Churchill, a credit union volunteer from North Battleford, Saskatchewan, in Tanganyika. Churchill followed Norm Riley from the Coady Institute, who had worked in Tanganyika during the first few months of 1961.[157] Riley had helped to prepare legislation, and had conducted a series of classes on credit unions and other co-operatives.

In 1963 and 1964, the Michigan League, also a long-time supporter of the international programme, provided $20,000 annually to allow its assistant managing director, Jack Dublin, his wife Selma and their children to go to Africa. Dublin had become interested in international work because of visits to Michigan by overseas leaders and because of meetings with Paddy Bailey and Al Charbonneau. In 1962, after Dublin had finished helping devise the plan for Latin America, he moved with his family to Tanganyika. Tanganyika was selected by WED because it had a brief history of involvement with credit unions, a supportive set of networks through the Catholic and Lutheran churches, and a government interested in expanding the movement.

TANGANYIKA

The great leader of Tanganyikan independence, the man who would found the new country of Tanzania, was Julius Nyerere. A visionary and a revered leader, Nyerere was determined to push his country rapidly into the industrial age. He was convinced that it had to make the same progress in one or two generations that some European countries had taken a century to achieve. He undertook a mammoth restructuring of his country, called *ujamaa*, which saw the formation of entirely new villages operated through quasi-co-operative structures. It was an approach widely applauded at the time and supported by considerable outside funds, particularly from Scandinavia and Canada.

Nyerere initially placed great emphasis on co-operative organizations to carry out his revolution. He particularly stressed savings and thrift co-operatives. By themselves, these co-operatives represented a revolution in a country where some people, especially in rural areas, still buried their savings in the ground, and where many families measured their wealth in cattle. With his government's encouragement, savings and credit co-operatives developed rapidly as many members

The books of a credit union being checked in public by the Supervisory Committee. (COURTESY OF CUNA)

brought in their coins and paper money, often still in the tin cans that had been concealed under their huts or in their gardens. Others brought their money because they had grown tired of losing their savings in fires or, if stored carelessly, to rats and termites.[158] Credit unions could obviously play a role in those circumstances.

While it is difficult to generalize about a continent as large and diverse as Africa, there were some ways in which the experience in Tanganyika/Tanzania can be seen as typical. It was essentially a rural country with coffee and cotton as its chief export crops. This meant that many of the credit unions were based on small rural communities and had to adjust to a cash economy based largely on a single crop that was typically vulnerable to dramatic price shifts on international markets. There was a well-differentiated class system divided between Europeans and Africans and among different groups of African peoples; this meant there would always be important cultural and social dimensions to the credit union movements that emerged. The politics of the period added further complexities — the Dublins arrived, in fact, during a mutiny. It would take some time before they, like most North Americans and Europeans, understood African political systems.

As in other African countries, the political cultures of northern industrialized societies had been poorly imposed upon the Tanganyikan people. The ideologies of nineteenth-century Europe had certainly had an impact, especially the different forms of socialism, but they were far less important than the inherited politics of clan, family, language and nationality; even these would be overwhelmed by struggles among individuals and groups for the possibilities of power. Within any given community and region, all of these elements were far more important than the political rhetoric and ideological schisms simplistically applied by some people from northern societies.

In parts of Tanganyika, as in other countries of Africa, western styles of education were inadequately implemented. Illiteracy was a common problem, especially in rural areas. Moreover, even where there were educational systems similar to those in Europe, the United States and Canada, the prevalent kind of teaching emphasized rote learning rather than independent thinking. It did not prepare students well for operating financial institutions. By and large, students were not educated in such "mundane matters" as keeping books, taking minutes, mobilizing people and chairing meetings, all skills essential in the operation of credit unions. Imparting these skills, therefore, became a priority for the Dublins and all credit union leaders, native and foreign, who helped the movement's development.

At the same time, the complicated restructuring brought about by the withdrawal of the European powers greatly disturbed the fabric of the colonial societies. It would take two or three generations before the African peoples could build the new economic and political infrastructure they needed to manage their own societies effectively. During the turmoil of the independence period, there was an optimistic yet frantic search for position and opportunities among people newly free. For credit unions this meant immense demand for credit, memberships drawn from a public service confronting reduced incomes as imperial funding declined and pressure on credit unions from some politicians and businessmen for unsecured loans, advantageous terms and forgiven payments. All too often, it could mean memberships that were dominated by the unemployed and those who could not, or would not, save as economies worsened.

The migration of peoples associated with the economic restructuring typical of the independence period further challenged the developing credit union systems. Cities started to grow quickly; traditional economic activities were replaced by specialized production, especially in agriculture; large families continued to be commonplace, even increasing in size as the incidence of some diseases was restricted by northern medicines; and gender roles began to change.

One common problem was that many men lost their traditional status: removed from customary roles by the decline of hunting and the limitations of herding, they were diverted to an often fruitless search for permanent jobs in industry and mining. When those kinds of jobs failed to materialize, disappeared or declined, the result was reduced incomes, unemployment and low self-esteem. For credit unions, that could mean men who wanted loans not for "providential" purposes but for purchasing beer to "forest the table" (buying the drinks) when one's turn came.

As for women, they had a traditional role as "savers" in many African societies. They were involved in credit unions from the beginning, in that, while seldom participating directly in organizational and early meetings, they sat on the outside of the circles of people trying to understand the concept. Their applause and "boos" could be as important as any formal votes that were taken. Moreover, women were among the first to join the credit unions and to use its services. In many communities, too, where men worked away from home or had unreliable incomes, it was the women with small but regular incomes who were the stable base for credit union growth. Very quickly, some women became secretary-treasurers, partly because they had gained the necessary education and training, partly because so many men had to travel away to work, and partly because, unlike some parts of the developing world, it was culturally acceptable for men to borrow from women lenders.[159]

In its early phases the Tanganyikan movement was concentrated in rural areas; gradually, though, it moved into the cities. In other countries, such as Zambia, Ethiopia and Ghana, the emphasis was more on urban areas from the beginning of WED involvement. Considerable success was achieved in the cities among the same kinds of groups that had brought much stability to the American, Canadian and Latin American movements: teachers, public servants, police and armed forces — in other words, groups with regular salaries and sufficient expertise to operate credit unions with relatively little training. In those countries, credit unions could be financially strong from the beginning.[160]

As the African movements developed, the World Extension Department expanded Paddy Bailey's role to include responsibility for Africa. Bailey made his first visit in 1961, calling upon co-operative banking leaders and credit union enthusiasts in Ghana, Kenya, Liberia, Malawi, Nigeria, Sierra Leone, Tanzania, Uganda and Zambia. As a result of his visit, conferences were held in 1963 and 1964, one in Dar-es-Salaam, Tanzania, and the other in Lagos, Nigeria. Both were subsidized by the World Extension Department. Similar conferences were held in various African cities in four of the next five years.[161]

In 1964 the department began exploring the possibility of attracting USAID support for its growing African involve-

A.A. "Paddy" Bailey (bending down behind children) with farming people in Southern Rhodesia, 1963. (Courtesy of CUNA)

ments. It proved to be somewhat more difficult to secure than had been the case in Latin America. The United States did not contribute as heavily to Africa at that time, and there was less sympathy for credit unions among the original USAID officers in Africa, a problem that would disappear in time. Eventually, however, the department did gain USAID and Peace Corps assistance for general African programmes and for national initiatives in Tanzania, Kenya and Uganda between 1964 and 1969.

ASIA

At the same time, the department began to explore seriously what it could do in Asia. In May 1961, it opened an office in Manila that helped organize, in November of that year, an Asian regional conference for credit union leaders, held in Baguio City, the Philippines. Financed largely by the Asia Foundation, the conference drew fifty participants from Japan, Korea, Vietnam, Hong Kong, Singapore, Formosa (now Taiwan), Thailand, New Guinea and Ceylon (as Sri Lanka was then called). It was a significant catalyst for the development of credit unions in nearly all of the countries represented.

Much of the early leadership in the Asian credit union movement came from the Philippines. The sources of that movement lay in the problems encountered by farm families struggling to enter the market economy. An agricultural credit system was introduced in 1915, and various government schemes for rural credit had subsequently been attempted. Credit unions, first organized during the 1940s, grew to an estimated 400 by 1961; many of them had become stagnant, however, and they lacked a central organization until 1960.

As in other Asian countries, one of the reasons for the emergence of credit unions in the Philippines was fear of the rise of communism. American observers and Roman Catholic leaders within and without Asia were increasingly preoccupied with Vietnam and the so-called "domino effect", whereby it was believed that communist movements would systematically sweep through Asia. Within the Roman Catholic Church the Jesuit Fathers of Asia were particularly concerned, and they created the Socio-Economic Life of Asia (SELA) to promote the social and economic improvement of people in Asia. Like many Americans at the time, they believed that the best way to combat communism was through expanded educational activities that enhanced economic opportunities. In 1963 SELA organized the Social Action Leadership Course, sponsored by the Asia Foundation. For the remainder of the decade the leadership course, offered in several centres, would be an important training vehicle for individuals interested in the development of credit unions.

One of the movements affected by the leadership course was the Taiwanese or Nationalist Chinese movement. Four delegates from Taiwan attended the first session of the course. They were from the Association for Socio-Economic Development in China, organized by the Roman Catholic Church to foster the creation of credit unions. In 1964, the association sponsored its own training programme in Taipei. That same year Taiwan's first credit union was organized in the Hsinchu Catholic Church.

Taiwan was fertile ground for the development of credit unions. At the time, the island was economically weak and overpopulated for the number of economic opportunities then available. The bulk of the population did not have access to savings and credit facilities, especially those people who were on the island when the Chinese nationalists arrived in large numbers during the late 1940s. Once started, the movement spread quickly through northern Taiwan and then, with the help of the Presbyterian as well as the Roman Catholic Church, through the central portions of the country.

Among the Catholics, Father Albert O'Hare, Father Jess S. Brena and Cardinal Yu-Pin played important roles in the formative years of the Taiwanese movement and particularly assisted in gaining popular as well as government support. WED/CUNA International, CUNA Mutual Insurance Society and the Michigan Credit Union League provided some outside funding for the movement. Between 1964 and 1968, over eighty credit unions were created, and in the latter year a league was formed. Within a few years, it became a dynamic and influential movement. In common with several other Asian movements, the Taiwanese movement evinced a deep concern for broad socio-economic issues. It embraced health programmes as well as community development and adult education, all issues that were commonly espoused by Roman Catholic activists in the region.

In South Korea the tragic relocations of the Korean War were still being felt. A flood of homeless people was looking for ways to enter the economy in the aftermath of the war, either in the industrializing cities or the often economically marginal rural areas where most recent arrivals lived. Like the Koreans who were already there, the newcomers found access to credit difficult and usurious: loans could cost 60 percent, even 120 percent per annum from the lenders in the so-called "curb market". Koreans therefore had a strong reason to embrace credit unionism.

These circumstances formed a propitious environment for Sister Mary Gabriella Mulherin and her band of credit union enthusiasts, notably Augustine Kang, Lee Sang Ho and Park Hee Sup Ho. Together, they built a national movement that grew from its first credit union in 1960 — the Holy Family Credit Union in Pusan — to over 100 in 1965. By 1970, the movement had 507 credit unions, 81,000 members and savings of over $2,500,000US. The largest single type of membership came from closed-bond credit unions, but there were also credit unions with memberships from among small tradespeople, farmers, labourers, and fishing people. Indeed, the most common reason for loans was the funding of small stores.

The expansion was not without its strains. As in many other countries, the original "Catholic" vision of credit unions was to create small, comparatively informal organizations based on parish networks. It placed great emphasis on the ethical side of credit unions, their role in the struggle for social justice, extensive continuing educational activities, and the importance of volunteers. In the case of Sister Gabriella, it also meant, in the tradition of Antigonish, an integrated approach to community development using a wide range of co-operative organizations.

Many of the dynamic early leaders, like Sister Gabriella herself, were powerful individuals with a natural desire to shape the movement according to their own lights. By 1965, she found herself being gradually replaced by other leaders more committed to larger credit unions and concerned about a higher degree of professionalism within the movement: leaders not as committed to other kinds of co-operative enterprise and more interested in expanding beyond the Roman Catholic base. The result was that Sister Gabriella withdrew the Cooperative Education Institute she had started from the

President Rod Glen presents Sister Mary Gabriella Mulherin with a framed citation, a special Founders Club pin and a donation of money from CUNA International for her pioneering work in Korea. (COURTESY OF CUNA)

Korean League. Sister Gabriella's estrangement was brief, but she never again played the role she had earlier, and the movement went in the directions the new leaders wished without rejecting the importance of the Catholic vision. It was a story that would be repeated in other countries in different ways over the following decade or so.

Nevertheless, the Korean movement, partly because of the influence of the Antigonish heritage, devoted considerable time and resources to credit union education. All members, not just the elected leaders, were expected to study the principles, practices and structures by attending seminars that could last two or even three days. One of the reasons for the emphasis on education was the need to overcome a long history of domination by the Japanese, as well as by local landlords. Encouraging people to take control of their own destinies had a different dimension in Korea and many other Asian countries because of recent history and because of the traditional views people held of authority. Those traditions and needs would help to shape movements with somewhat different values and bonds of association than were readily apparent elsewhere. They would also help to explain the successes many of the Asian movements would achieve.

In Hong Kong, the rapid population increase and intensive economic growth ushered in with the 1960s provided fertile ground for credit union development, originally, as in so many other Asian countries, under the leadership of the Roman Catholic Church. In 1961 the Committee for Socio-Economic Life sponsored a workshop on credit unions; as a result of that workshop, an American Jesuit, John Collins, was freed from his other responsibilities to explore the ways in which credit unions could be developed. Through a grant from the Asia Foundation, Collins visited credit unions in Fiji, the Philippines and Australia in 1962.[162] Upon his return to Hong Kong, he found several supporters, notably Andrew So, Father Harold Trube and Francis Kwok, and formed the Credit Union Voluntary Centre, which became the Hong Kong Credit Union League in 1966. The first member organization, St. Francis Credit Union, was formed in 1964; there were thirty-three by 1970 and fifty-one two years later.[163]

Although Collins remained heavily involved, a feature of the Hong Kong movement, and one shared with other Asian movements, was the speed with which a national leadership emerged. Andrew So was particularly important in the Hong Kong movement, becoming managing director of the league in 1968, the year in which a special credit union act was passed.[164] So, a keen student of the evolution of credit unions, sparked the expansion of the movement until 1973, when he joined CUNA Mutual.

In Thailand, the movement was born in Bangkok's meanest slums, in an area called Huay Kwang, during the later 1950s. It developed from the social action of a number of concerned Roman Catholics, including a priest, Father Alfred Bonnongue, a doctor, Chavalit Chitrankroh, and an academic, Prkhin Xumsasl, and grew out of a centre they helped start and in which several community activists worked, including Wasini Prakokit and Amporan Watthanawongs. Amporan would go on to become one of the most important leaders in the Thai movement. It was not until 1965, however, that the country's first credit union was formed. One of the main reasons for the relatively slow development was that the incorporation of credit unions was difficult to secure; the registering authorities were using an old co-operative act that did not meet the needs of financial co-operatives and specifically did not provide adequately for the formation of central co-operative bodies. In fact, one of the other main problems for the Thai movement in the early years was that the credit unions were organized among very scattered groups of people with "no strong relation to each other and without any feeling of belonging to a world-wide movement".[165]

The organization of the first Thai credit union coincided with the second Asian regional credit union training conference held in Bangkok. That meeting inspired considerable interest, and the movement expanded steadily thereafter, reaching 23 credit unions with over 2,000 members by 1970. During the same years, there were also eleven pre-credit unions in the process of formation and seven junior credit unions.[166]

In Japan, the movement emerged out of experiments with co-operative banking that went back to the nineteenth century, the traditions of Christian co-operativism associated with Toyohiko Kagawa, and the important roles co-operatives played in reconstruction after World War II. Carlos Matos visited Japan in 1960 and helped make Sophia University in Tokyo a centre for the study and promotion of credit unions. The first credit union was established that same year in a Catholic parish in Saebo City by Father Clair Yaeck, a Scarboro missionary from Canada who had studied at Antigonish. Other Scarboro priests helped organize credit unions among girls and young women working in the textile industry, while Augustinian and Maryknoll missionaries helped create credit unions in Shiroyama and Kyoto. Priests from Quebec, with the assistance of the Desjardins movement, helped form credit unions in northern Japan; they were particularly successful at organizing credit unions with a high commitment to community building, an important theme in post-war Japan.

Leadership within the Japanese movement soon passed to Japanese priests, many of whom received training through Socio-Economic Life in Asia. In 1968 they organized the Japanese Credit Union League, which included 25 credit unions with just over 3,000 members.[167] By 1970 they had successfully promoted the passage of a credit union law that combined features of Quebec and American credit union legislation. The Japanese movement remained very much a Roman Catholic movement. One of the challenges of the 1970s — and later decades — would be to expand beyond that rather narrow base to other groups in modern Japan.

In Indonesia, a co-operative banking network patterned after the Raiffeisen system and with a history stretching back to the beginning of the century, encountered difficulties in the mid-1960s. The country was thrown into turmoil during that decade by the overthrow of President Sukarno by anti-Communist forces and by rampant inflation. In 1967, as stability returned, Paddy Bailey visited the country and, at a series of meetings, helped spark a renewed interest in co-operative banking. Shortly afterwards, Father K. Albrecht, a Jesuit, started to organize credit unions. The movement would expand quickly in the 1970s.

In total, and largely through initiatives within the countries involved, the Asian movement made remarkable strides during the 1960s. It had been accepted to varying but significant degrees within the cultures of several countries. Most obviously located within the diverse and dynamic Roman

Catholic traditions, it reflected Buddhist dimensions as well, particularly in Thailand. The movement had developed by attracting a wide diversity of people: residents from the poorer districts of Hong Kong and Kyoto; police forces, public servants and teachers in many countries; girls working in the factories of Ichinomiya and low-income people in the markets of Bangkok.

WED played an important role in the early development of the Asian movement by contributing directly to the development of credit unions in Korea, Taiwan, the Philippines, Hong Kong, Vietnam and Thailand. Starting in 1966 it increased its allocations to the region, and the first USAID/Peace Corps contracts began in 1966. Asia nevertheless represented a daunting challenge for the organization. The size and complexity of the region were intimidating, and the cultural traditions remarkably diverse. It was abundantly clear from the beginning, however, that the ethical as well as the economic interest of the credit union movement (indeed the larger co-operative movement) resonated well in many Asian countries. In some ways, too, many parts of Asia, especially as economies started to boom, did not need much assistance. There were others, though, that did, and they would be the focus of growing attention in the 1970s.

NEW ZEALAND

The idea of credit unions also gained momentum in New Zealand during the late 1950s and early 1960s. The first credit union had actually been formed in 1942 by the International Order of Oddfellows, a friendly society, using advice from CUNA. Over the next twenty-five years another eight had been organized within lodges of the order. The movement was not generally promoted until 1955, when Father Marion Ganey visited the North Island. His leadership inspired many leaders within the Roman Catholic Church, especially Tom Mitchell and Father H. Boyd. The first credit union started by the Roman Catholic Church, called St. Joseph's (Matata), was among the Maori. Shortly afterward, another credit union, St. Mary's, was formed in Hamilton.[168] In 1961 Father Ganey once again visited New Zealand on one of his Pacific tours promoting credit unions.[169] His visit led to

Colin D. Smith, the founder of the New Zealand movement. (COURTESY OF NEW ZEALAND ASSOCIATION OF CREDIT UNIONS)

the formation of a league and stimulated a drive for the creation of more credit unions. Within a decade there were over 100 throughout New Zealand, an increasing number of them outside the Roman Catholic Church.

The driving force behind the New Zealand movement was Colin D. Smith, an accountant who became the first secretary of the New Zealand Credit Union League. Smith became the league's first full-time employee and its most prominent spokesperson until his death in 1986.[170] He would have a long and colourful career, within both the New Zealand and international movements.

AUSTRALIA

The Australian movement made substantial progress during the 1960s. In some years, credit union memberships increased at the phenomenal rate of 25 percent each year. The leading credit union in the country, ironically enough, served the employees of the Commonwealth Bank of Australia.[171] In 1960 bank employees succeeded in securing payroll deductions from the bank and started to deliver its services to employees outside Sydney; by 1964, the credit union was serving over 7,000 members.[172] As word about this and other credit unions spread, more people became interested in the possibilities the movement afforded. Within New South Wales, where the movement was strongest, credit unions tended to follow the American model and to be organized among employee, religious and ethnic groups. In Victoria, where the next strongest movement emerged, credit unions tended to be influenced more by the Canadian model, and community credit unions were the norm; in fact, some of them were closely tied, as in Canada, to consumer co-operatives.

The growth of these larger credit unions aggressively engaged in the marketplace opened up an intensive debate that became understood in Australia as a struggle between the traditionalists and the modernists.[173] While there were shades of opinions in this debate, it became sharp and continuous in Australia, as it did under different circumstances in the United States and Canada. It can also be seen as an inevitable kind of tension whenever credit unions change their cultures from populist to managerial institutions. As elsewhere, the debate focused on issues of democracy, the decline of "character" as a

Kevin Yates, the foremost pioneer of the Australian credit union movement.
(COURTESY OF CUSC)

sufficient guarantee for a loan, the desirability of rapid growth, and the changing role of volunteers.

Despite the divisions, the Australian movement made considerable progress and even began to encourage credit unions in nearby countries. Attracted by the example of Marion Ganey, the Australian movement turned first to finding funds to support the educational programmes of the Fijian movement. In 1967 Stan Arneil was primarily responsible for the establishment of the South Pacific Association of Credit Unions. Its purpose was to bring together the Australian, New Zealand and Hong Kong movements with those of the Pacific islands in a strong Pacific movement.[174] It was a daunting task, but one that demonstrated a strong Australian interest in the region and a commitment to the international development of credit unions.

THE PACIFIC

Within the islands of the South Pacific the example of Fiji and the powerful personality of Father Ganey remained prominent, even dominant. By 1963 Fiji had 175 credit unions. Widely recognized throughout the country as the most important initiative for increasing local control over the economy, they developed democratically within a society that had been dominated by chiefs, and did so with very little apparent difficulty.[175] They were essentially small credit unions serving small communities and employee groups. They relied extensively upon the work of volunteers and were almost entirely within the emancipatory phase of development.

One of the most important needs for the development of the Fijian movement was the training of leaders, a typical problem for credit unions in the formative stage. Starting in 1958, Father Ganey had begun teaching about credit unions to small groups of Fijians in his home. "There was no structured program at that time and the main teaching tool was the blackboard. The facilities were scant — there were no beds, and the dining room was a table on an open porch. The house was small and was on stilts because of the marshy land all around."[176] The school grew. By 1964 Ganey and his assistant, Ioane Naisara, had developed a structured programme with several mini-courses. In that year enrolment reached 42 and the class had to be moved to a vacant church nearby. A more permanent solution was found the next year when Gladys Bergengren, the widow of Roy Bergengren, visited Fiji. Seeing the problem, she donated the beneficiary money she had received from CUNA Mutual upon her husband's death to the development of the school. Ganey used the funds to purchase a house that he named the Roy F. Bergengren Credit Union Training School.

The school, which was dedicated in 1970, became the centre for the educational and training activities of the movement in Fiji and other Pacific islands.[177] The courses focused on bookkeeping and accounting as well as leadership training, public speaking, and credit union history and philosophy. Courses lasted from one to six weeks. Most of them were taught in Fijian, with a few in English. In addition, the instructors frequently travelled to visit credit unions, where they taught short courses, reviewed the financial records and helped committees carry out their work. When they found difficulties they stayed as long as necessary, sometimes "sitting with the people around the kava bowl until well into the morning."[178]

Father Marion M. Ganey with Fiji credit union members. (COURTESY OF CUNA)

Gladys Burroughs Bergengren, whose self-sacrifice made possible the work of Roy Bergengren and who supported credit unions throughout her life.
(COURTESY OF CUNA)

IRELAND

Meanwhile, half a world away, the Irish movement made remarkable strides during the 1960s. In 1960, when the Irish League was established, there were only four credit unions; its affairs were managed in Nora Herlihy's living room, as they would be for a number of years. Five years later there were 113 credit unions, and they were of all types: occupational, parish, community and organizational.

One of the reasons the movement grew so quickly in Ireland was that the Irish League successfully negotiated distinctive legislation for the Irish movement. The process, which took three years to complete, came to an end in 1966, when the bill unanimously passed the Irish Parliament, or Oireachtas. It became law in August 1966, as a proud band of Irish leaders watched Eamon de Valera, president of the republic, sign the bill.

Another reason the Irish movement grew so quickly was a particularly successful booklet written by Nora Herlihy. Entitled *The Credit Union Question Time* and first published in 1962, it was a compilation of Herlihy's answers to the most frequently asked questions she had encountered in advising local groups on starting credit unions. Within four years more than 20,000 copies were distributed, outside of Ireland as well as in her homeland.

Rather remarkably, given the tensions of the times, the Irish movement embraced both Protestant and Catholic groups and existed in both the south and the north. Wherever they were, the Irish credit unions were very much built upon the original and continuing contributions of volunteers. Even as they grew larger, they still relied upon volunteers to do most of the work, and their commitment to education did not waver. They were proud manifestations of commitments to workplace, parish and community. Unlike too many of their counterparts in the United States and Canada, they continued to manifest deep

President Eamon de Valera of Ireland prepares to sign the national credit union act handed to him by Nora Herlihy. (Courtesy of CUNA)

concern about how to maintain a very strong sense of member ownership and control.

From its earliest successful days, the Irish movement was drawn to international activities. Father Gallagher visited the American movement several times, as did Nora Herlihy. Perhaps most importantly, the Irish movement became aware early in its history of the challenges, difficulties and possibilities of credit unions in developing countries. It also had some influential allies; in the mission fields of Africa, for example, Irish priests were common, and active in the movement. Many of them would help develop credit unions, especially during the 1960s and 1970s. Not surprisingly, the credit unions they tended to favour were in the Irish mode: clearly led by volunteers, strongly committed to education, and deeply rooted in the communities they served.

UNITED KINGDOM

Across the Irish Sea, the years following World War II saw a steady and continuing migration of people from the West Indies to Great Britain. During the 1960s many of these immigrants living in London organized credit unions like the ones they had known in their native lands. By the later years of the decade, West Indians and others were organizing credit unions in the Midlands, northern England and Scotland. In 1969 the Credit Union League of Great Britain was formed and began to lobby for appropriate legislation. The existing legislation, the Provident Societies and the Companies Act, restricted credit unions to being little more than savings clubs, meaning that many credit unions did not even register, thereby creating an image problem, particularly if they encountered financial difficulties.[179] Achieving permanence and stability would not be an easy matter for the British movement.

THE CARIBBEAN

Meanwhile, in the Caribbean region from which so much impetus for the British movement had come, credit unions continued to grow, although the region generally was experiencing some difficult times. The economies of many of the islands were stagnant, and the growth of credit unions had consequently slowed. Nevertheless, between 1962 and 1969, the number of affiliated credit unions increased from 500 to just over 600. The number of members increased from 86,000 to 135,000; assets grew from $6,115,000US to $23,000,000US.[180]

The largest movements continued to be in Jamaica and Trinidad and Tobago, and they expanded, although they had difficulty in creating strong central organizations. A remarkable credit union movement was evident in Dominica (or the Dominican Republic, as it was more commonly called at the time), where the work of Sister Alicia De Tremmerie helped attract over 40 percent of the island's population to credit union membership. She gathered a band of people around her, including Edward Elwin, Joffre Robinson and Theophile Waldron, who helped build the movement in subsequent years.

A similarly dynamic movement had begun in British Honduras (now Belize), which tended to be closely associated with the Caribbean credit unions. That movement had been started by Jesuits in 1944, and had grown steadily on a parish basis. From early in the movement's history the largest credit union was Holy Redeemer Credit Union; Jane Usher, who would become its manager, and her husband Henry, who played an important role in the fishing co-operative associated with it, became particularly prominent leaders within the national, Caribbean and international movements. Other leaders who played prominent roles in the formation of the national movement were Norrin Meighan, Harry Stanley and Edward "Ned" Pitts.

During the 1960s the movement spread to other countries in the region. The first credit union was organized in Guyana in 1963 and in St. Kitts and Nevis in 1965, in both instances among public servants. In some countries, such as Grenada, St. Vincent and the Grenadines, the movements began earlier, but it was in the 1960s that they started to gain significant momentum. In nearly all instances, however, the movements and the credit unions were small, making it difficult to achieve the financial resources needed to create stability.[181]

Nevertheless, the Caribbean movement played an important role in the deliberations of the international movement. That was partly because Paddy Bailey brought the perspec-

tives of the region to the department. It was also because of the work of Lorrell Bruce. Bruce, who had learned about credit unions from Father John Sullivan, had a distinguished career as secretary for the Prime Minister of Jamaica. In addition to providing leadership for credit unions in the region, Bruce served for many years on the Credit Union World Extension Committee, a group of representatives from the various movements that helped provide direction for the overseas programme. His diplomatic skill and understanding of views from outside the United States were instrumental in bringing about many of the positive changes within WED, CUNA International and the World Council from the late 1960s onward.

The role of the Caribbean as the first region to which the American and Canadian movements attempted to export the credit union idea was significant in the selection of Kingston, Jamaica, as the site for a particularly important conference in the history of the international movement; it was held in October 1966, and chaired by Rod Glen, then the president of CUNA International. The conference attracted several leaders from the Caribbean and Latin American movements and drew representatives from the American and Canadian movements, the French, German, Israeli, Indian and Swiss co-operative banking movements, the International Co-operative Alliance and the International Labour Office. It was an important step in establishing the presence of the credit union movement within the international co-operative movement.

All told, as the 1960s came to an end, the leaders of the international credit union movement had considerable reason for pride and optimism. The credit union idea had shown remarkable resilience and appeal throughout the world. What started out as a very small operation in 1954 had become a promising network of enthusiasts, distributed widely throughout countries in all of the world's continents. That progress had been achieved by a devoted band of employees and volunteers; it had been supported by growing contributions from the American and Canadian movements; it had received an immense boost from the labour of many religious leaders, especially in the Roman Catholic Church; and it enjoyed growing support from the international development community.

The credit union "idea" that moved around the world in those years was strongly influenced by the culture of populist credit unions. It reached out to marginalized people in many parts of the globe, championing the cause of farm families and mobilizing the urban poor. It spoke to "the little man" under the umbrella, only now the "man" had many different skin colours, wore different costumes and could be a woman.

The predominance of membership and community, however they appealed at home and overseas, almost by necessity invited increased attention to managerial and institutional concerns. How to stabilize the immense number of credit unions that had been created? How to develop the necessary management skills? How to organize credit unions as they became larger and more complex, particularly, but not only, in North America? How to structure credit union organizations on a national and regional basis? These questions were more difficult to answer than they might appear. They were questions that could not be ignored as the 1960s came to an end.

Chapter Six

Matters of Structure: The Beginnings of Regionalization
1963-1970

BY THE EARLY 1960S, MANY PEOPLE WITHIN CREDIT union circles wanted to reconsider how the international movement might be most effectively organized. Their desire to do so stemmed from many changes within the international movement: a wish to be a significant player as international development circles embraced co-operatives; a search for more effective ways to manage credit unions, both in developed and developing movements; the rationalization of the established movements; the need to resolve the long-standing insurance issue; and the desire to bring the Global Projects Office in Washington closer to the CUNA International office in Madison. What might appear as a simple matter of institutional reform was in reality the consequence of considerable ferment in credit union circles from Michigan to Nairobi, Vancouver to Panama City, Sydney to Seoul.

The increased opportunities to promote co-operatives as a major vehicle for international development owed a great deal to the efforts of the United Nations. As part of its International Development Decade, the United Nations designated 1964 as "International Co-operative Year". It issued a set of commemorative stamps and a medallion to acknowledge the co-operative heritage, while it encouraged UNESCO and development agencies to foster co-operative movements. This initiative helped to awaken interest in development issues and co-operatives specifically in the international community, particularly within the governments of industrialized countries.

Naturally enough, the international credit union movement wanted to take advantage of this trend. By 1964 credit union movements in some sixteen countries had joined CUNA,[182] partly so they could participate more actively as donors and suppliers or as recipients of aid for credit union development. The prospects were attractive: in addition to the general support of the United Nations and the promising beginnings with USAID, there were profitable developing partnerships with the Food and Agriculture Organization, the International Labour Office, the Caribbean Commission, the Pacific Commission and the Asia Pacific Foundation. Relations continued to be excellent with religious organizations interested in development, most notably MISEREOR and the Catholic Relief Services. Within countries like Canada and Australia, there were looming possibilities as governments began seriously to engage their international responsibilities for economic development.

To take advantage of these possibilities, the international movement had to have stable and capable organizations that governments could trust. That meant addressing at length the problem of structure, one of the most difficult and persistent issues within the international movement. Moreover, it was an issue that not only affected the developing movements but was deeply entwined with changes sweeping the more developed movements in the United States and Canada.

During the 1960s the American and Canadian movements expanded significantly in members and assets. The creation of new credit unions was slowing down in many parts of the two countries, and in some areas, particularly in Canada, had stopped. Instead of encouraging new organizations, the more aggressive credit unions were starting to diversify their activities or to amalgamate in order to build membership, secure efficiencies of scale, and provide a wider range of services to their members. Significantly, they were not expanding the movement through the fostering of new credit unions. They were reflecting the expansionist strategies common to managerial credit unions.

This kind of expansion, however, was concentrated in an increasingly more powerful minority of credit unions. At a local level in both countries there were many credit unions that were steeped in populist cultures. Many of those serving specific, limited groups of people preferred to continue in the ways established by Bergengren and Filene — and they could afford to do so. The result was a differentiation between small and larger credit unions that became steadily more significant.

One aspect of the differentiation was that larger credit unions, especially, became more professionalized, from the service representatives to secretary-treasurers/general managers. It was this increasingly professionalized group that led the process of restructuring credit unions at the local, state/provincial and national levels. They would do the same at the international level.

As local credit unions expanded, the need for more complex, expensive and jointly owned services also grew. Because of their community credit unions and the greater interest in providing members with mortgage and chequing services, the Canadian movement led the way in this area. It had organized a series of provincial centrals in the 1940s and a national central, the Canadian Cooperative Credit Society, in 1953. These centrals looked after cheque-clearing as soon as it was practical, held the movement's statutory and surplus liquidity, and made some larger loans. In the United States, interest in forming centrals began to grow at a state level in the 1960s, but it grew slowly because of the greater American emphasis on limited and simpler services to the membership.

In essence, what was happening was that a new generation of managerial talent — employed by credit unions or drawn from other business activities to positions on boards — was gaining influence within the American and Canadian movements. These managers often became associated with each other through the ICU Committee which became very active in the later 1960s, meeting whenever CUNA conferences were held and maintaining links in the interim periods through smaller conferences, task forces and informal contacts.

The new generation of leadership was very concerned about achieving greater state or provincial economies of scale and rationalization. It brought those same concerns to the international movement as some — people like Rod Glen — began to take an interest in the issue during the late 1960s and especially the 1970s. They were determined to create at once a more broadly based and yet more tightly run organization at the international level. In doing so, they were, in many respects, replicating what they had been doing at home.

The new managers of the 1960s — and many elected leaders of the time — generally were convinced exponents of formal planning procedures as a way to bring about institutional changes. Such programmes as "management by objectives" and annual planning cycles for managements and boards became more common and expected. Indeed, by the late 1960s several state and provincial movements had invested heavily in planning activities. They were recognizing a need to understand more completely the diverse nature of memberships. It was no longer possible to rely only upon common knowledge of member needs; it was essential to find ways to understand members systematically and to provide a wider range of services to members.

The trend toward planning soon caught on within the international movement. The Global Projects Office, for example, embraced the planning mode early and incorporated it into its activities; by the 1970s it was deeply committed to the practice.[183] In Latin America Herb Wegner and Tony Schumacher became well known for their planning skills. USAID encouraged planning activities in the projects it funded, and by the end of the decade there were few national movements that were not engaged in planning exercises. "Planning" was becoming a common, even central, activity

A credit union manager's office in 1961. (COURTESY OF CUNA)

within the international movement. By its very nature, planning would also lead to reconsideration of how the international movement should be restructured.

Planning was particularly important in the international field because of the complexity of development programmes. Carrying out projects in the field required a clear understanding of what was intended among donor agencies, receiving peoples and their governments, not to mention the people working for Global Projects and in Madison. Moreover, as grants from government became more important, it was necessary to have clear objectives and measurable results, both of which required care in formulating projects and allocating resources. It was a different approach from the way in which credit unions had emerged in North America.

Another reason for the growing importance of planning within the international movement was that the American and Canadian movements were facing some very difficult problems in the 1960s. To overcome them, a greater degree of planning and co-ordination was necessary. In the United States and, to a lesser extent, in Canada, the movement was under attack by banks and insurance companies over a supposedly privileged

taxation position. Responding effectively to these changes meant that the movements had to augment parts of their national programmes, bring together legal resources, maximize their ability to speak to government, and mobilize support for legislative positions. Inevitably, this meant that increased attention was paid to the structures within which the national, and ultimately the international, movement functioned. Few issues draw credit unions — and other kinds of co-operatives — together more readily than relations with governments, be it for taxation or legislative change.

Indirectly, the taxation issue and the growing importance of national organizations helped the international programmes in three ways. First, it meant that it was comparatively easy to include promotion of the international programme at well-attended annual and special general meetings; the result was more support for international programmes. Second, it meant that the American and Canadian movements became increasingly adept at dealing with governments, and the resultant skills would help them in developing programmes for overseas development. Third, it was a natural step for some of the best minds of the movement to move their attention from their own movements to the broader and, for many, intensely interesting domain of international credit union development.

The other crucially important issue in the 1960s that affected the structuring of the international movement had a more home-grown origin: the continuing feud between CUNA and CUNA Mutual. From the vantage point of thirty or forty years later, it is difficult to appreciate the bitterness of that dispute. Throughout the 1950s and 1960s it dominated most of CUNA's annual conventions, divided leagues, and encouraged cliques. The dispute was far more than an American feud. Delegates from the credit unions in overseas countries were selected or courted on the basis of whether they supported one "side" or the other. One can only guess at the humour they must have found in the annual political struggles and rituals the Americans and Canadians persisted in inflicting upon themselves for so many years.

In Australia and Canada the "insurance" issue created divisions that would last for two generations. Some of the debate in the two countries was the consequence of conflicting personalities who always seemed capable of marshalling two camps of supporters of relatively equal size. Much of the debate was about business — the burgeoning credit union movements around the world represented potentially an immense insurance market if the limitations of varying national regulatory systems could be overcome. The business could also produce substantial reserve and investment funds. The question was how those funds would be deployed, and by whom. They were not low stakes.

In Australia the "insurance" storm swirled around Stan Arneil, a convinced and powerful exponent of the views of CUNA Mutual. He believed there should be a single global insurance company for credit unions, and that associations with other co-operatives should be discouraged. In 1965 Arneil, who became manager of CUNA Mutual in Australia, started to work on incorporating the company in Australia. That action angered the leadership of the National Co-operative Insurance Services, which was providing loans insurance. There was, however, a need for bonding insurance, and that was the need CUNA Mutual sought to meet. The result was a bitter public debate that would deeply divide the Australian movement until the early 1970s.[184]

In Canada, the debate revolved around the development of two insurance companies, one headquartered in western Canada, the other in Ontario. Nationalistic in outlook, owned partly by other co-operatives as well as credit unions, needing to expand their business bases, they were both interested in entering the credit union insurance field; that led to more than a decade of competition and acrimony between supporters of the two different ways to meet the insurance needs of the Canadian movement.

These intense debates in Australia and Canada echoed through CUNA and reinforced old fears about the power and potential domination of CUNA Mutual. More importantly for the international movement, they encouraged leaders to consider creating a more independent international organization, one that had clear accountability to national and regional groupings of credit unions, that was linked to CUNA Mutual but possessed autonomy in its operations. Some of this sentiment could be found in Australia; more was evident in Canada. It could also be found in Latin America and Africa, where the leadership of several national movements was starting to assert itself. Leaders on those two continents, soon to be joined by a growing number from Asia, wanted more opportunities to talk among themselves at CUNA meetings. They also wanted more influence in the daily decisions of the international programme.

Nevertheless, it was the Australian and Canadian movements that took the key leadership roles in pressuring for the reconstruction of CUNA. They were joined by some American leaders who also believed changes would be advantageous. Many Americans, for example, were resentful of the time taken at the CUNA meetings to discuss international issues. Even more importantly, many Americans wanted to have complete control over CUNA. They did not appreciate the fact that others, especially the generally more liberal Canadians, could cast decisive votes on issues the Americans thought were essentially the business of the American credit unions.

The CUNA board struck a committee in 1962 to review the structure of the organization. Chaired by R.W. Eckart of Ohio, but greatly influenced by Harold Carpenter of Alabama, the committee flirted with the idea of creating a new independent international organization made up of national and regional associations. The idea proved too radical at the time, and support for it, originally strong, faded quickly. The committee therefore recommended, in early 1964, the creation of three forums, one made up of representatives from the American movement, another for the Canadian delegates, and the third for representatives of movements from all other countries. The forums would convene independently before CUNA meetings and deal with matters of exclusive concern, such as national legislation, central funds and share insurance.

The committee recommended that the overall structure of the organization remained essentially the same. At that time, the membership of CUNA consisted of 77 leagues from seventy countries around the world. Each league was entitled to elect from one to five directors, dependent upon its size. The leagues were organized into twelve districts, nine in the United States, two in Canada, and one for the rest of the world. This allocation to some extent reflected membership; it certainly reflected the dues paid by member organizations. The president was elected by the membership, and each region elected a vice-president.

The innovation of the forums was at first broadly acceptable, and it was linked to a renaming of CUNA to CUNA International. These recommendations were approved at a CUNA meeting in May 1964. That change suited American views and honestly indicated where the vast majority of the funding came from, but it did not please leaders in other countries. For some, the very name smacked of increased interest by CUNA Mutual in international insurance possibilities, while the "National" in CUNA clearly referred to the United States. It was not a name choice that would placate the desire for further change.[185] Nor was the compromise reached in 1964 one that would have a long life.

Despite the debates over the best structure for the organization, CUNA International was in basically a strong position during the 1960s. The Global Projects Office in Washington had worked out how to administer overseas contracts efficiently. Harry Culbreth turned sixty-five in 1970 but he agreed to stay on for a year so that his replacement, Paul Hebert, could be adequately trained. A native of Fall River, Massachusetts, the community with the highest penetration of Roman Catholic credit unions in the state, Hebert had come from the Washington Telephone Credit Union in 1969. Before that, he had been manager of the District of Columbia Credit Union League. An ebullient and decisive leader with a penchant for clarity and a capacity for tough bargaining, and a committed advocate of planning, Hebert came from a strong Roman Catholic background and possessed a deep commitment to social justice. He was also an efficient administrator who would manage the Washington office with care and ingenuity; in the process he would build a strong team of employees around him after he assumed control in 1971.

In some ways, the Madison office was in a more difficult situation. By necessity, the largest programmes, those funded by USAID, were operated out of Washington. Direct involvement by Madison officials in the Latin American programme, therefore, seems to have been minimal, although Paddy Bailey remained active in the Caribbean and increasingly in Africa. Bailey also spent considerable time travelling around the United States and Canada, promoting the international movement at meetings of leagues and centrals. In those settings, his obvious commitment and oratorical gifts made him an important spokesperson for the international movement.

Bailey became assistant managing director of CUNA International in 1968. Orrin Shipe remained as managing director while also acting as managing director of CUNA. Unfortunately, Shipe became a very controversial figure as the 1960s came to an end. He was in a difficult, and probably for most, an impossible situation.

To keep his position as managing director of CUNA, Shipe had to be ratified each year by the CUNA board. Because of the continuing tensions with CUNA Mutual and the ingrained personality rifts, his job was annually on the line. In some years, he was sustained by only one or two votes at annual meetings and at some board meetings. That situation naturally made Shipe rather insecure, meaning that the Madison office, charged with dealing with the American and Canadian movements, had to be cautious, low key and uncontroversial, not an easy or desirable situation for an organization engaged in international development. On the other hand, Shipe was a committed supporter of the international programme. Between Washington and Madison, it made substantial progress during his tenure, not least of all because of his genuine interest and leadership.

From an external perspective, there were many positive aspects of the work to be seen by the later 1960s. In addition to many successful projects in some diverse and difficult circumstances around the world, WED/CUNA International had built up an extensive workforce that varied between fifty and seventy people, and it had created some very effective ways to communicate "the credit union message". In 1967 CUNA International succeeded in having the movement declare October as Credit Union World Extension month. That gave the organization an opportunity to prepare a film, arrange for visits by people from overseas or those involved in overseas work, and print posters for distribution among credit unions.[186] These activities did much to promote the international programme and, not unimportantly, to encourage those involved to feel proud of what they had accomplished.

Despite these positive developments, the issue of how best to structure the international movement would not go away.

In fact, the successes arguably made it necessary to revisit the issue almost as soon as the 1964 compromise had been accepted. There was too much growth, too much change, for there not to be a constant rethinking about how best to organize internationally. There was another reason for the concern: the system as amended in 1964 was very expensive to maintain. It meant bringing together 250 directors for annual meetings, costs that represented between one-quarter and one-third of the annual budget. In an organization concerned about the plight of the poor in many parts of the globe, that was hardly an acceptable situation.

As the 1960s came to an end, leaders within the international movement reconsidered the possibility of regional associations or confederations. The idea had even been tried: the West Indies had pioneered in that institutional innovation in 1956, although the West Indies Confederation had made slow progress in its first decade, largely because of limited funds. It also benefited from natural, spontaneous and growing support from national movements around the world. For their own reasons, various movements at the state/provincial and national levels were becoming increasingly interested in working more closely together on a regional basis.

One of the regions in which a confederation seemed to make sense in the later 1960s was Latin America. There, the regional confederation grew naturally out of a committee made up of the presidents and managing directors of each national federation in the region. That committee, which started to meet in 1964, was essentially charged with advising the Latin American Regional Office. It was an easy, even natural, step for this committee to evolve into a more formal and independent confederation. It did so in 1969, when eighteen national movements came together to form La Confederación Latino-americana de Cooperativas de Ahorro y Crédito (Latin American Confederation of Credit Unions, or COLAC). The member countries were Bolivia, Colombia, Ecuador, Brazil, Peru, Venezuela, Panama, Costa Rica, Guatemala, Nicaragua, El Salvador, Mexico, Dominica, the Netherlands Antilles and Honduras.

The situation in Africa was more complex, but the idea of a confederation also had great appeal, partly for distinctive African reasons: it reflected the proud sense of Africanism that had become so apparent as one African country after another gained independence. Further, it satisfied the growing desire of African leaders to meet regularly to exchange ideas and plan joint projects. Finally, it was the result of increasing pressure for services from a growing number of African countries. By 1968, CUNA International had responded to requests from movements in Tanzania, Liberia, Sierra Leone, Nigeria, Ghana, Cameroon, Congo, Malawi, Zambia, Botswana, Lesotho, Swaziland, Ethiopia, Sudan, Mauritius, Kenya, Somalia, Uganda, Rhodesia (now Zimbabwe) and Zambia.

Partly, too, the idea was attractive because it suited the needs of CUNA International. First, a continental confederation would make it easier to attract funding from aid agencies by facilitating the development of a clear, inclusive plan for the region. Second, CUNA International was much influenced by the fact that a strong, well-financed central leadership had made possible the beginnings of the American movement under Filene and Bergengren; although the circumstances were different, the model still made sense a continent away and thirty years later. Third, a strong, centrally organized programme had apparently worked well in Latin America. With USAID and Peace Corps help, Latin Americans had increased the number of credit unions from 432 to 2,496 in four years; they had also increased membership from 124,000 to over 630,000, and savings from $4,200,000US to $49,000,000US.[187] If a co-ordinated approach had worked so well in one region, why not use it in another? In that sense, the African confederation was just another, even more co-ordinated, it was hoped, approach to regional development.

The possibility of an African confederation, to be called the African Cooperative and Savings and Credit Association (ACOSCA), was discussed at conferences in Lesotho and Kenya in January and August 1968, and formally created the following September. It started with a budget of $2,500,000US, almost all of which came from twenty national and international aid agencies. Membership included ten national associations of credit unions and another fourteen national promotion committees. With headquarters in Nairobi, the association worked through five training centres, two each in "Anglophone" and "Francophone" Africa, and one in Cameroon, which, in terms of European languages, was bilingual.[188]

The idea of creating regional confederations also resonated well in some circles in Australia and Canada, as neither country had been able to develop a strong national voice. In their case (as in the American), however, the confederation was national, not continental in scope, a structure that reflected the size of the three movements.

In Australia, any move toward a strong national confederation was difficult, for a number of reasons: the weakness of leagues outside of New South Wales and Victoria; the impact of the insurance debate; and the strong local and regional feelings typical of the Australian experience.

Nevertheless, in 1966 the Australian movement created the Australian Federation of Credit Union Leagues. Much of the leadership for the federation in its early years came from Stan Arneil, perhaps unfortunately, because it meant that the insurance issue could never be far from the surface. The federation did unite, however, largely through the efforts of Ken Miller, in pressuring for a reconsideration of how CUNA International was organized. The Australian movement was unhappy with being lumped in with the "rest of the world" within CUNA International. It wanted its own district so that it could meet independently and elect its own director to CUNA's board. It also wanted a greater voice in how the movement was developing in the Pacific.

The structure of CUNA International was one issue on which many Australian credit unionists could agree. Their support was particularly important in the discussions on international restructuring in the later 1960s. Ken Miller, Dermot Ryan, Beresford Calverley and Graham Benson, all key Australian leaders, became important participants in the debates over the future of CUNA International.

In Canada, the National Association of Credit Unions, created in 1958 and theoretically consisting of CUNA members, met regularly to consider issues of national importance and to prepare for CUNA meetings. Because of the divisions over insurance, ideology, regionalism and personalities, however, the Ontario and New Brunswick leagues were not members, while other provinces, at different times, were unhappy members. During the 1960s, a new generation of leaders, especially George May, Rod Glen, Chris Hansen, Les Tendler and Peter Podovinikoff, tried to forge a stronger national presence. They reached out to leaders in the Desjardins movement, who briefly seemed to share the vision of creating a truly Canadian movement. They sought to placate the leadership of the two estranged provinces. Their efforts would lead to an invigorated national focus within the English-Canadian movement as the decade came to an end.

Coincidentally, the same leaders and others were restructuring provincial movements by bringing together leagues and centrals to create stronger provincial organizations. They did so to cope with major technological challenges which seemed to require revamped provincial and national organizations. This enthusiasm for restructuring, based on a perception that the credit union movement had to adjust to new circumstances, spilled over into CUNA International. In particular, Rod Glen and George May played major roles, roles far greater than the size of the Canadian movement would have warranted, in the restructuring of the international movement.

The demand for reconsidering the structure of CUNA International reappeared not too long after the well-intentioned reform of 1964 was introduced. The focus for much of the discussion outside the United States and Canada was the grouping of the "rest of the world" into District Twelve. The Australians were publicly unhappy with this situation; so too were the Latin Americans. At the 1965 annual meeting of the CUNA board, Latin American representatives requested their own forum where they could speak Spanish and Portuguese. They also requested, as did the Australians, the formation of a thirteenth district — but the Latin Americans wanted it so that they could elect their own representative to the CUNA International board. In addition, they wanted a review of the Latin American Regional Office to ensure that it was meeting the best needs of the region. Perhaps above all, they wanted increased attention from CUNA International, aside from the continuing involvement through the Global Projects Office.[189]

Similar feelings were beginning to be expressed in the African and Asian movements, while the Canadian movement continued its struggle toward a greater degree of national integration. In the final analysis, it was the support of many within the Australian and Canadian delegations that made the reconsideration of CUNA International's structure necessary and possible. In 1967 CUNA's Planning Committee, particularly because of the intervention of Australia's Ken Miller, was asked to consider the future of CUNA International. At the time, the committee was co-chaired by R.C. Morgan from Texas, one of the movement's most respected leaders, and Rod Glen, who had earned the movement's general respect despite his left-wing politics.[190] They were an effective pair and led the process with remarkable skill and foresight.

The Canadian support for reform was partly because it agreed with the positions increasingly evident in Latin America, Australia and Africa. It also fit in well with the attempt to restructure and revitalize the Canadian movement. The reconsideration could help, for example, in bringing the recalcitrant leagues into membership in the National Association of Canadian Credit Unions; it might even stimulate the amalgamation of NACCU with the Canadian Co-operative Credit Society. A few even hoped it would assist in bringing the *caisses populaires* and credit union movements together in some loose form of a truly national system.

Following presentations and discussions in 1968, the committee reported in June 1969 and called for the creation of an independent international organization, the World Council of Credit Unions. The committee recommended that the American and Canadian movements, already meeting as forums, evolve into "regional confederations" because of their size and because of the dues they paid; it encouraged other regions to form confederations, and particularly urged Australia to do so; it encouraged District Twelve to create appropriate confederations as soon as it was convenient to do so. The committee did not assume that the existing confederations in the Caribbean, Africa and Latin America would automatically become "confederation" members in the new organization. It did, however, suggest that freestanding leagues could be members if they came from regions with limited credit union movements or regions that could not support an independent confederation. The committee recommended proportionate voting that gave enhanced control to those paying most of the dues, and it developed a complicated formula for dues based on average per capita income of member countries. It recommended that between 50 and 60 delegates would represent the leagues around the world at triennial meetings; this was a sharp reduction from the prohibitively expensive pattern of having 250 directors gather annually.

The committee recommended the creation of a fifteen-person board made up of nine individuals from the United States, two from Canada and four from the remaining member countries. The board would be responsible for the operation of the new organization, using in the first instance funds raised by dues. It was a dramatic reconstruction, but a necessary one.

At the end of the day, the decision to create the World Council ultimately rested with the Americans, as it had in the early 1960s when the idea of regional associations or confederations had first been floated and rejected. The Americans had most of the votes, they paid most of the dues, and they made most of the annual special contributions. They even owned Filene House in Madison, a valuable piece of property that housed CUNA International and which the committee proposed handing over to the new organization.

The possibilities for deadlock or filibustering were almost endless. There were some difficult legal issues; the voting pattern was obviously a compromise; a cumbersome six-year period of adjustment was proposed; the budgetary system was complicated; the balance of power in the new organization was a matter of conjecture; the kind of internationalism the new organization seemed to represent was not widely supported in the United States; the issue of Filene House represented a significant investment and a fiduciary responsibility to the many individuals and organizations that had contributed to its development.

The key debate took place at the meeting of the CUNA International Board on February 9-10, 1969. Formally, it lasted one long afternoon and most of the following morning; informally, it consumed much of the night in between. The debate was occasionally passionate, but the kind of acrimony that had appeared in the past over the CUNA/CUNA Mutual issues did not surface. A few diplomatic and skilful American leaders, especially R.C. Morgan and the president of the day, R.C. Robertson, and some representatives from other countries, notably the Australian Dermot Ryan and the Canadian Rod Glen, headed off any attempts to undermine the compromise that had been achieved. The vote was unanimous. A new, more appropriate structure — the World Council of Credit Unions (WOCCU) — had finally been found for the international movement.

CHAPTER SEVEN

SHAPING A GLOBAL MOVEMENT
1971-1978

THE WORLD COUNCIL OF CREDIT UNIONS (WOCCU) came into existence as an incorporated company in the state of Wisconsin on January 1, 1971. It was a benchmark in the history of the international movement, the culmination of a dream that had stirred enthusiasts from two generations of credit union leaders.

By 1971, the dream had some basis in reality. Between 1962 and 1970, the credit union movements in the United States, Canada and Australia had generally started the systematic expansion of the international movement. The enthusiasm emanating from that expansion would last for most of the 1970s. The slogan for WOCCU's first annual meeting in 1971, in fact, was "Dare to Look Ahead", a phrase taken from one of Edward Filene's writings; it was embraced with gusto by many of the world's credit union leaders.

The optimism was important. It was a prerequisite for anyone engaged for long in international development work. After all, people coping with the challenges of extreme poverty, low educational levels, local politics and cultural tensions need confidence. They must assume that their work can make a significant difference, or they would not be able to continue doing it. They must believe in their own capabilities and, more to the point, have faith in the abilities of people they often hardly know. It was, as it always would be, difficult work, often frustrating, but tremendously rewarding when it succeeded.

Moreover, the world of international development was animated by several major debates in the 1970s. These debates were generated by significant differences of opinion over such issues as the primacy of agricultural as opposed to industrial development; the relative importance of transportation systems; the role of health and development programmes; the significance of housing policy; the importance of education and training; the role of government; the kinds of technology that would be appropriate in different parts of the world; and the importance of planning by both governments and private-sector institutions. To complicate matters further, almost all of these debates were inevitably cast in an ideological framework at a time when most people responded compulsively and simplistically in matters of ideology.

The credit union movement was caught up in these debates, both in North America and overseas. It inherently possessed, however, a point of view shaped by generations of co-operative thought, the North American experience, and particularly the American model of credit unionism. The movement favoured gradual development within small groups, generally "from the bottom up"; it championed educational and human development; it focused on communities defined by workplace, community, religious and social bonds of association; it was suspicious of any widespread and complicated efforts to transform societies quickly and fundamentally; it believed in the capacity of almost any group to mobilize savings, then a rather heretical idea in development circles; and it was resistant to government control but would seek distinctive and enforced regulatory structures from both government and its own institutions. This point of view would always have difficulty finding environments in which it could naturally thrive, but it was an approach with much to recommend it.

Statistically, the overall results achieved by 1971 were impressive and encouraging. The rapid growth would continue until 1978. In 1962, just over 29,000 credit unions were affiliated with the leagues belonging to CUNA and therefore served by the World Extension Department; they had 17,400,000 members and $8,860,000,000US in assets. At the end of 1970 56,000 credit unions around the world were affiliated through national federations and freestanding leagues with the World Council; they had 40,000,000 members and assets of $23,500,000,000US. By 1978, there would be 44,692 credit unions, 11,300 fewer than seven years earlier, largely because of amalgamations in the developed movements, but they would have over 56,000,000 members and assets of more than $85,000,000,000US.[191] All told, it was a pattern of remarkable growth, in many cases under difficult circumstances, and in a short period of time.

In keeping with the context in which the World Council was created, and reflecting the growth of management cultures, the leadership in the 1970s placed considerable emphasis on planning. In October 1971, WOCCU's Planning Committee met in Scottsdale, Arizona. There it drew up the purposes for the new organization, and it was an ambitious list: assisting member confederations in their development programmes; expanding credit union services around the world; enabling national federations and the confederations to achieve technical and financial self-sufficiency in the shortest possible time; maximizing the distribution of technical support services; fostering closer relations with kindred organizations; ensuring the autonomy of federations and confederations from government control; and assisting member organizations with the national economic programmes within their own countries.[192]

The committee devoted considerable time to discussing how the organization should carry out its development activities overseas. It stressed planning at all levels of the international movement and called for all federations and confederations to undertake the preparation of five-year plans; all of them did so within a short period of time. The committee also emphasized participation in credit for agricultural production, co-operation with kindred organizations and increased participation in government and United Nations programmes.

In addition to discussing the work in developing countries, the plan clearly accentuated the role of the World Council in promoting international co-operative banking activities: that is, bringing together established co-operative banking organizations in an integrated framework able to compete in a financial world being transformed by technology. It was a perspective the World Council would struggle to retain as it dealt with the myriad challenges of developing the new and newer credit union movements. It was also arguably the ultimate challenge for the council over the long run.

The early 1970s saw several changes in the staffing of the international programme. In 1971 Orrin Shipe's rather controversial career as managing director of CUNA came to an end. He moved on to become managing director of the Arizona League until his retirement in 1977. Even after the move to Arizona and into his retirement, Shipe retained his genuine interest in the international movement, most particularly by serving as an advisor for the Thai movement in the early 1980s.[193]

Shipe's replacement as managing director of CUNA was Herb Wegner, who continued the practice of simultaneously holding the position of managing director of the World Council until 1975. In 1971 Paul Hebert took over as manager of the Global Projects Office and other Washington-based WOCCU activities, inheriting the responsibilities of Harry Culbreth. Paddy Bailey was variously the assistant managing director and acting managing director of WOCCU until he was appointed permanent managing director in late 1975, the first person to hold that position exclusively.[194]

As for the makeup of the World Council, the American movement was still by far the largest. Indeed, much of the growth in the period took place in the United States, reversing a trend that had started in the 1960s, when the rapid development of credit unions in Latin America and Africa had sharply reduced the American percentage share of the numbers of credit unions and of members within the international movement. It had not, however, significantly altered the massive dominance in total assets that the Americans enjoyed.

During the 1970s, the growth, in membership and assets, of American movement more than kept pace with that of the international movement. In 1962 the American movement had 72 percent of the affiliated credit unions, 80 percent of the members and 80 percent of the assets. In 1970, because of the growth overseas, its share of credit unions had dipped dramatically to 41 percent and membership to 55 percent, but it still accounted for 74 percent of the assets of the global movement. In 1978 the American movement had 49 percent of the credit unions, but, because of the movement's growing popularity in the United States, it had increased its membership to 72 percent, while its share of the assets remained relatively constant at 73 percent.[195]

The size of the American movement meant that it continued to play a powerful role within the international movement. Financially, it was crucially important: American sources provided close to 90 percent of the World Council's annual budget of approximately $2,000,000US (exclusive of funds from agencies for projects overseas). Just as significantly, through its connections with USAID, CUNA had negotiated the projects undertaken with USAID support in the 1960s on behalf of the American credit unions; it would continue to play that role during the years that lay immediately ahead. All told, by the autumn of 1971, the funds pledged from development and charitable organizations, with USAID the most important donor, amounted annually to between $6,000,000 and $6,500,000US.[196]

While the American participation was of greatest importance, it is also true that the Canadian and Australian contributions were increasingly significant. Until the 1970s, the Canadian participation had been through small (but important) contributions from some leagues, the direct involvement of Canadian volunteers overseas and, most importantly, the continuing strong support of Canadian leaders within WED/CUNA International. That involvement would increase, but it would remain largely with a few centrals: along with the Australians, Canadians would contribute more in the 1970s, particularly as their governments became more involved in external aid.

Despite this support, WOCCU was not a wealthy organization and had to scramble annually for funds to carry out its activities. Its core funding initially came from a dues structure that required each confederation to submit 1½ cents per member, and each freestanding league to submit 10 cents per member. In 1973 this amount was changed to a flat 1½ cents in an effort to help the smaller and, for the most part, newer movements. Almost invariably, though, new movements, such as some in Africa, were unable to pay their full amounts, thereby making the American contributions even more important.

It is not surprising, therefore, that most of the key elected leaders in the new organization came largely from the United States. The first president of the World Council was R.C. Robertson from Arizona, who served until the St. Louis meeting in 1973. A widely respected, deeply committed credit unionist, Robertson had done much to bring about the formation of the World Council. Other important leaders elected from the United States in the early 1970s included Harold Carpenter from Alabama, Joseph Medeiros from Hawaii and Dominic Allessio from Washington.

Along with the American leadership, however, a few from other countries played important roles. The most prominent Canadians were Harold Braaten (president from 1973 to 1975), Rod Glen, George May and Al Charbonneau. The most prominent Australians were Graham Benson, Ken Miller and Jack Coyne. Lorrell Bruce from Jamaica was another particularly important, even pivotal, figure in the 1970s. Bruce played a crucial role in his capacity as chairman of the "Overseas Forum", and he was ideally suited to bridge many of the cultural gaps in the international movement.

Institutionally, WOCCU was closely tied to CUNA. It purchased a number of services from the larger organization, including those of the managing director as well as accounting, public relations, education and personnel. It also depended upon good relations with CUNA Mutual Insurance, which provided expertise on insurance issues, offered its products outside the United States when it was feasible, and contributed funds to overseas development.

Despite the obvious dominance of the Americans, there was an oft-expressed, generally widespread desire — in the United

States as well as elsewhere — to expand the ownership and involvement of people in other regions of the world. It is easy to criticize how well these good intentions were carried out during the 1970s. Indulging in such criticism, however, would lose sight of how incredibly difficult it was — and always would be — to achieve a truly international perspective. It also underestimates the challenge of developing an equitable control structure that spanned the world. Doing so was particularly difficult for North Americans, then at the height of their economic ascendency and conditioned by capitalist perceptions to allocate power primarily to those who were essentially paying the piper.

One way to test the commitment to building a genuinely international organization is to consider the energy and resources expended in creating effective confederations, including those in countries with well-established national movements. At the time of its formation, the World Council consisted of three national "confederations" — the United States (CUNA), Australia (the Australian Federation of Credit Union Leagues or AFCUL) and Canada (the National Association of Canadian Credit Unions or NACCU) — and freestanding leagues from several countries. The American confederation was the easiest to adapt to the new framework; it was necessary only to reorganize CUNA into an exclusively national organization. In some ways, it was liberating for American credit unionists to focus more clearly upon the considerable challenges confronting the American movement: for example, protecting the taxation position of credit unions, resolving the long-standing and debilitating feud between CUNA and CUNA Mutual, placating the larger credit unions, and warding off growing competition from larger banks and savings and loans banks.

It was more difficult, but more than overdue, for the Australians and Canadians to wrestle seriously with the structural challenge of creating effective national organizations. In Canada, the 1970s witnessed the remarkable growth of large community credit unions, especially in western Canada. In some ways they forced the expansion of central credit unions to meet their growing technological needs and to press for legislative reform in order to provide more services for their members. In other ways, they weakened the capacity of

centrals to speak on behalf of the entire movement, because in several instances they were insistent that new financial "products" be designed and delivered at the local level, thereby depleting the power of centrals.

Most importantly, however, the centrals and the larger credit unions were concerned about how the national financial system was developing in Canada. Until the 1970s the few major banks in Canada had dominated government relations; the evolution of the Canadian payments system, which started to undergo dramatic change in the 1970s, was a case in point. During the decade, therefore, the credit union system, through the Canadian Co-operative Credit Society, joined with the Desjardins movement to gain a place for the co-operative banking system in the evolution of the system. Indirectly, this national effort helped the Canadian international initiatives, because the more energized CCCS paid more attention to the topic and promoted it among centrals and local credit unions more effectively.

In Australia, though the Australian Federation of Credit Unions had been in place since 1968, it was more promise than reality. Until the 1970s, the national movement was dominated by the New South Wales movement and that dominance had some negative features. First, in the political and social culture of Australia, New South Wales, as the largest and most powerful state with by far the largest city, was always looked upon with some suspicion by people in other states. It was a fact of Australian life. Second, and more importantly, the movement in New South Wales was in a fractious period, divided between CUNA Mutual and nationalist advocates on the insurance issue, between large and small credit unions, between advocates of populist and managerial credit unions, and between idealists and hardliners. Third, and most important, the movement was beset by a major liquidity problem in 1974-1975, which preoccupied most of the state's leaders for much of the middle of the decade.[197]

At the same time, the movement in the rest of the country was progressing rapidly, and it was naturally preoccupied by its own affairs and growing pains. The movement in the state of Victoria went through a boom period, reflecting a strong commitment to the nationalist side of the insurance issue, advocating close contacts with other kinds of co-operatives and showing a greater commitment to community credit unions. In other parts of the country — Queensland, South Australia, Western Australia, the Northern Territory and Tasmania — the movement was in an early stage of development but growing fast. In fact, its demands raised the question in some circles of whether whatever resources the Australian movement possessed should be devoted to its own promotion rather than sent overseas.

Thus, the advocates of a strong Australian federation and, by implication, of strong support for the international movement faced an uphill struggle in the 1970s. Nevertheless, Dermot Ryan and his supporters in this matter — Graham Benson from Victoria, Beresford Calverley, Ken Miller and Jack Coyne from New South Wales — persisted in promoting the national and international movements. In the process, they played significant roles in the annual gatherings of the World Council and in advancing a distinctive Australian view — a strong dose of pragmatism mixed with a deep concern for the Pacific region — within the international movement.

In other parts of the world, the formation of confederations was hindered essentially by the shortage of funds and the immaturity of national movements. Nevertheless, according to the vision of the time, it was in Latin America, Africa and Asia that confederations were most needed. The remarkable statistical and real success of the development programmes of the 1960s suggested that central organizations could attract funds from external agencies and foster extensive credit union growth. Moreover, the creation of confederations overseas would demonstrate emphatically that the movement had expanded beyond its North American roots, and that credit unions in other parts of the world had at least started to be accepted at "the table". It would also conform to the common views that credit unions were a flexible form of organization shaped by the economic and social needs of the society in which they existed: they were not convenient structures imposed by external organizers, but manifestations of local and regional pride.

For all these reasons, there was a strong determination among many World Council leaders in the established and emerging movements to promote the development of confed-

erations as much as possible. By May 1971, confederations had been formed for Asia (Asian Confederation of Credit Unions, or ACCU), Latin America (La Confederación Latino-americana de Cooperativas de Ahorro y Crédito, the Latin American Confederation of Credit Unions or COLAC), and Africa (African Co-operative Savings and Credit Association, or ACCOSCA). That left freestanding leagues for other parts of the world, including at that time New Zealand, Trinidad and Tobago, Fiji, British Honduras, the Eastern Caribbean Council, Great Britain, Guyana, Ireland and Jamaica.

Like the formation of the council itself, this restructuring was a major development in the history of the international movement, although in retrospect it may also have been premature. It was a frank and generous recognition by credit unionists in the established movements, but especially by many in the United States, that it was time to make a clear move toward creating a genuinely international credit union structure based upon as much local, national and regional control as possible. As *The International Yearbook* for 1971 stated: the newly created confederations "are now assured that local leadership will occupy a proud place in the international arena as representatives of one of the largest human resource development organizations in the world".[198]

Behind these transformations the support networks upon which the movement relied had started to change in the 1960s. They would continue to do so in the 1970s. The work originally undertaken by WED, and even much of that undertaken by CUNA International, had depended largely upon volunteer international networks provided by the Christian churches, most importantly the Roman Catholic Church. The close association with religious groups would continue during the early 1970s.

In fact, the association with religious groups was cemented by special international forums in 1970 and 1975 aimed at co-ordinating the support of Roman Catholic and Protestant churches and at welcoming the involvement of Buddhist leaders from Asia and Moslem leaders from Africa. An international working group was formed in 1970 to co-ordinate the work of the churches in support of credit union development around the world. The group sponsored three working parties, one each in Africa, Asia and Latin America, and sponsored regional training conferences for interested clergy and lay people to help the development of credit unions in their respective countries.[199]

Increasingly, however, there were tensions with church leaders in Korea, Japan, Fiji and Latin America, where some clerics sought to retain control over credit unions even though other, more secular leaders had started to emerge, and more professional management was necessary.

In some instances, the lingering control by religious leaders reflected the depth of their commitment and the extent of their past sacrifices. In others, the instinctive and deep commitment to "populist" credit unions by church leaders conflicted with those who wished to force them to evolve into more managerial cultures. In still other instances, the issue was politics, as some religious leaders were deeply influenced by liberation theology and wished to see their credit unions become agents of direct political, as well as economic and social, change.

At the same time, the World Council, like CUNA International before it, sought out associations with other international organizations engaged in international development. The inevitable corollary was that it would have a growing need for specialists, especially to administer projects from the Global Projects Office, not for the kinds of idealistic generalists who were common in the early years. Thus, the council employed more people experienced in international development work; it continued to use effectively the services of such organizations as the Peace Corps; it gradually developed its own cadre of continuing employees, an increasing percentage of whom were technical experts. The council also worked with a range of international organizations, some with church affiliations, such as MISEREOR and the Catholic Relief Services, some with co-operative connections, notably the Raiffeisen movement and the International Co-operative Alliance, but an increasing number of them with ties to government and United Nations agencies.

Starting in the early 1970s, World Council officials regularly and systematically visited major international funding agencies, such as the Canadian International Development Agency, the International Raiffeisen Union, MISEREOR, the Asia Foundation and the Konrad Adenauer Foundation, in search of funds for credit union development in southern countries. They were very successful in making contacts and ultimately in encouraging funding either directly to WOCCU or to national movements and regional confederations.

The council's association with the international development community would grow. In 1972, WOCCU opened an office in Geneva to be closer to many of the international development organizations. In that year it also invited the International Raiffeisen Union, the International Co-operative Alliance and the Desjardins movement to attend its meeting in Halifax, the first time it had sought to engage outside organizations in its key deliberations. Also in 1972, WOCCU was invited to become a full member of the Committee on Social and Economic Development of the International Council of Voluntary Agencies. It also began to work closely with the Joint Committee for the Promotion of Agricultural Co-operatives (COPAC), an agency supported by FAO, ILO, UNESCO, ICA and UNICO. And, in its own house, WOCCU became more open to outside influences in 1973 when it created associate memberships so that groups such as thrift and credit organizations could play a role in its deliberations.

As the World Council programme unfolded, several trends were evident. One of them concerned a problem shared by most other kinds of co-operatives within the developing world: establishing appropriate relationships with the state. Credit unions were particularly vulnerable to unwanted attention from the governments of developing countries; they were one of the few effective ways of raising capital and could become, therefore, very valuable tools for countries in desperate need of financial resources. On a local level, too, they could become "targets" for politicians seeking popular support or even financial resources. Just as dangerously, governments were prone to enlist credit unions in the delivery of state funding for any number of projects, from agricultural support to health programmes. If not managed properly, this kind of attention could create artificial prosperity for a given credit union organization and work against the development of effective management techniques.[200] Credit union leaders could be lulled into adopting uneconomic practices if they became too reliant upon fees generated from government agreements.

Fundamentally, there was the problem of deciding what governments should do to foster growth of credit union movements. There was no doubt that government support was necessary for the development of co-operatives, including credit unions, in the early years. The challenge was to get governments, like all good parents, to realize when it was time to let their co-operative children accept responsibility for their own development. That problem would be particularly acute in Africa, but it was found in Asia and Latin America as well. Indeed, it could be found in more muted forms in some states and provinces in the United States, Canada and Australia.

In short, the long tradition of insulation from undue government influence in European and North American co-operative banking circles would not be easily replicated in all parts of the developing world. In many countries, it would be difficult to establish a situation in which the state provided appropriate legislation that allowed credit unions to function effectively in the marketplace; that ensured they were not discriminated against in any way in government policy; that provided adequate statistical, supervisory and research support; and that considered sympathetically how credit unions might help alleviate economic disparities.[201]

A second trend that became evident during the 1970s was an increasing concern for resolving many of the problems confronting rural areas around the world. Partly, this was in response to trends within the international development community. Starting in the late 1960s, USAID and CIDA, for example, both placed a steadily higher priority on development projects that assisted rural areas. WOCCU, the American movement and their Canadian partners responded positively to this mandate.[202]

The common way to address rural dilemmas was to use government resources, frequently delivered through co-operative supply and marketing organizations, to expand the credit possibilities to farm families. Such programmes, which were widespread in many parts of the developing world, had a mixed history. In some places, for example, Japan, they functioned reasonably well and met their original limited objectives satisfactorily: they assisted in the development of strong farming sectors and vibrant rural communities. In other places they did not function as well; they invited corruption, created dependency, and sustained production units that were ultimately incapable of competing. Such situations posed a problem for credit union movements in various countries. Should they collaborate? Should they accept government funding? If so, under what terms? In reality, the movement was grappling with one of the most difficult issues of the industrial and post-industrial eras: how to provide for healthy and sustainable areas outside of the economically dominant urban/industrial metropolitan centres.

In the 1970s, the World Bank, recognizing the failure of many of its previous efforts in rural areas, sponsored numerous studies in an attempt to understand what could be done to alleviate the lot of the absolute poor, many of whom lived in the countryside. The plight of rural women was particularly bad. As Robert McNamara, then president of the World Bank, pointed out in 1973, these women spent most of their lives gathering firewood and fetching water. "Women in Development" would become a priority for credit unions by 1975.

Underlying the World Bank's concern was a growing recognition that many of the 1950s and 1960s development projects had been limited successes at best. For all the good intentions of most of the individuals involved, many of the projects had stressed massive manipulations of the environment or advocated technologies that worked well in some northern climes but were inappropriate in subtropical and tropical regions. The result had been several poorly developed agricultural projects based on machinery that was misapplied, planting and harvesting techniques that were too expensive and water drainage systems that were too exploitive.

An alternative approach, one that became more fashionable by the late 1960s and the early 1970s, emphasized smaller projects better suited to host environments. This approach stressed the importance of mobilizing funds at the local level, something earlier development projects had deemed improbable. It argued that if the situation confronting a growing population of rural poor was going to be improved, then ways had to be found to increase rural production incrementally. In many cases this meant the purchase of low-cost seeds, fertilizers and other supplies; in other words, the encouragement of selective aspects of what was then widely called the "green revolution", all of which required mobilizing local savings, a strategy in which credit unions could be immensely valuable.

There were also some more general political reasons — both "at home" and globally — for emphasizing rural development overseas. The worsening plight of the rural poor, especially in war-torn southern countries, became one of the great social and economic problems of the day. It was not a problem that could be readily avoided; increasingly, more pervasive modern media made it impossible to do so. Nor would the problem become easier: the adoption of preventive health measures, especially a better water supply, improved dietary practices and inoculations, reduced the incidence of early childhood deaths, and extended life expectancy. Thus, as the years went by, increased population pressures made the problems even greater.

Moreover, protest movements in southern countries often had their origins in rural areas, many of them taking on the Marxist overtones that were so unwelcome among national elites and northern observers, including many credit union leaders. There were many reasons why northern countries wanted to pay more attention to the growing problem of the rural poor in the developing world.

While it could never be a complete solution to the difficult problems of the rural poor, the credit union movement was an attractive partial answer. For that reason, governments and donor agencies were increasingly willing to invest in credit union development. WOCCU, along with associated credit union development programmes emanating from Canada and Australia, would be able to attract support for overseas projects. Credit unionism resonated well with most people interested in international development in the 1970s.

By 1973, therefore, WOCCU had developed its priorities for credit union development around the world. First, it would help low-income farmers; second, it would encourage interlending between credit unions in the developed and developing parts of the world; third, it would promote credit union growth through development agencies; and fourth, it would improve communications among credit unionists around the world.[203]

Carrying out these objectives required considerable support from credit union movements in the United States, Canada and, increasingly, Australia and Ireland. One way to achieve this goal was through the use of films both at home and overseas. In the 1970s the most popular films were those that had been made by Fenton McHugh during the previous decade: the perennially popular "Small Miracle of Santa Cruz", along with "The People of Kolevu" and "Building Tomorrow Together". The former was about the Fijian movement, while the latter two marked the tenth anniversary of the Africa Cooperative Savings and Credit Association.

In addition, the print material emanating from Madison, especially *The World Reporter* and the *Newsletter*, became steadily more professional and attractive. These periodicals, along with a wide range of publications for training sessions, were available in a growing number of languages for use around the world. Pamphlets, a medium that staged something of a comeback in the 1970s, were also used extensively; they were integrated into the adult education activities of the period and became an effective link between the established and developing movements.

The most colourful and memorable activities associated with the World Council, however, were its forums. These forums, which featured a parade of flags from all the member countries at both the opening and closing celebrations, were presented with a growing sense of occasion marked by speeches from important dignitaries, movement leaders and guest experts. Each of the national organizations presented information on recent experiences. The evenings were given over to special entertainments reflecting the host country and to visits in the homes of local credit union leaders. On one of the evenings, gifts from delegates were auctioned off to raise funds for development projects. In the best meaning of the words, the forums were educational and social events. They helped greatly in creating a sense of the international movement.

One reason why such links were important was the growing significance of credit union foundations. The foundations were important, first, because of the funds they raised for the overseas programmes. Second, they were viewed by government funding agencies as indicators of the support of ordinary citizens for the work being carried out overseas. Third, for the ordinary credit union member, they were useful because they made clear how funds would be spent and because they provided tax receipts for donations.

When the World Council was formed, it inherited the CUNA International Foundation, which had been established in 1965 as the charitable arm of CUNA International and was used primarily to offer tax relief to individuals who had donated to overseas development. In addition to helping in development projects, the foundation served as a way in which credit unionists could donate to disaster relief, especially disasters affecting credit unions. In 1974 WOCCU changed the name to the Worldwide Foundation in anticipation of being able to serve credit unionists around the world. Doing so proved to be difficult, however. Some national movements preferred to organize their own foundations in the belief that their nationals would rather donate to them. Moreover, the national organizations wanted to control how the funds they collected were disbursed so as to ensure they would be spent in ways applauded back home. This meant that the Worldwide Foundation was forced to place even greater emphasis on disaster relief during the later 1970s, a charitable activity largely funded by national foundations willing to donate 5 percent of their annual contributions.

In Canada, the Co-operative Union of Canada had organized the Co-operative Development Foundation of Canada in 1947. The foundation languished until 1958, when Alexander Laidlaw,[204] the CUC's General Secretary, encouraged its expansion so that it could contribute to the development of co-operatives in the Canadian North and overseas. During the 1960s some funds were found through the foundation to assist in the development of credit unions and other co-operatives in the West Indies and Guyana. The amounts raised were small but they were very helpful in developing credit unions and fishing co-operatives, particularly in the Caribbean.

In 1972, Canada's taxation laws were changed and credit unions started to be taxed much like other businesses; this made the foundation more important because it could issue tax receipts for charitable donations for overseas activities. In 1974, the National Association of Canadian Credit Unions designated the foundation as the channel through which credit unions should contribute to international credit union development. In doing so, it also hoped to qualify for increased support from the Canadian International Development Association, which, like USAID, was drawn to the grassroots success of co-operative endeavour both at home and overseas.

By 1977, the Co-operative Development Foundation of Canada was funding eleven projects worth $275,000 overseas; the amount jumped dramatically to $683,000 in 1978, $1,560,000 in 1980 and $3,500,000 in 1983. Given this track record, and concerned to attract more funding from the Canadian government, the Canadian Co-operative Credit Society transferred all of its limited overseas activities to the foundation, whose projects were administered by the Co-operative Union of Canada.

The Australian Credit Union Foundation was formed in 1971 by the Australian Federation of Credit Unions. Its focus was the institutional development of credit union movements in Asia and the Pacific. Like the Canadian foundation, it had a dual mandate: to meet needs both at home and overseas. At home it provided assistance to aboriginal peoples interested in forming credit unions. Overseas, it used the interest on its investments to fund specific projects, such as the Bergengren school in Fiji and helping the Tongan movement to develop an accounting system. The Australian foundation worked consistently within the WOCCU system, unlike the Canadians, who would undertake programmes on their own initiative.

The connections with the American, Canadian and, as the decade wore on, the Australian movement, also took place on a more subtle level. There was a tendency in those three countries — then and later — to think that their movements were considerably different from those in developing countries. In reality, that was not the case; it has never been the case. Nevertheless, leaders from the three movements found they had much in common when they met at international gatherings. In fact, the main trends in the American, Canadian and Australian movements almost immediately affected the way in which their leaders viewed developments overseas.

Within those three countries the variations among credit unions by the 1970s were quite remarkable. A growing number of credit unions were deeply embedded in "managerial" cultures and had become very sophisticated organizations. In some instances, they were pace-setting institutions within the banking industry, pioneering in hours of opening, innovative lending and a range of services. The larger credit unions were exploring new technologies, particularly the computing systems that would revolutionize the financial industries during the 1970s and 1980s. In doing so, some of them were increasingly less comfortable within the state, provincial and national credit union structures that had been created; they sought new technologies and new approaches either independently or through groups of like-minded credit unions. Characteristically, and too single-mindedly, their critics argued, these credit unions were preoccupied with their bottom lines and aimed for business efficiency, both at home and overseas; their notions of membership and communities were becoming very different from those found in populist credit unions.

During the 1960s, American, Canadian and Australian credit union leaders, for the most part from the larger credit unions, were particularly concerned about improving the level of management expertise and the use of technology within the two national movements. Their concerns had led to the formation of ICU Service Corporation in 1966. The corporation initially marketed credit union money orders and sold travellers cheques, but it soon offered an investment service for credit unions and facilitated interlending among credit unions.

Eventually, all these developments affected the World Council. WOCCU participated in the early development of CUNADATA, but, as in Australia and Canada, enlisting the full support of the movement and settling upon software acceptable to most credit unions proved to be difficult, frustrating work. Nevertheless, the fascination with new technologies was in principle well placed, in that machines would transform the banking industry by the later 1980s. They would also find their role within the international movement, a process tentatively begun during the 1970s.

The divisions within the American, Canadian and Australian movements were also echoed overseas. In the early 1970s there were still many credit unions in the three countries manifesting populist culture: they were largely dependent upon volunteers and close to their members. In the "overseas" countries, the populist credit union was the norm, if it wasn't universal. For credit unionists from the three countries who came from, or who were sympathetic to, that culture, work in the developing countries could be exhilarating. In fact, it could be the reaffirmation of a lifetime's work. For those who came from credit unions imbued with management culture, it could be very frustrating; they could have great difficulty avoiding the trap of

dismissing too lightly what they saw, or of assuming they were "at the same stage we were years ago". One of the perpetual challenges confronting the World Council was how to bridge the various gaps created by such diversity.

Despite such complexities, the expansion of the overseas movement during the 1970s was exhilarating. It was a time for exploring an apparently unending set of possibilities, and for creating new support networks in both the old and new movements. It was a time to confront new issues, to reach for a truly international perspective. It was a time to consider seriously what was involved in creating a global movement and to understand more thoroughly the scale of the issues associated with international development.

The Executive Committee of the World Council, 1970-1971. From left to right: Charles F. Bernard, J. Orrin Shipe, Harold Braaten (president), Robert C. Robertson and Harold B. Carpenter. (COURTESY OF CUNA)

CHAPTER EIGHT

BUILDING MOVEMENTS AROUND THE WORLD
1970-1982

Credit union philosophy is in tune with the philosophies of developing countries and will have its economic development policies conditioned by local sociological and cultural concepts. WOCCU has no political ax to grind on behalf of any country; but simply seeks to be a catalyst for the development of new co-operative services. It will work with the public and private co-operative sector of the economy and will not be limited by restricted outlooks.

"A Report on the Planning Committee Meeting" 1971

... unless we begin to help our individual members understand that they are the backbone of our Movement, not just members of Credit Unions, we cannot proudly say that we have built a movement with a good cause and a common philosophy, a movement for constructive change, a movement to give people meaningful participation and an opportunity through ownership to become masters of their own destinies.

Andrew So

LATIN AMERICA

THE EXPANSION OF THE OVERSEAS MOVEMENT DURING the 1970s was a time for building new structures. As in the 1960s, the greatest efforts, until at least the middle of the decade, were expended in Latin America. Indeed, one of the primary tasks of the World Council in the early 1970s was to establish a strong basis for the new Latin American confederation. It was a task that required both the building of an effective management system and the establishment of a strong financial foundation. Neither task was easy.

The first step on the management issue was to work out an appropriate relationship between the Latin American movements and the Latin American Regional Office (LARO). The leaders of the Latin American movements had started to assert themselves in the later 1960s, and in 1969 asked LARO to carry out a feasibility study on the creation of a regional financial system. The study, completed in 1970, led to the formation of COLAC in August 1971.[205] Shortly thereafter, the board of COLAC became the board responsible for LARO, at that time managed by Henry Cruz. This meant that most of the staff employed by WOCCU and the new confederation were located in Panama. On average, over the next few years between forty and fifty regional specialists would be regularly employed by LARO to improve operational techniques within credit unions, including financial innovations, insurance programmes and, increasingly, the agricultural programmes of the credit union movement. For the most part, they were technicians able to advise on the more common business problems that credit unions encountered.

In 1972 all administrative, management and programme responsibilities were transferred from the LARO director to the

COLAC director. The shift coincided with the adoption of a five-year development plan for the years 1972 to 1976. The plan placed considerable emphasis on developing credit unions in rural areas, and it advocated strengthening the administrative and economic efficiency of local credit unions. Above all, it called upon the Latin American movement to set itself the goal of self-sufficiency.

Once COLAC had responsibility for the office, it sought greater control over WOCCU's programme in Latin America. By April 1, 1974, it had gained complete responsibility for the technical assistance programme: USAID agreed to turn over all the funds it was providing for credit union development in Latin America. This was a significant milestone for the international movement, since it indicated a high degree of confidence in the leadership groups that had been formed in less than a decade.

The creation of a strong financial base was a more complicated matter, involving the negotiation of a series of loans from international agencies. WOCCU and LARO had a successful track record in this regard, and in 1971 arranged loans worth $7,500,000US. The loans were to be used to provide income for COLAC and national federations, but ultimately they were intended to expand the lending capital of local credit unions.

In 1975 the Global Projects Office negotiated a $1,000,000US loan from the Inter-American Foundation in order to kick-start a programme for expanding loans to rural credit union members. The loan, which was intended to expand rapidly the lending capacity of COLAC, was imaginatively developed so as to help stabilize COLAC, a primary challenge for the regional movement. One policy of the loan required that each Latin American federation invest a minimum of $250,000US per year in COLAC; another required each national federation to purchase shares equal to a further 1 percent of all outstanding loans with COLAC. Following these policies meant that COLAC would quickly have a $2,000,000US equity capital base; in turn, these funds could be leveraged to borrow up to $10,000,000US, to be loaned to credit unions, through their federations, for the use of rural borrowers. In the context of the time, and given the newness of the organization, it was a significant fund and

demonstrated the possibilities if credit unions in the region could work closely together.[206]

In 1974 WOCCU developed the International Lending Program largely through the efforts of Angel Castro. The programme offered loans of $100,000US or more to qualified credit union confederations through the recently formed United States Central Credit Union. The loans were ultimately to be used at the local level to help members whose credit needs surpassed the capabilities of the depositors, and were guaranteed by the Overseas Private Investment Corporation, a U.S. government agency created to stimulate American investment in developing countries. The earliest loans were made in Latin America in 1975, and the programme soon expanded to include Asian and African credit union movements.[207] It remained, however, primarily a Latin American programme.

In 1975 the Inter-American Development Bank made its first loan — $9,000,000US — to assist COLAC in developing credit unions. The funds were used to enhance credit unions in Bolivia, Colombia, Costa Rica, Ecuador, El Salvador, Guatemala, Mexico, Nicaragua, Peru and the Dominican Republic.[208] Since this loan and others that followed were also leveraged to make funds available to members at the local level, they represented a significant expansion of the lending capacity of credit unions in the Latin American region.

Throughout the negotiations for these loans it became clear that the priority — from the viewpoint of both donors/lenders and Latin American countries — was the countryside. The reasons for this emphasis are clear enough. Between 70 and 80 percent of the population in most countries still lived in rural communities. The credit union movement as it existed, however, was predominantly urban: in 1971, for example, only 43 percent of the credit unions served rural people, the remaining 57 percent being in urban locations.[209]

There was also a successful model that could be employed in rural areas. The Directed Agricultural Production Programme (DAPP) started by Percy Avram in Ecuador in 1965 had proved to be a success, and Avram had moved to Panama in 1967 to develop the programme regionally. By 1972 WOCCU was funding DAPP initiatives through COLAC in Bolivia, Colombia, Costa Rica, Ecuador, El Salvador, Honduras, Nicaragua, Panama, Paraguay and Dominica.

As the managerial structure was created and funding was found, COLAC developed an ambitious programme for the region, in retrospect perhaps too ambitious a programme. In addition to its efforts at stabilizing and expanding existing movements, it devoted considerable energy, with mixed success, to attracting support from co-operative banking groups in unaffiliated areas. COLAC was particularly interested in developing credit unions in parts of the Cono Sur, as Brazil, Argentina, Uruguay and Chile are commonly called. In those South American countries European immigrants, mostly Germans, had started Raiffeisen or Schultze-Delitzsch banks early in the century, but there was also interest in creating credit unions. The dream of COLAC's leaders was to create an integrated regional movement that would span the continent.

The dream was not easily achieved. In many ways the Mexican situation displayed the kinds of problems that confronted all of the national credit union movements in the period. In the late 1960s and early 1970s, the Mexican movement took on new life. From its beginnings in the 1950s, it had gradually grown to include a number of regional federations that loosely blanketed the country; these federations were, in turn, loosely associated in a national confederation located in Mexico City. The groupings, however, suffered from an overreliance on outside and charitable aid, and they lacked a strong managerial core. Overall, the movement showed early promise, but it was held back by serious organizational difficulties and limited managerial resources.

The World Council, through the efforts of Dick Robertson, found sufficient funds in 1971 to bring in a U.S. technician — Ed Palenque — who could help reorganize the movement and promote more grassroots activity. Palenque also helped redesign the Mexican confederation, which had been developed, in keeping with earlier suggestions from American advisors, on a rather grandiose scale. The smaller, more efficient office that resulted was much more effective in building strong connections with regional federations and the local credit unions.[210]

At the same time, the Mexican credit union movement was suffering from an overreliance on the church connection and a predilection for charitable as opposed to self-help activities. In particular, it did not embrace all the useful opportunities to develop credit unions among working-class people through trade unions and peasant organizations. Doing so was difficult; it was also politically dangerous. Nevertheless, it was only by serving those groups and the small business interests that the movement could thrive. The movement would need considerable time to work out a sound structure and a clear, focused approach to its activities.

There were other, more general, reasons why the Latin American movements were encountering significant challenges in the 1970s. The cultural and political divisions in the region were enormous, far surpassing the variations met earlier in the United States and Canada. Throughout the decade, too, the continent was caught up in political turmoil, partly because of the complexities of the political economies of the countries involved, partly because of the machinations of outside nations extending their political and military competition into Latin America.

The Latin American national economies, in some instances often poorly managed, were also buffeted by international commodity prices and fluctuating interest rates. It was not uncommon to find interest rates in the hundreds; in a few instances they soared over 1,000 percent per annum. It was nearly impossible to run stable credit union systems under these circumstances.

The Latin American movements also had some problems related directly to the way in which they had developed. One of these was that growth, to some extent overheated by the injection of aid funding, outpaced the capacity of local credit unions to grow naturally and soundly. The result was a shortage of trained personnel at both the local and federation levels, especially for accounting and statistical support. One of the most important priorities for COLAC, therefore, was the operation of training programmes normally carried out through national federations. It was a matter of running hard barely to keep up.

A second problem was that many credit unions were expected to carry out a wide range of member and community purposes, meaning that the leadership, both elected and employed, was strained beyond its training. Many credit unions were closer to the Canadian model of community-based enterprises rather than the more narrowly focused American model. This was potentially dangerous unless there were strong management practices to protect the integrity of the banking activities.

Even early success could be harmful. For example, it could encourage credit unions to embrace more broadly based economic growth or to engage in social programmes they could not afford; in turn, that would lead co-operatives and other organizations to expect them to play roles for which they did not have adequate resources, financial or human. Such activities can be undertaken, but only prudently and gradually, and always in a businesslike fashion. That was not always possible in Latin America, given the problems of the region.

Third, national credit union legislation could limit the development of credit unions. In some countries, the "predominant economic groups", notably large land owners, successfully lobbied governments to restrict the capacity of credit unions to attract deposits.[211] In some instances, too, credit union regulators placed statutory restrictions on credit union development: for example, by limiting the percentage of interest that could be paid on deposits or charged on loans. That particular restriction was intended to protect members, to continue the original practice as developed in American and Canadian credit unions and to conform with the basic co-operative principles then advocated by the International Co-operative Alliance. However, it severely restricted the development of credit unions, especially when interest rates soared later in the decade.[212]

Fourth, the credit union movement sometimes became caught up in the political turmoil of the period in certain Latin American countries. Some governments sought to intervene directly in the affairs of credit unions. A few even tried to place them and other co-operatives under direct state control. There were also examples of political groups, on both the right and the left, who tried to dominate national credit union movements through controlling their boards.[213]

Fifth, some governments — such as in Peru, Ecuador, Bolivia and Guyana — wanted to use co-operatives as direct agents for the implementation of their policies. As in other parts of the world, this could be advantageous, but more often than not the association brought trouble: minimally by creating dependency, more seriously by leading to government domination.

All of their problems, combined with adverse economic times, meant that a number of Latin American movements encountered difficulties in the 1970s, including, at various times, Venezuela, the Netherlands Antilles, Nicaragua, Peru and Colombia. Nevertheless, national movements also made progress throughout the period. Increasingly, too, they did so on their own. The direct aid provided by WOCCU to the original national federations was declining by the 1970s, in keeping with the 1960s objective to emphasize national responsibility for credit union stability. In fact, in the early 1970s the World Council was extending direct aid to only three of the original participating countries; by 1975 it was not extending aid to any national movement. While that did not mean there were no significant problems on the national level, it did mean the movements themselves were learning how to deal with the problems that emerged. It was not easy, but it was progress.

AFRICA

WOCCU's work in Africa was somewhat similar to that undertaken by CUNA International in Latin America in the 1960s. At first glance, its work was largely with ACOSCA, but in reality it was also closely associated with various national movements. In its efforts with ACOSCA, WOCCU assisted in the very difficult task of securing funds to help the confederation operate its office in Nairobi and to carry out its most important activities throughout the region: supporting national organizations, operating five training centres, and sponsoring annual conferences on "the mobilization of savings".

In carrying out their work, WOCCU, and particularly ACOSCA, were facing the daunting task of providing training for an expanding number of elected people and professional staff in a steadily growing number of countries. That meant finding the financial and human resources to reach out across the vast expanse that is sub-Saharan Africa. That meant creating training materials that could be used in a wide variety of circumstances and among very diverse groups of people. All of this demanded more than ACOSCA or the World Council could produce and strained the resources of the international and African movements to the limit.

A particularly important change within ACOSCA during the 1970s was the increasing importance of African peoples whose first European language was French. In 1972, Togo, Dahomey and Tunisia joined Senegal and Cameroon to make five members in which French was extensively spoken. Their addition made associations with French-speaking movements in the developed world — the Desjardins movement in Quebec and Crédit Mutuel in France — important, and meant that the ACOSCA office in Nairobi had to expand its capacity to provide service in French. The addition of Tunisia was also regarded at the time as being particularly important as a first step in expanding the movement within Moslem/Arab countries. Three missions were sent to the Arab countries of the north, but progress was slow, partly because the needs of sub-Saharan countries were soon consuming all the resources available.

WOCCU funded its activities in Africa partly through dues from its members and partly through grants from a wide range of donors. The Global Projects Office became increasingly more active in the continent, starting with the provision of a technical assistant for ACOSCA in 1970. It became particularly involved in farm production credit programmes, beginning with projects in Lesotho and Cameroon in 1974. The World Council also became adept at mobilizing support from private organizations, including the Catholic Relief Services, MISEREOR, the Konrad Adenauer Foundation, the Ford Foundation and Rabobank of the Netherlands. It collaborated with technicians sent into the region by the Canadian movement through funding secured largely from CIDA. During the early years, the Canadians worked primarily in countries that were part of the Commonwealth. By the middle of the decade, however, they were also active in the vast areas of Africa in which the dominant European language was French.

By the early 1970s there were between twenty and thirty fieldmen (no "field women") in Africa. Most were employed in projects funded largely by USAID through the Global Projects Office, but many were also supported directly by the World Council or co-operating agencies. Some were funded by credit union leagues in North America. They included some Peace Corps volunteers but increasingly the fieldmen were technician volunteers who had been released for short-term assignments from the North American and Irish movements.

The most common activity in which ACOSCA and WOCCU were engaged during the 1970s was the sponsoring of training events. Typically funded by church, international development and co-operative organizations these events were usually held in ACOSCA training centres located in Bobo Dioulasso in Upper Volta, and Bakvu in the Congo (both of which catered to French speakers), Buea in Cameroon and Maseru in Lesotho as well as in Nairobi in Kenya.

Like other education programmes for credit unions in the formative stage, the early emphasis was on the general education of volunteers; the priority soon switched, however, to technical training, for example, bookkeeping and lending policies. Planning these events was time-consuming and sometimes difficult because of the distances involved and the complexities of organizational details; it seemed to consume much of the time of the Nairobi office.

The basic approach continued to be "train the trainers" and, overall, it worked effectively, especially in terms of starting credit unions.[214] Ensuring their effective survival was another matter. In fact, the expansion in Africa during the 1970s, based on statistics that were in some instances estimates, was remarkable. From 1970 to 1978 the numbers of affiliated credit unions grew from 3,400 to nearly 11,000, while membership increased from 194,000 to 1,330,000. The most significant increase, however, was in assets, which grew from $2,460,000 to $161,500,000US.[215] This growth, spread over more than twenty countries, placed enormous demands upon ACOSCA and WOCCU to provide the necessary training and support services. In some ways, it was perhaps too much, too soon, for the limited resources that were available both within the countries and from the international development community.

While outsiders tended to credit this growth to the work of development agencies, Africans naturally adopted a more "homegrown" explanation. The African movements viewed their support for credit unions in the context of widespread participation in informal mutual aid organizations. In the days when bartering was the most common form of exchange, most African peoples used one system or another of storing first goods and then money; the accumulated wealth would be distributed, usually on a rotational basis, among members of a given association. Variously called *ndjonu, gameya, tontines, sanduk, esusu* and many other names, these associations were deeply embedded in most African societies. When credit unions appeared, therefore, they tended to be seen as an elaboration of an African tradition, extensions of what had been, not imports from another place. As the writer of the official booklet for the tenth anniversary of ACOSCA wrote:

> It must be stated here that the co-operative savings and credit "seed" could sprout, take root and grow, only because of the existence of the right kind of soil — authentic traditional African social systems which through centuries and generations had functioned in a co-operative way to provide needed "credit" to its members. The co-operative savings and credit idea was presented to African peoples prepared, both in mind and heart, to adapt its philosophy and practices.[216]

One example of the remarkable African growth was the movement in Cameroon. From its beginnings in 1963 the movement had spread throughout most of the country's provinces and reached out to people whose first European language was French or English. By the late 1970s the

Members, staff and board of a thrift and credit co-operative in Ghana, 1977. (COURTESY OF CUNA)

movement was serving over 50,000 families through 200 credit unions, with assets of $8,000,000US. This represented considerable progress when one remembers that Cameroon was one of the poorest countries in the world and that the credit unions were serving people not being served by other financial institutions: that is, some of the poorest people in the country. By the late 1970s, the movement had developed, as in other African countries, a significant agricultural production credit programme through funds provided by USAID.[217] It was, at the time, an excellent example of what could be accomplished in mobilizing credit in a situation where the dominant development approach of the time would have dismissed it as impossible.

By the late 1970s, however, the Cameroon movement was creating managerial cultures and encountering a series of problems that would be typical of many movements in Africa and, indeed, elsewhere. As it moved from the formative stage into activities and services that required more managerial expertise, it encountered needs that were difficult to meet. It required more trained staff in the national organization, a more advanced planning system, better liquidity management and improved operating standards. Making the necessary transition to meet these needs would prove to be difficult, more difficult than in economically developed countries, for a number of reasons: for example, the limited numbers of trained people within the society, the economic uncertainties of the period, and the tendency of governments to interfere. It would not be easy in Cameroon or any other African country to forge the management cultures required to operate large and sophisticated credit unions.

As in the previous decade, the African movements depended extensively upon sympathetic networks for growth and development, and as in the past, the churches continued to be the most important of these networks. During the early 1970s, for example, an effective partnership was worked out with the Catholic Relief Services to provide resources for ACOSCA. The goal was to create "a continent-wide association, crossing many barriers in Africa, bringing people to work together in a co-ordinated program for the mobilization of savings."[218] WOCCU built upon this partnership to bring together a number of development agencies. A co-ordinated programme was developed, attracting $2,000,000US in aid funding, most of it from North American leagues, CIDA, MISEREOR, USAID and the Konrad Adenauer Foundation as well as the Catholic Relief Services.[219] Numerous other organizations, such as CUNA Mutual, the Dutch Raiffeisen movement, ICA, OXFAM, ILO and FAO, contributed smaller amounts. It was an exercise in co-ordinating international activities that seemed to indicate significant possibilities for the future. It also clearly established WOCCU as a key participant in the international development community.

Another network that assumed growing importance in the period was trade unions. Between 1972 and 1975 the Ethiopian trade union movement sponsored an educational programme promoting credit unions. In Kenya the Central Organization of Trade Unions hired two field workers for the promotion of credit unions starting in 1974. The Zambia Congress of Trade Unions began its involvement with credit unions in the early 1970s, sponsoring educational programmes and providing day-to-day support for credit union activities.[220] It was a promising connection that helped bring credit unions to the attention of a significant force in many African societies.

There were, however, several problems that confronted the African movement. In many countries, travel and other forms of communication were slow or difficult. The growing importance of agricultural credit meant that the demands for loans fluctuated frequently over the course of the year, creating periodic shortages of funds alternating with "gluts" of deposits for short periods. Moreover, many of the agricultural programmes depended upon funds extended by government, either directly through the credit unions or indirectly through farmer members. On occasion, if political upheavals occurred or if governments were short of funds, there could be delays, causing serious liquidity problems.

Everywhere, there was a shortage of trained personnel for accounting and office management. The African education systems were not producing such people in sufficient quantity, and governments and the private sector, which could often pay better salaries, tended to secure those who were available. That meant that local credit unions had difficulty developing a management culture and relied upon volunteers extensively. Creating national institutions was even more problematic than

in other parts of the globe; arranging for interlending among credit unions, for example, could be difficult, in some cases impossible, because of the lack of expertise.

Another general problem, one that was almost pervasive, was relations with government. The state played a unique role in most African countries; it was the instrument through which independence was won; it was the tool expected to shape the new societies that had been created; it was the employer that many people, especially the educated elites, looked to for jobs, status and power. Thus the state was intrusive, and in many instances had to be so, if the economic infrastructure was to be developed to permit participation in international marketing activities. This meant that most states embraced co-operative enterprise as extensions of state policy, particularly the more numerous and originally more important marketing co-operatives.

Credit unions — all forms of thrift and credit co-operatives, in fact — tended to be seen in the same light. For that reason, credit union movements had to struggle to secure their own legislation, regarded as a necessity by credit unionists schooled in North American practice, which meant they had to undertake continuous efforts to educate public servants and politicians. The matter was complicated, and confusing even for the public servants, because at the same time credit union leaders were typically calling for certain kinds of support from government. For example, they wanted regular, dependable inspection from governments and they sometimes wanted government to provide some advisory services, notably in those countries where the movements were too small to provide them for themselves. The relationship was a subtle one, as it was in more economically developed countries. In Africa, though, especially when there was political instability and desperate need, the possibilities for inappropriate government interest and action were much greater.

UGANDA

There were also some problems that were specific to individual countries. In Uganda, for example, the tumultuous politics of the 1970s created what might have been an impossible situation. In 1972 Idi Amin took over the government and there followed six years of economic turmoil, political

A meeting of board members and staff of the Uganda Co-operative Savings and Credit Union, the apex body for the Ugandan movement, in September 1980. (Courtesy of CUNA)

crises and frequent violence. The exact numbers of lives that were lost will never be known. The economic costs of the almost perpetual conflict will never be totalled. Remarkably, the credit union movement not only survived, it even made modest gains. In 1970, for example, there were 30 credit unions; by 1975 there were 120.[221]

The Ugandan movement survived partly because some credit unions became "lenders in kind", meaning that they loaned members money so that they could buy or rent bicycles, equipment and tools from the credit union. In other words, they assumed a role often taken on by credit unions amid economic crises — they became leaders in the informal economy. Partly they survived because in the midst of the disruptions they were more secure than many informal and even formal banking organizations. Partly they survived because they became an important conduit for funding from development and relief organizations, including credit union/co-operative networks in the northern countries.

TANZANIA

Tanzania was another unusual case. In 1975, the government of Julius Nyerere undertook a massive restructuring of society that reached into nearly all communities in the country,

with the exception of Kilimanjaro, where tribal solidarity and geography inhibited drastic government-led change. The policy, called *ujamaa*, was in keeping with an approach to rural revitalization common at the time; it amalgamated, by coaxing and sometimes by coercion, smaller villages and clusters of population into larger regional communities. In theory, doing so would permit greater production of farm commodities, the rationalization of equipment and other input costs, and the facilitation of social services delivery, notably education and health. It was a rather extreme example of an approach that could be found in different forms at different times in locations as diverse as the Soviet Union, China, India and Newfoundland.

In Tanzania, *ujamaa* meant a social and economic restructuring of traditional society. It meant the rather abrupt disruption of traditions and associations of importance that had been in place for as long as anyone could remember. It meant direct lending to the poor through what became an impossibly large and complex bureaucracy. It meant increased costs as well intentioned government programmes sought to serve villages equally across the nation.[222] It meant interference in social and class relationships, always a certain stimulant of social and political unrest.

Ujamaa attracted the criticisms of the "free market" advocates in the remainder of the world even as it attracted the support of some, especially Scandinavians and Canadians, who were drawn by its moral fervour and idealistic purpose. It also elicited mixed reviews from the co-operative world because of its drastic impact upon the co-operative movement. Smaller co-operatives, including many savings and thrift societies, were closed down or amalgamated to meet the demands of government policies. In the process, some savings vanished amid the bureaucratic restructuring, meaning that many people lost confidence in their organizations.

Moreover, all co-operative endeavour was amalgamated within multi-purpose co-operatives, an approach that requires very careful business management and clear lines of responsibility between the members and the leadership. Unfortunately, this was not always the case. All too often, the driving priority of the multi-purpose co-operatives was marketing or some other economic activity, meaning that funds raised from the membership were not always dealt with in a prudent and directly accountable manner. The result was that the autonomous thrift and credit movement in Tanzania, once so promising, entered a fifteen-year period of slow growth.

In 1978 ACOSCA celebrated its tenth anniversary. It was a happy occasion. Over 500 delegates gathered in Nairobi. They came from the thirty-one countries that possessed affiliated movements. They were proudly aware of what they, with outside assistance, had accomplished. They had worked through two five-year plans with considerable success. They had produced a generation of leaders — people like Joseph Mutayoba of Tanzania, Benedict Mukong of Cameroon, Joseph Muletta of Ethiopia and Ade Adebiyi of Nigeria — who had helped spark a remarkable burst of expansion. They had strong advocates from the churches and the international movement — people like Joseph Van den Dries, Paddy Bailey and Paul Hebert— whose support promised continued outside assistance. It is little wonder that the meeting and most of the activities of the middle and later 1970s were characterized by extensive optimism.

Unfortunately, the optimism underestimated the complexities involved in developing managerial expertise capable of meeting member needs. In addition, the African movements would be buffeted by adverse economic situations in the later 1970s. One problem was inflation, a general world problem in the period, but magnified in Africa where global trends were compounded by widely varying national inflation rates. This situation led to the devaluation of currencies, always a traumatic event for any savings institution, and prompted governments to borrow to their limits to pay off accumulating national debts, some of them for development loans. The result was increased taxation and increased direct government control.

Inflation created havoc for African credit unions, causing even more problems than it did for credit unions in more economically developed countries. Most national movements were limited by statute as to the interest they could charge on loans, usually 1 percent per month on the diminishing balance, an impossible restriction when inflation rates and general interest rates exceeded 20 percent. Most confronted liquidity crises caused by inadequate member savings and slow payment of government funds, pay or grants to memberships;

few possessed the expertise at national levels — or the requisite loyalty — to invest funds effectively. As the economic problems mounted, the international banking community, especially the International Monetary Fund, began to apply pressures on African governments to adopt more rigorous budgeting practices, to forsake interventionist programmes, and to reduce the size of government. This rigorous realignment of political and economic forces in African societies, usually referred to as structural readjustment, was a complete reversal of the way in which African governments had tended to operate since independence. The cost, measured in increased unemployment and reduced services over an indefinite period, was high and painful.

To these problems were added unusually frequent natural disasters, most notably drought in savannah regions. As in the special cases of Uganda and Tanzania, however, the amazing outcome of the period of great difficulties in Africa was that credit unions survived as well as they did. Although criticisms became commonplace — as they always do when times are difficult — the movements, whether because of the effectiveness of the leaders and their advisors or because they were so natural to the African experience, survived and adjusted as needed.

ASIA

Of all the regional movements, the Asian was in the best position for sound expansion in the 1970s. Geographically, it was the largest region; culturally, it was the most diverse; socially and religiously, it had community traditions that would be sympathetic to co-operative forms of organization; economically, many of its countries were on the verge of dramatic growth, often a propitious time for co-operative banking. During the 1950s and 1960s, the development of credit unions had been significant in absolute terms but, in light of the potential growth, just barely a beginning. By 1970, the Korean, Philippine and Hong Kong movements had made impressive beginnings; the Indonesian and Thai movements were on a good footing; the Japanese movement was stable but still restricted largely to the small Christian minority as were the movements in Bangladesh, Pakistan and India.

In the spring of 1971, shortly after the council's formation, the leaders of the Asian national movements met in Oro City, the Philippines, to organize the Asian Confederation of Credit Unions. The member organizations came from Korea, Japan, Taiwan, Hong Kong, Indonesia, Malaysia, Vietnam, Thailand and the Philippines. They represented over 3,300 credit unions with 310,000 members and nearly $12,500,000US in assets.[223] The primary purposes of the new organization were to build unity among credit union leaders in Asia and to secure financial and human resources for expanded training programmes.

Many national leaders — for example, Robby Tulus, Hoichi Endo, Somchit Varangknangyubol, Andrew So, Matthew Wang, Michael Lee and Bill Griffin — played important roles in the early development of the confederation. The most important early leaders on a regional level, however, were Andrew So, who became the first president, and Augustine Kang, the first general manager. Augustine Kang's role was particularly prominent throughout the 1970s. He believed strongly in the need for national movements to progress steadily and in keeping with their own momentum, their own cultural needs and their own economic requirements. Kang was also a strong believer in the need to keep credit unions distinct from other co-operatives, a view that fitted well into American assumptions about credit unions, but one that was not shared universally within the Asian or other movements. For his efforts, Kang received the Ramon Magsaysay Award for International Understanding in 1981.[224]

During the 1970s the confederation sponsored two major training programmes each year, many of them financed in part or entirely through grants from the World Council, CUNA Mutual, the Asia Foundation, the Co-operative Development Foundation of Canada and the Australian Credit Union Foundation. Religious groups also played a role in assisting the confederation, especially the Catholic Relief Services and MISEREOR. CUNA/USAID was also supportive throughout the 1970s, providing funds for specific projects and working with Peace Corps volunteers to promote credit unions in the region.

As in other parts of the world, the primary role of WOCCU in Asia was to support the work of the confederation. During the 1970s, a number of WOCCU employees contributed significantly to the development of the confederation and to

A meeting of Asian credit union leaders. (Courtesy of CUNA)

many national movements. Percy Avram, for example, helped start the Laos movement early in the decade, when he introduced the Directed Agricultural Production Programme.

While the 1970s were a tumultuous decade in many Asian countries because of the continuing, although eventually diminishing, impact of the Vietnam War and its associated geopolitical tensions, the Asian movement made considerable progress. From 1968 to 1978 the number of credit unions increased from 2,200 to 3,600; the number of members grew from 560,000 to 1,400,000; and assets expanded from $82,000,000US to $290,000,000US.

Korea

Among the national movements, the Korean movement grew at close to a record-breaking pace: the number of credit unions increased to nearly 900, with almost 600,000 members and over $172,00,000US in assets. Indeed, the 1970s were something like a golden age for the Korean movement. Following the passage of national legislation in 1970, credit unions emerged in nearly all districts throughout the country, filling clear needs for thousands of people who otherwise would not have had access to credit. While many of the new credit unions were employee-based, a growing number were linked to the "New Community Movement", part of the intense drive in the country to build stable communities as the turmoil of the war years gave way to a long, if often threatened, peace.

TAIWAN

Other movements grew, too, although at lesser rates. The Taiwanese movement continued to expand, despite being restrained under the too close supervision of government through the Association for Social and Economic Life in the Republic of China. The Hong Kong movement became noted for its innovation, particularly as a pioneer in interlending and new technologies.

Toward the end of the decade the Sri Lankan movement started to make significant gains. There had been a thrift and credit co-operative movement since 1906, patterned after the Indian experience. It suffered from too close identification with government, however, in fact often appearing to be little more than an extension of government departments. The movement also declined sharply in the early 1970s because of the emergence of a national savings bank that drew away many members.

In 1978, Augustine Kang and Andrew So went to Sri Lanka and joined P.A. Kiriwaneniya on visits to thrift and credit co-operative societies. Kiriwaneniya, trained as a social worker, had turned from Sarvodaya Sramadanya, a Gandhian community development movement, to work with thrift and credit co-operatives. Regional and national seminars were organized, followed by six two-day residential seminars, each attracting 350 delegates. In 1979 work began on the formation of the Federation of Co-operative Thrift and Credit Co-operatives Union Ltd.

Using the base of many of the old thrift and credit co-operatives, Kiriwaneniya sparked a revitalization of the Sri Lankan movement and drew it steadily away from government domination. Seminars were organized, membership campaigns were undertaken, and central services were developed. It would become one of the most dramatic credit union movements in the world in the 1980s.

INDONESIA

In Indonesia the movement picked up momentum under the leadership of the Credit Union Counselling Office (CUCO). Organized in 1970, and led by Robby Tulus, CUCO developed an extensive education and training programme that first concentrated on trained field organizers and then on elected officials and secretary-treasurers. Between 1970 and 1978 nearly 340 credit unions were organized, and at the end of the period there were 125,000 members and nearly $25,000,000US in assets.[225]

Like most Asian movements, the Indonesian movement had its own distinctive philosophical base. In the 1970s it formally adopted the PANACASILA state philosophy with its emphasis on a "Belief in God, Humanity, Nationalism, Democracy and Social Justice." It emphasized human resource development and the social goals of credit unions, although it was also one of the pioneers of the Asian movements in some technical activities, such as interlending. It was a movement that was deeply involved in the development of its communities, generally managing very effectively to mix social and economic purposes in its daily activities. In that respect, it was a movement that did not conform nicely to Augustine Kang's and the general American view of how credit unions could best develop.

This commitment to social and economic goals was important because, as the international movement developed, many leaders, especially from North America, were preoccupied with growth. A natural tension ensued — one that was also known in North America — between those who saw the future in terms of size and technological change and those who believed it was essential to retain the distinctive qualities of credit unionism. In truth, the wisest course was to find the most appropriate path within the continuum represented by those two viewpoints. The Asian credit union movements, in part because of their associations with Buddhism, Confucianism and Christianity, pursued their own solutions to those dilemmas.

In April 1975, the World Council held its annual meeting in Hong Kong, the first time the organization had met outside of North America. It was also a memorable meeting because it was one of the first opportunities to bring together a representative group of credit unionists from many countries so that a successful planning meeting could be convened. Under the leadership of Tony Schumacher, then CUNA's organization development director, a three-year plan was developed for the region. The plan called for a more intensive educational and expansion programme using fieldmen, and it concentrated on the need for developing a more appropriate legislative framework. The meeting also provided many North American leaders with their first chance to visit the Asian movements, particularly those in Korea, Taiwan and Japan. Some seventy representatives from the American, Canadian and Australian credit union movements visited credit union and political leaders in the three countries, and carried back to their own credit unions and countries enthusiasm for the new movements and an enhanced understanding of international credit union trends. They had visited a region that would become arguably the best hope for rapid, sustained and stable growth in the years that lay ahead.

THE CARIBBEAN

The move to develop an effective confederation in the Caribbean faced a different set of difficulties. At the beginning of the 1970s, there were two credit union federations in the region: one was the Caribbean Conference of Credit Unions (CCCU), the regional educational institution; the other was the Eastern Caribbean Conference which brought together the movements in the seven associated states of the Eastern Caribbean and Barbados. The CCCU, which was formed at a meeting in Dominica in 1972 and owed much to the leadership of Lorrell Bruce and Paddy Bailey, was essentially an evolution from the West Indies Confederation of Credit Unions. In the first few years, the headquarters for the CCCU were in Port-of-Spain, and management systems were created for local credit unions. In 1975 the World Council and the Co-operative Union of Canada collaborated in securing funds from USAID and the Canadian International Development Agency to help expand the Caribbean movement. Nearly $2,300,000US was secured, the largest percentage from Canada. It was used to help local credit unions expand their

membership bases and to create development projects and management training programmes for leagues in the Caribbean region.

Although constantly restricted by limited funds and frequently faced with the problems of drawing together island movements, CCCU made steady progress in the 1970s. It worked with government officials and trade unions in several islands to organize groups in their workplaces, and especially in their communities. In the mid-1970s seven members of the public service in the Cayman Islands formed a credit union, which within ten years grew to include more than 18,000 people and $2,745,000US in assets. In several islands useful alliances were made with trade union movements. In Barbados, for example, the largest trade union, the Barbados Workers Union, and the National Union of Public Workers gave considerable impetus to the movement, as did seamen and waterfront workers in Belize and Granada. In Montserrat, the Allied Workers' Union established the Montserrat Co-operative Credit Union in 1982, one year before the Bermuda movement was started by the Bermuda Industrial Union.[226]

The 1970s, however, were difficult years for the people of the Caribbean: economies suffered as sugar prices fluctuated; protective governments gave way to free market regimes under prodding from the international banking community; tourism ebbed and flowed amid political uncertainties and social unrest. Moreover, managerial abilities were limited because of the nature of the education system, better career prospects outside of the movement for well-trained people, and the small size of most credit unions. All of these factors, plus the perennial problems of achieving unity among the islands, made the work of CCCU difficult.

UNITED KINGDOM

The freestanding leagues also generally made progress during most of the 1970s. In the United Kingdom, the movement was badly needed; in the early 1970s there were still 2,500 registered moneylenders who charged interest rates that varied between 50 percent and 100 percent per annum to the large number of people who had no other non-familial way to borrow money. Unfortunately, the movement was restricted in its development

United Kingdom credit unions — the Caribbean connection. Many of the early credit unions were started by immigrants from the Caribbean. Father John Sullivan, the most prominent early leader in Jamaica, is shown at a meeting with Frank Villiers and Lloyd Bascom, two early leaders of the British movement. (COURTESY OF WOCCU)

systems found in most parts of the pre-industrial world. Consequently, many people who organized credit unions did not register them, thereby creating an image problem for credit unions, especially when one found itself in trouble. Registered or not, however, the few credit unions in existence had managed to attract some 8,800 members by 1979.[227]

A Labour Member of Parliament, John Roper, embraced the cause of creating appropriate legislation. Aided by the Irish League, which was concerned about the growth of the movement in Northern Ireland, Roper spearheaded the passage through Parliament of legislation that would allow for the specific incorporation of credit unions. The legislation, however, was quite restrictive, limiting memberships to employee groups or "properly constituted" associations. The

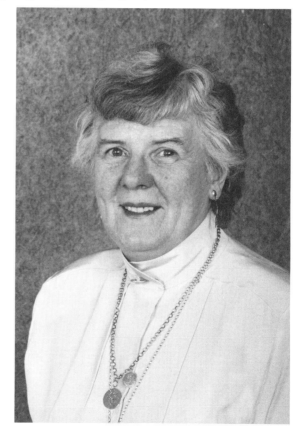

Rose Dorman, one of the early leaders of the Scottish credit union movement, 1997. (COURTESY OF WOCCU)

by structural problems, some of them of its own making, some caused by inadequate relations with the state. The original movement was centred in London and had been led by the National Federation of Credit Unions (NFCU). It grew slowly over the years, attracting support from credit unions sympathetic to the Raiffeisen tradition, but it suffered from some managerial problems in the early 1980s. It was also reluctant to work closely with the Association of British Credit Unions, Limited (ABCUL), the larger World Council affiliate formed in 1975. They differed because of personalities and, particularly, over ABCUL's support for CUNA Mutual. In that respect, the division echoed similar debates in Canada and Australia.

Credit unions in the United Kingdom were also significantly restricted by the provisions of the Industrial and Provident Societies Act and the Companies Act, under which they were regulated. In fact, they could be little more than savings clubs, an industrial variant of the informal savings legislation also limited the deposits to £5,000, a considerable sum at the time, but an amount that would seriously limit future growth.

Relying largely on the work of volunteers and using help extended by the Irish movement as well as the World Council, in the 1970s the Credit Union League of Great Britain turned its attention to industrial credit unions. Using some funding provided by the Irish League and CUNA Mutual, the league, under Len Nuttall, developed some larger credit unions among workers in Manchester, Liverpool and Glasgow.[228] In fact, the movement made remarkable strides in Scotland, where it well met the needs of public and company employees in the Strathclyde region.

IRELAND

The Irish movement, one of the most individualistic in the international movement, retained its deep commitment to the concept of volunteer service and involvement. It resisted efforts to develop professional management groups and worked hard at retaining local control essentially through small credit unions. This approach was not without controversy in Ireland, and it often questioned the assumptions of the American, Canadian and Australian movements. Nevertheless, it was a system that worked well in Ireland in the 1970s. It was not a perspective that argued against technological change in all respects, nor did it deny the necessity for strong central support systems.

In the mid-1970s the Irish League created a league stabilization reserve, offered seminars on risk management to local leaders, and established a central financial service to meet movement needs. It developed its own insurance company in 1976 to provide loans and savings insurance, a move that sparked considerable controversy at the time. It helped credit unions develop computerized information systems; it also hired technical assistants who could help credit unions in difficulty. The league began to reconsider the credit union act in Ireland, and it worked with its member credit unions in Northern Ireland to create a better legislative framework in the United Kingdom. The result was an improved Irish act in 1979, and a better regulatory regime for British credit unions.

By 1978 there were 220 credit unions affiliated with the Irish League, nearly 390,000 members and $14,700,000US in assets. The league leadership — and much of the membership — was deeply committed to the international movement and was always supportive of expanded programmes overseas, especially among the poor.

NEW ZEALAND

The New Zealand movement also made progress. By 1979 it had over 100,000 members in 235 credit unions, with $26,000,000US in assets. It too was moving quickly into the computer age and in the late 1970s developed its own computing system based upon credit union needs, a feat that eluded many other supposedly more sophisticated movements. In 1973 the New Zealand movement established an insurance department in collaboration with CUNA Mutual. It successfully escaped the British system of legislation, basically the same system that had held back the British movement, and in 1979 celebrated the passage of a credit union act. The league hired a field staff to work with local credit unions, and it was an advocate of self-regulation. On an international level, the New Zealand league devoted most of its efforts to supporting the Bergengren school in Fiji. It provided scholarships that allowed Fijian and Tongan leaders as well as New Zealanders to attend sessions of the school.

THE PACIFIC

The Fijian, Tongan and Papua New Guinean movements were small in absolute terms compared to other movements, but they were important and growing movements in their own countries. The Papua New Guinea federation was formed in 1972, with considerable help from the Australian and New Zealand movements. As in the other two Pacific island nations, its movement consisted largely of small credit unions operating on a village basis. The Tongan movement also had its beginnings in the 1970s; by 1979 it had 60 credit unions with 4,500 members, but only $190,000US in assets. Unfortunately, it was not able to remain as an affiliate of the World Council.

The most important of the movements in Oceania was still Fiji. In 1979 it had 378 credit unions with 61,000 members and $7,000,000US in assets and was clearly the focus for work in the Pacific islands because of its long history and the operation of the Bergengren centre. In fact, its leaders dreamed of creating a confederation that would bring together the credit unions and similar organizations in the region. Given the size of its own movement, the economic problems many of them encountered in the later 1970s and the preliminary stages of development elsewhere, this was a dream that could not be immediately realized.

The freestanding leagues and the confederations represented a considerable accomplishment by the end of the 1970s. The dreams of WOCCU's founders at the start of the decade may not have been fully realized, but arguably those dreams were unrealistically ambitious in the first place. The reality had been a period of steady growth, in some parts of the world remarkable growth. Growth had meant change; so had developments in the banking industry, on both national and international levels. Moreover, the euphoria of beginnings and rapid organization were giving way to concerns about achieving stability, to the recognition that it might be better to build more securely and less rapidly. It was time, once again, to consider mission and organization, to rethink the structure of the international movement.

An officer of the Registry of Savings and Loan Societies, Fiji, explains the benefits of credit unions to prospective members. (COURTESY OF CUNA)

A Credit Union Photograph Album

THE INTERNATIONAL MOVEMENT HOLDS ITS FORUM; PEOPLE COME FROM ALL OVER THE WORLD.

clockwise from top left: Scotland, Australia, Korea, Ghana, The United States, Indonesia; centre: Ukraine

clockwise from top left: Togo, Jamaica, Romania, Panama, The United Kingdom, The Philippines

YOUNG PEOPLE ARE IMPORTANT IN THE DEVELOPMENT OF CREDIT UNIONS IN MANY LANDS, OFTEN HAVING THEIR OWN SAVINGS PROGRAMS.

clockwise from top left: The United States, Grenada, Sri Lanka, Fiji; centre: China

clockwise from top left: Russia, Thailand, "Pre-members" from several Asian countries, Nicaragua

CREDIT UNION BUILDINGS LOOK DIFFERENT FROM THE OUTSIDE AROUND THE WORLD.

clockwise from top left: Kenya, Honduras, The Philippines, Guatemala; centre: Bolivia

clockwise from top left: Indonesia, Surinam, Malawi, Guyana

AND THE BUILDINGS ARE DIFFERENT ON THE INSIDE TOO.

clockwise from top: Honduras, Guatemala, St. Kitts, Poland, The United States; centre: Grenada

clockwise from top left: The Philippines, China, Bangladesh, Sri Lanka; centre: Taiwan

CREDIT UNIONS BRING PEOPLE TOGETHER.

clockwise from top left: India, Sri Lanka, Indonesia, Lesotho, Malawi, Lithuania, Surinam, China

clockwise from top left: South Africa, Nepal, Mozambique, The Philippines, Sri Lanka, Niger; centre: Romania

Chapter Nine

This Should Not Alarm Us: Redesigning the World Council
1979-1984

So here we stand … watching the "sagging seventies" slowly giving way to what may well be the "agonizing eighties". Energy, food, population and environmental problems are crowding upon us. High expectations are giving way to apprehensions. The basics of human survival — food, clothing, shelter, security — are again moving high upon the list of priorities.

Rod Glen

In the past few years, our credit union systems have been challenged as never before by change. Old formulas have fallen by the wayside as new ones are created. This should not alarm us. It is a sign of our vitality. As long as these changes take place in the context of our principles, we will retain this vitality while acting in the best interests of those whom we seek to serve.

Chris Baker

I N RETROSPECT, THE 1970S WERE A TIME OF MIXED BLESSINGS for the international credit union movement. On the one side, there was growth and development. That growth had led to confident planning and optimistic predictions. On the other side there were problems, such as slowing expansion as the decade ended and growing concerns about the stability of many movements. These disappointing aspects led to a narrowing of focus and to a search for greater discipline and better lines of accountability.

In the more established movements, growth had tended to concentrate in the managerial credit unions and to be reflected in the "mainstreaming" of credit union organizations. It had been driven by the increasing sophistication of services offered to members and by the development of managerial cadres at the local, state/provincial and national levels. Growth had required increasing co-ordination among credit unions in order to put together the funds needed to pay for the new technological systems. It had meant increased emphasis upon government relations so that credit union interests would be protected in the rapidly evolving financial industry. In short, the momentum for change coming from the more established movements meant that the World Council was forced to react to the constant pressures of modernization and to consider what they meant for credit unions in the developing world.

Equally, the World Council was responding to growth in the new movements, which almost invariably were caught up in the challenges typical of the early stages of development. They were facing the problems endemic in educating large numbers of new directors, training secretary-treasurers or managers, lobbying governments for appropriate legislation and finding the money to fund national and regional organizations. While none of these challenges was easy, meeting them, if done effectively under positive conditions, usually produced a kind of optimism, even euphoria.

Moreover, because of the way in which most of the new movements were started, their leaders generally possessed a deep commitment to the ethical values of credit unionism. Thus, the momentum of the developing movement was normally positive and enthusiastic, impatient and optimistic. It was a contagious viewpoint that looked constantly toward growth, most commonly manifested in the creation of more credit unions.

Indeed, the most outstanding feature of the international movement by the end of the decade was that it was large, especially given its relative youth. Between 1970 and 1979 the number of credit unions affiliated with the World Council increased only 11 percent, at first glance not a large amount until one remembers that the process of amalgamating smaller credit unions had become widespread, particularly in the developed movements. More obviously impressive were the numbers of members and the growth in assets. Membership had nearly doubled to 28,900,000, and assets had grown over 300 percent to nearly $93,000,000,000US,[229] a considerable increase even given the impact of inflation.

Geographically, too, the movement had expanded significantly, one might even say dramatically. By 1979 the membership roll of the World Council included sixty-seven countries, the vast majority of them classified, in the jargon of the day, as developing countries. Although there were some troublesome aspects to the way the movement had developed, this global growth invited dreams of creating an integrated international co-operative financial system. It raised in the minds of at least some leaders what is arguably the ultimate credit union goal: the creation of an international financial system able to influence the way in which the international economy functions.

Much of the early interest in this goal came from the International Association of Managing Directors (IAMD), as a result of growing business contacts with European co-operative banks. The Canadian movement, because of the restless vision of George May while he was in British Columbia, and, latterly, the support of John Nicholson, an emerging charismatic national leader from Sydney, Nova Scotia, pioneered in opening relation-

ships with the European co-operative banks. May started to meet with leaders from the European co-operative movement in the middle 1970s. Under his leadership the British Columbian movement negotiated a series of loans from the European banks, notably the Deutsche Genossenschaftsbank (DG) and Rabobank. That experiment soon attracted the interest of American credit union leaders, some of whom were searching for capital to carry out the kinds of expansion they thought necessary for survival.

The growing interest in the United States stemmed partly from significant legislative and technological changes. In 1977 federal legislation was passed, expanding the capacity of credit unions to offer mortgages and to move funds easily from one credit union to another, indeed, across movements. At the same time, the American movement was making progress on share draft legislation (in effect, the capacity to deal with third-party transactions) and was entering the world of electronic funds transfer. These initiatives, along with the already developed programmes to invest funds from American credit unions in overseas credit unions, all suggested that the American movement, at least, was nearing the stage when it could become a factor in international finance.

The interest was reciprocated in Europe. DG had entered the international banking field fairly aggressively in the 1970s and, in fact, had invested in the International Credit Union Services Corporation. It was more than willing, therefore, to join with the American and Canadian movements in creating a committee to explore the possibilities of developing more extensive international collaboration among co-operative banking institutions. The committee, chaired by George May, included Paddy Bailey, Ulrich Brixner from DG, Richard Ayers from the U.S. Central, and Angel Castro, who had pioneered the Latin American/American interlending programmes. The committee used COPAC to carry out its first studies, which explored how funds could be moved from developed co-operative banking systems to thrift and credit co-operatives in other parts of the world. If followed, their proposals would lead to close financial collaboration and even joint ventures between the North American credit unions and the European banks. It was an imaginative undertaking that promised much in 1978 and 1979, just at the time when the structure of the World

Council was being considered in earnest. In a way, it was the final dream flowing from the expansionist impulse that started in the 1950s and gained so much momentum in the 1960s and 1970s.

On the other side, some problematic issues at the end of the 1970s also encouraged reconsideration of the way WOCCU was organized. Growth was slowing in several countries, notably Latin America and parts of Africa, for the first time in twenty years. In those movements, and in others such as in Canada and Australia, where growth continued but income declined, financial health began to deteriorate, as did the capacity to serve their members.

Most of these problematic developments stemmed from economic/social/political adjustments caused by change in the global economy. The aftermath of the oil crisis created profound dislocation in the industrialized world and helped trigger inflationary spirals unparalleled in this century. Banking institutions, including credit unions, were particularly affected by these occurrences; all too often, credit unions were forced to attract deposits at rising rates, while their income was restricted by long-term low rates on the bonds, loans and mortgages in which they had invested.

More fundamentally, the technological revolution caused by the advent of computing was changing forever the business world in which credit unions operated. Capital markets, while they had been international in their reach for generations, now had the immense advantage of being able to transfer funds instantaneously. In some countries around the globe stock markets were open at all times of the day, and they were easily accessible for investors nearly everywhere. The demand for capital, especially as parts of Asia started to boom, exceeded any peacetime period in the past. The pressures, as well as the opportunities created by these changes, would challenge national and regional credit union movements as never before. The financial marketplace was starting to change with bewildering speed, a trend that would gather speed during the 1980s and become a blur in the 1990s.

The technological revolution also brought its challenges to credit unions on the local level. Like all sophisticated financial institutions, larger credit unions with appropriate managerial expertise could tailor a wide range of financial products for

The emergence of the "modern" credit union in North America — in this case, Rohr Federal Credit Union in Chula Vista, California, January 1977. (COURTESY OF CUNA)

their members — on both the deposit and lending side of the ledger. In fact, their traditional closeness to members could be a significant advantage, providing excellent opportunities to respond more directly to needs and preferences. Wise managers and thoughtful boards used that advantage to make their credit unions trendsetters in the financial industries.

Embracing the new technology, however, was expensive, in both financial and human terms. It also strained the political structures of credit union movements around the world: it required degrees of co-ordination that credit unions built on local control and limited financial resources sometimes found difficult to embrace. The resulting uncertainties and tensions helped create an atmosphere in which the structure of the international movement, like those of many national movements, became a subject of concern and debate.

To complicate matters, most credit union leaders had never been faced with the types of problems that began to appear as the 1970s came to a close. In the past, credit unions had generally responded to whatever problems they had encountered by trying to "grow" out of them: that is, by attracting more deposits to generate returns to cover current needs. It was an approach that, if followed in the context of the late 1970s and early 1980s, could lead to disaster. New ways to meet adversity had to be found. New disciplines and different skills had to be developed and instituted.

At the same time, governments began to deregulate financial institutions, opening up nearly all areas of the financial industry to increased competition. They removed the state, provincial and national barriers that had previously protected credit unions and many other financial institutions from some forms of competition. In part, this development was a manifestation of ideological change as governments became more conservative, but it was also a consequence of technological change. By using computers, financial institutions could expand their services and reach out to different kinds of people, including, in the industrialized countries, the lower-income groups that credit unions had traditionally served. To carry out these expanded activities in most jurisdictions, however, they needed more powers from the regulators.

Finally, the apprehensive feeling was connected to at least three concerns about what was happening to the World Council as an organization. First, there was some unease throughout the movement about whether enough had actually been accomplished. Partly, this uncertainty was the result of the exuberance of the 1960s and early 1970s, when many credit unionists had seriously underestimated how difficult it was to start credit unions and, even more, to make sure they became viable. Too many had forgotten the decades it had taken to build the North American movements. Too many had assumed that skills taken for granted in well-educated populations and purchasable by mature institutions could be quickly replicated elsewhere. Too few had recognized the enormity of what was being undertaken.

Second, the support of the established movements in the United States, Canada and Australia, while important, had not achieved the levels anticipated by enthusiasts a few years earlier. Even more discouraging, interest in the developed movement was not as high as was desired or had been anticipated. In other words, the activities of the World Council were not being featured as prominently within the regular activities of the state,

provincial and national credit union organizations as proponents wanted. For those who could not understand why such a good idea as credit unionism did not catch the enthusiasm of everyone, these slow developments were frustrating.[230]

Third, there were increasing questions about the operation of the Global Projects Office, although its overall competency and effectiveness were not questioned, and its established record was widely appreciated. The statistics speak for themselves.

From its first grant through 1979, the GPO had negotiated fifty-one grants from USAID for the projects of CUNA International and the World Council. These grants, totalling $13,306,345US, had helped movements in twenty-one countries.[231] Within the norms of American international development efforts, the office had done well; undoubtedly, much of the growth around the world during the decade was the result of the work it had done. The problem was that the Global Projects Office seemed to some to be rather aloof from the national, even the American, movements. Contradictorily enough, others thought it was too closely watched and influenced by CUNA and CUNA Mutual, a charge vigorously denied by its leaders. Others believed it was unduly aligned to American interests overseas, a problem in any country when government assistance is accepted, but a particular problem in a country as large and powerful as the United States. This charge was also strongly rejected by the Global Projects Office.[232]

Some of these problems, apparent or otherwise, were natural enough, given the circumstances. Much of GPO's business was with USAID, not directly with the credit union movements, while CUNA, not the World Council, had the ultimate responsibility for the contracts that were signed. Moreover, the board of the World Council had little formal influence on the operations of GPO, even, it appeared, on the development of its policies.

Starting in 1974 there had been several attempts to integrate the two offices, and the problem was still not resolved when Paddy Bailey was appointed managing director of the World Council in 1975. There were several issues that made integration difficult and, for some eight years, impossible. There was, for example, some uncertainty for a period of time as to whether USAID would provide funds, or as many funds, to an international organization not completely controlled by

Americans. There was some competition between Paul Hebert and Paddy Bailey over who would have final authority. Ultimately, however, the board of directors was for some years unwilling to address the issues, as it arguably should have done.

The situation was particularly difficult for Paddy Bailey after he was formally appointed managing director. He never could create the seamless management system any manager would have desired. The Global Projects Office was solidly entrenched in its own activities and led by a committed, effective and confident management group. GPO had control over most of the funds available for international development, and it carried out most of the key negotiations for overseas projects. Inevitably, its focus was outward: across the oceans, to the projects it was administering, and across the city, to USAID and its priorities for international development. It did not help that Bailey's customary office was more than a thousand miles away, in Madison, and consisted of fewer personnel with a much smaller budget. To make matters more difficult, his duties as a kind of international "ambassador" for the movement drew him out of the country for long periods each year.

Thus, there were abundant reasons — general and specific — why the structure that made sense in the late 1960s was not making as much sense a decade later. An impatient international credit union movement, now liberally sprinkled around the world, wanted a more cohesive system in which the ultimate accountability lay with its elected leaders. Moreover, the gathering complexities of the international movement led some of its more thoughtful leaders to conclude that a more systematic approach was needed, that first principles should be revisited. It was time to assert once again the importance of planning.

The commitment to planning, in fact, had grown steadily throughout the movement, most particularly as the American, Canadian and Australian movements sought to deal with changing circumstances. It had also become an integral part of the way the World Council did business. Shortly after the establishment of the World Council in 1970, the board had created a planning committee which became a central part of the organization's activities. By 1975, largely through the efforts of this committee and the support of such individuals as

Paul Hebert, Herb Wegner, Tony Schumacher and Chris Baker, planning had become widespread in the international movement, although its strongest advocates were not satisfied that it was being carried out as continuously or professionally as was required.

Aside from whatever merits planning exercises carry with them, there were special reasons why it was an important activity for the World Council. Arguably, it is a mode of institutional behaviour always of utmost significance to an international organization that has many stakeholders, tries to absorb views from around the world, needs a strong consensus to carry out its work, and has to be able to communicate effectively to a diversity of people and institutions. Moreover, by the 1970s, the only way to survive, let alone prosper, as an international development organization was to identify basic objectives, consider alternatives and proceed with care. To do otherwise was to risk disaster; governments had little time for organizations that did not demonstrate precise objectives, organizational efficiency and clear accountability.

Indeed, the world of developmental assistance was beginning to undergo extensive change as the 1970s ended. Some governments were becoming influenced by the kinds of conservative ideology that looked skeptically on international aid. Others had been disappointed by the lack of success of many forms of aid, particularly those based upon extensive economic and social intervention in recipient countries. Almost all governments, affected by the decline in funds after public debt charges were paid, were becoming more demanding about how the agencies they sponsored accounted for their expenditures. Thus, when delegates to the fourth credit union forum came to order in Sydney, Australia, in May 1979, the questions of how best to organize the international movement and to plan for its future were at the forefront. There were abundant reasons — both positive and problematic — why they should consider whether or not the basic organizational structure of the World Council was the right one.

The location of the 1979 forum was also significant. The Australian movement had just gone through a difficult time because of a serious liquidity problem earlier in the decade. Earlier than the Canadian and American movements, it had become aware of how the changing economy and regulatory regimes were altering the framework within which credit unions had to operate. For that reason, the issue of how best to plan for the future of the international movement had a strong resonance among the numerous Australian delegates in attendance.

Australians were also particularly interested in how the international movement would be structured, because it reflected upon their own situation. Some of the debates that had divided the movement in the earlier years were subsiding, and the need to organize an effective national institution was becoming clearer. The small band of enthusiasts for a strong national system and a significant voice in international credit union affairs was being heard by a growing number of people. Following lively discussions, therefore, the delegates at the forum instructed John Nicholson, the incoming president, to appoint a special planning committee to provide the organization with a clear picture of its broad purposes. It would be asked to indicate how those purposes might best be fulfilled by identifying strategies and priorities and establishing how resources should be raised and allocated.

The planning committee was chaired initially by George May and latterly by Eugene Farley from Virginia; its membership, which also changed slightly, included Angel Castro and Augustine J. R. Kang, both long-time participants in international activities, Augustine "Gus" Murray and Gerald Mulhern from Ireland, Jim Williams from Texas (the president of CUNA), and Wilbur Wormer, also from the United States. Paddy Bailey and Paul Hebert provided support, and Christopher Baker was staff liaison officer. Baker, a native of Michigan, had grown up in Cuba, was fluent in Spanish and had spent considerable time in Costa Rica as a graduate student. He had been employed in the Global Projects Office since 1974, where he was originally engaged in planning and evaluation; subsequently he was involved in administering some of the Latin American projects, and he also participated in efforts in the later 1970s to bring about greater integration between the Washington and Madison offices. Baker became a pivotal figure in the work of the committee and would play a major role in the World Council in the following years.

The first stage of the committee's work was the preparation of an overview analysis essentially carried out by a task force of three technical experts: Brad Murray and Tony

Paul Hebert (left) and Chris Baker, 1996. (COURTESY OF CHRIS BAKER)

Schumacher from CUNA and Charles Spooner from the Canadian Co-operative Credit Society. The task force prepared, distributed and analyzed a questionnaire that was sent out to all the movements around the world. It also interviewed influential leaders and studied the numerous key documents relating to the development of the international movement in the previous decade.

The overview analysis prepared by the task force was taken to a meeting of the board in Jamaica in February 1980. While paying tribute to earlier work, the analysis stressed that the World Council needed to project a stronger vision of the possibilities of the international movement. It needed to "become more proactive and dynamic in conceptualizing and carrying forward" its mission. It needed to become clearly recognized "as *the* world credit union organization, truly international in its scope, objectives, representative and professional in its scope, objectives, operations and attitudes".[233] The World Council also had to mobilize resources from the credit union movements around the world, expanding the roles of volunteers and developing national foundations to increase contributions to new movements from the older, wealthier movements.

Above all, the overview analysis argued for enhanced conceptual, administrative and operational resources at the managerial level within a completely integrated framework. It called for the full merger of the Global Projects Office and the Madison office, and for the appointment of a chief executive officer responsible exclusively to the board of the World Council. Further, it recommended that the contracts formally held by CUNA and administered through Washington be transferred to the World Council. While it advocated maintaining a reduced office in Washington to continue managing the overseas projects, the analysis insisted that its manager would report to the chief executive officer of the World Council, who would work out of Madison, where most of the employees would also be located.

One relatively minor reason why Madison was suggested was because it was thought useful to create some physical distance between WOCCU and Washington, given the concerns expressed by some overseas credit unionists about undue government influence. Another reason was that the American movement was completing a large complex in Madison to bring together the offices of CUNA Mutual and CUNA in a group of buildings, and the World Council could secure premises in the International Building of the World Credit Union Center in the complex at reasonable rates. The most important reason, however, was that sharing premises with the other credit union organizations would permit closer contacts with the mainstream of the American movement, thereby encouraging the kinds of synergistic activities that are so important in any co-operative enterprise, but particularly in multi-national co-operative organizations.

The board accepted the recommendations on the amalgamation of the two offices which took place on January 1, 1981. Shortly thereafter, most of the staff from the Washington office moved to Madison. The board also accepted the recommendation on the need for a single manager responsible for all of WOCCU's activities. The search for the new

chief executive officer began in the summer of 1980; the person ultimately selected was Howard Helman from the Organization for Rehabilitation through Training, a private European organization specializing in manpower development. Helman possessed extensive experience in Asia, Europe and Africa, and was the American representative on the Club of Sahel, an organization of donor agencies and African nations concerned with drought in the Sahel. He appeared to be an appropriate choice for leading the organization.

In particular, Helman brought a good understanding of the European co-operative situation, then still a matter of considerable interest to the WOCCU board. In fact, the board had authorized the opening of an office in Geneva, Switzerland, in 1980. Under the direction of Dean Mahon, its chief task was the establishment of closer contacts with European co-operative organizations, the International Co-operative Alliance and development agencies. It was the most obvious statement of WOCCU's interest in becoming more integrated into the international development and the international co-operative communities.

Despite his credentials, Helman's tenure with the World Council, as it turned out, was brief. He was replaced within a few months by Al Charbonneau, from the small Francophone community of La Fleche in Saskatchewan, Canada. A dynamic, affable and committed credit unionist, Charbonneau started with his local credit union in 1952. His rise in the provincial movement was rapid, and he became manager of the Saskatchewan Credit Union League in 1959, when he was only thirty-three years old. Subsequently, he served the credit union movement in a variety of positions, including stints as managing director of the Michigan League and as chief executive officer of the Ontario Central during a particularly difficult period.

Charbonneau brought to the World Council, therefore, both considerable understanding of the dynamics of league/central politics and the limitations of the two largest national movements within the World Council. He also brought a well-honed interest in the international movement. Charbonneau had been drawn to the international programme initially by the enthusiasms of Paddy Bailey and Rod Glen. He became involved in some of the projects funded by the

Saskatchewan, Michigan and Ontario movements and worked briefly as assistant managing director of CUNA International in the 1960s. Partly because he came from a francophone background in Canada, Charbonneau had a deep understanding of the cultural dimensions of credit unionism. Partly because of his Canadian roots, too, he was empathetic to the movement's broad co-operative background. He would provide considerable leadership in expanding the linguistic capabilities of the World Council and in expanding contacts with European movements.

Once the task force's overview analysis was completed and accepted by the board, the planning committee undertook extensive personal consultation with most of the movements around the world. Teams of members from the planning committee travelled to all the confederations and most of the freestanding leagues to review the previously circulated questionnaire and to consider issues specific to each organization. The result was an inventory of global, regional, national and local needs as well as a catalogue of specific issues affecting the World Council as an organization.

Several generic issues emerged as this process unfolded. One was the need to articulate a clear vision of the purpose of the World Council and the beliefs upon which its work was based. This clarity was necessary in order to give coherence to the diversity of experiences scattered across so many countries around the world, to distinguish credit unions from other kinds of co-operative banking organizations, and to present a unified position to governments. The committee therefore embarked on the difficult process of elaborating a mission statement for the organization and of creating a statement of beliefs for the international movement. The mission statement that was finally adopted read as follows:

> The World Council of Credit Unions is the international organization of credit unions and similar co-operative institutions. Its mission is to assist members to organize, expand, improve and integrate credit union and related institutions as effective instruments for the economic and social development of people. The World Council of Credit Unions shall serve as a forum for the exchange of ideas and information, provide services for its members, promote membership development and growth, represent members' interests, and extend co-operative financial services to areas where people want and need such services.[234]

The statement of beliefs that was ultimately developed affirmed the movement's commitment to expansion around the globe regardless of race, nationality, sex, religion and politics. It envisioned credit unions as vehicles of social, economic and human development, for both individuals and communities. It called for credit unions to encourage the prudent utilization of local savings and to work with other credit unions in the interests of their members. It called upon all credit union organizations to become self-sufficient institutions controlled through effective democratic processes. It encouraged credit unions to develop the best human resources, whether elected officials or paid employees.

STATEMENT OF BELIEFS

* We believe the credit union movement should extend the opportunity to participate in the services and benefits of credit unions to all who want and need these. Such services and benefits should be provided with neutrality relative to race, nationality, gender, religion or politics.

* We believe that credit unions should serve as effective instruments for human, social and economic development throughout the world.

* We believe that local, national and international credit union organizations should seek to contribute to the development goals and needs of their communities.

* We believe that the credit union movement should foster and practice the principles of co-operative pooling and utilization of resources for the ultimate benefit of the credit union member.

* We believe that all sectors of the credit union movement should strive for permanent viability through the attainment of financial and technical self-sufficiency.

* We believe that credit union leadership and management should embrace participation in the democratic process at all levels of the credit union movement.

* We believe that the credit union movement should attract and develop the best possible human resources at all levels to serve the leadership, management and staff of the movement.

* We believe that the credit union movement should adhere to the Credit Union Operating Principles defined by the World Council of Credit Unions.

The statement of beliefs was a forceful expression of what the credit union idea had become after some eighty years of experience. It possessed considerable cohesion while it explicitly and implicitly suggested the direction in which the movement should go. The emphasis on a free, independent movement that was operated democratically in the interest of the members was its most striking characteristic. Another important aspect was its implicit support of a unified system operating within a global framework; credit unionists attempting to carry out its mandate had little choice but to make the option available to anyone who might be interested in it.

Because the committee was concerned that the belief statement not remain just so many pleasant words on a document with little obvious relationship to what actually happened in the daily operations of credit unions, it started to develop a set of operating principles that would give credit union directors, managers and members some clear direction as to how their organization should be operated. After discussions during the consultation visits about operating principles, and after discussions by the board, Chris Baker drew up a draft statement of credit union operating principles that was circulated throughout the movement following the 1982 Toronto meeting. With minor revisions, the statement was adopted in 1984 at the first credit union forum, held in Panama.

The statement listed ten principles that should shape the activities of credit unions. These principles were derived partly from practices that had emerged over the years within credit unions and partly from the Rochdale principles that had been modified by the International Co-operative Alliance in 1937 and 1966. The ten operating principles for credit unions were:

open and voluntary membership;
democratic control;
limited deposits on equity capital;
fair rates of interest on deposits;
the return of surpluses to members based on their participation;
neutrality in race, religion and politics;

a commitment to high quality service to members;
support for ongoing education;
co-operation among co-operatives;
a concern for social responsibility.

INTERNATIONAL CREDIT UNION OPERATING PRINCIPLES

DEMOCRATIC STRUCTURE

* Open and Voluntary Membership
Membership in a credit union is voluntary and open to all within the accepted common bond of association that can make use of its services and are willing to accept the corresponding responsibilities.
* Democratic Control
Credit union members enjoy equal rights to vote (one member, one vote) and participate in decisions affecting the credit union, without regard to the amount of savings or deposits or the volume of business. Voting in credit union support organizations or associations may be proportional or representational, in keeping with democratic principles. The credit union is autonomous, within the framework of law and regulation, recognizing the credit union as a co-operative enterprise serving and controlled by its members. Credit union elected offices are voluntary in nature and incumbents should not receive a salary. However, credit unions may reimburse legitimate expenses incurred by elected officials.
* Non-Discrimination
Credit unions are non-discriminatory in relation to race, nationality, sex, religion, and politics.

SERVICE TO MEMBERS

* Service to Members
Credit union services are dedicated to improve the economic and social well-being of all members.
* Distribution to Members
To encourage thrift through savings and thus provide loans and other services, a fair rate of interest is paid on savings and deposits, within the capability of the credit union. The surplus arising out of the operations of the credit union after ensuring

appropriate reserve levels and after payment of limited dividends on permanent equity capital where it exists, belongs to and benefits all members with no member or groups of members benefitting to the detriment of others. This surplus may be distributed among members in proportion to their transactions with the credit union as interest or patronage refunds, or directed to improved or additional services required by members.

* Building Financial Stability

A prime concern of the credit union is to build financial strength, including adequate reserves and internal controls that will ensure continued service to membership.

SOCIAL GOALS

* On-Going Education

Credit unions actively promote the education of their members, officers and employees, along with the public in general, in the economic, social, democratic, and mutual self-help principles of credit unions. The promotion of thrift and the wise use of credit, as well as education on the rights and responsibilities of members, are essential to the dual social and economic character of credit unions in serving member needs.

* Co-operating Among Co-operatives

In keeping with their philosophy and the pooling practices of co-operatives, credit unions within their capability actively co-operate with other credit unions, co-operatives and their associations at local, national and international levels in order to best serve the interests of their members and their communities.

* Social Responsibility

Continuing the ideals and beliefs of the co-operative pioneers, credit unions seek to bring about human and social development. Their vision of social justice extends both to the individual members and to the larger community in which they work and reside. The credit union ideal is to extend service to all who need and can use it. Every person is either a member or a potential member and appropriately part of the credit union sphere of interest and concern. Decisions should be taken with full regard for the interest of the broader community within which the credit union and its members reside.

The operating principles, the belief statement and the mission statement represented a remarkable consensus, especially considering the diversity of credit union experience around the world. That they were developed in such a short time is a testimonial to the skills of the planning committee and the board. They were, in many respects, a manifestation of the historical tradition that situates credit unions within the broad sweep of co-operative experience dating back to the middle of the nineteenth century. Indeed, the statement of operating principles became an important model for the reconsideration of the principles upon which all co-operatives were based, a process undertaken by the International Co-operative Alliance in 1988 and completed in 1996.

The most obvious limiting factor in carrying out the more focused yet ambitious direction indicated in the plan as it emerged was a shortage of resources, both financial and human. As the overview analysis put it, the World Council was "a small organization trying to meet a wide range of expectations with a very limited resource base".[235] One partial answer to this problem was to streamline the structure of the World Council to make better use of its financial resources and, it was hoped, to ensure better communications with member organizations.

The changes proposed by the planning committee started at the membership level. The committee recommended the division of the movement into regional organizations so that resources could be better allocated around the world. It advocated the creation of different classes of membership, based on the dues organizations paid, their stage of development and whether they were like-minded organizations wishing associate or observer status. The committee also recommended that the board of directors be changed into a "membership council", an organization smaller than the board had been. It would consist of fewer representatives from the United States and Canada, but would include members from Australia, Latin America and other countries, notably Ireland and New Zealand. The membership council would meet annually, the governance of WOCCU in the meantime being carried out by an administrative committee of five persons elected from and by the membership council that would meet at least twice yearly.

To ensure meaningful contact with the movements around the world, the committee recommended the formation of two advisory bodies. One was the international credit union forum, which would meet every two years and was intended as an information-sharing and issue-oriented gathering involving representatives from the leagues and other co-operative and developmental organizations. The other was the chief executive officer's advisory committee, which drew together the chief executive officers from leagues and confederations. This recommendation came in the wake of a successful gathering of these officials during the meetings in Ireland in July 1981.

An important aspect of all these reforms was that member associations would be responsible for covering the expenses of those attending the various annual and biennial meetings, except for those persons who were on the membership council, whose expenses would be paid by the World Council. This provision greatly reduced WOCCU's "cost of democracy".

The identity statements and the revised structure for the World Council were part of a new corporate plan that also included objectives for the organization and for its programmes, along with elements covering policies, strategies, activities and financing. A detailed plan that amounted to a blueprint for the development of the international movement, it called upon WOCCU to undertake specific activities within nine general areas: providing philosophical direction for the movement; representing credit unions to other international organizations; fostering the growth of new credit unions around the world; assisting member organizations to mobilize human and financial resources; providing technical assistance to members as possible; disseminating information on credit unions; organizing training sessions; assisting member organizations financially as needed and as possible; and carrying out research. It was an ambitious list with a demanding set of activities associated with each element.

The plan was partly predicated upon continual government funding for development projects, expanded support from credit unions through foundations and increased self-suffi-ciency of member organizations. It also looked forward to attracting more support from co-operative organizations in other parts of the world. There were hopes of attracting the membership of *caisses populaires*, *cajas de credito* and unaffiliated co-operative thrift and credit organizations in Africa and Latin America. There was considerable room to grow.

When the delegates gathered at the fourth triennial meeting in Toronto in 1982, there was widespread support for the documents and the corporate plan. A new and popular chief executive officer was in place in the person of Al Charbonneau, the delegates were challenged as never before, John Nicholson forcefully chaired the proceedings and the supporting sessions dealt thoroughly with many of the key issues. In fact, the leaders of WOCCU had done remarkably well. They forged considerable unity of purpose and direction while re-engineering the organization of the World Council. How to create agreement, how to mobilize resources, how to build and maintain momentum, how to enlist the support of credit unionists right down to the grassroots level, how to project a clear, consistent vision of purpose — none of these was an easy question to answer, especially when resources were always limited and always uncertain.

The remarkable thing, though, is that the leaders involved had managed to do so well in bringing a consensus out of a movement that, like Topsy, had just grown. Above all, they had tried to direct the resources of the international movement toward the most significant possibilities. They had tried to elevate the momentum from the local and national to the greater good. As Chris Baker put it:

> The international credit union movement is one of great diversity. Such diversity at times may present us with temporary obstacles and communications difficulties. But it is from this diversity that we gain one of our greatest strengths. In the credit union world, the whole is indeed greater than the sum of its parts.[236]

CHAPTER TEN

LIVING WITHIN NARROWING LIMITS
1984-1992

> The basic responsibility and work of developing a credit union movement at both the local and national level is in the hands of the people themselves. Outside assistance, whether from the government or from development assistance organizations, can only help with that process. An inappropriate or too strong role by government or an outside organization will only hinder the development it seeks to support.
>
> Tony Schumacher

> It has become obvious that there are not only two economic options or models — the pure capitalist model and the centrally planned communist model, that between these two extremes there is a large number of intermediate schemes and that, in fact, they exist in the world with better results of well being and economic stability for the nations.
>
> *The COLAC System Development Strategies*

BY ANY MEASURE, THE 1980s WERE A DECISIVE DECADE in modern history. A complete list of the key changes during those ten years would be very long, but just a few suggest how much the world was transformed: the collapse of the centrally planned economies in central and eastern Europe; the economic rise of Asian countries, with its attendant growth of consumerism; the intensification of social, economic and political pressures for gender equality; the changing role of the state in all parts of the world; the increasing emphasis on individual rights over collective responsibility; the expanded impact of computerization and other aspects of the communications revolution; the widening gap between rich and poor in many parts of the world; a deepening environmental consciousness. The often vague concept of a "transitional period", sometimes used carelessly by historians, has particular validity when applied to the 1980s.

The credit union movement, both at the national level and globally, was profoundly buffeted by all the major changes of the decade. Indeed, credit unions are interesting and important organizations partly because, one way or another, they reflect any major trend affecting the societies in which they exist. For no period of time was that observation truer than during the 1980s.

On the one hand, there were the possibilities. The changes of the decade presented credit unions with increased opportunities, particularly because of the momentous changes in central and eastern Europe, but also because of the widening economic gaps between classes and regions: the value of credit unions is naturally more obvious when economic discrepancies are widening. Then too, the retreat of the state as a controlling force in society expanded opportunities for credit unions; it could mean increased powers and greater responsibilities for self-regulation. Technological advances fostered the growth of larger credit unions and expanded the services that credit unions could offer their members. The decline of national boundaries offered the possibility of closer contacts among national movements, although it was not an opportunity that could be easily grasped .

On the other hand, the threats and dangers were equally apparent; in some ways, they were the flip side of the possibilities. A sudden growth of interest in credit unions in central and eastern Europe would strain the resources of the international movement and draw resources from development in other parts of the globe. The social and class divisions would challenge how the movement could respond to the needs of those who were becoming poorer, not a simple issue of new uses of conventional banking approaches. In the more developed movements, it could raise the issue of whether that was any longer the role of credit unions. The decline of the state and the deregulation of financial industries meant increasing competition from banking interests, which almost invariably had a greater capacity to mobilize funds and resources. The same trend also meant a determination among government regulators to harmonize legislation affecting financial organizations, an objective that, when accomplished, could de-emphasize the distinctive qualities of credit unions. The 1980s were exciting times, sometimes too exciting, to be involved with credit unions.

CENTRAL AND EASTERN EUROPE

One of the most startling changes occurred in 1989 when the Berlin Wall was pulled down, the physical end to what the Iron Curtain had meant. The impact of this abrupt and dramatic change on the co-operative movements of the countries in central and eastern Europe was revolutionary. Although there had been some variation in countries and among sectors in the region, the record of co-operative development under communist rule had been uneven at best. The communist rulers had never transcended the ambiguities about co-operatives in Marx's writings and Lenin's policies; they had never shaken off the horrors of Stalin's rural policies; they had never allowed the co-operative movements to remain aloof from their own constant, often vicious, struggles for power. In general, they had viewed the widespread co-operative organizations as extensions of the state, as instruments for their own ends. In fact, in many instances the integration between co-operatives and the state had become complete. The Soviet period was tremendously difficult for those who sought to support meaningful co-operative enterprise in central and eastern Europe and for those from outside who tried to help them. It was, as Johnston Birchall has written, a "grotesque interlude" in the history of the co-operative movements of central and eastern Europe.[237]

Toward the end of the communist regimes, and in the early days of the transformation, some governments wrestled with efforts to create more genuine co-operatives. Their efforts achieved mixed results. The most important experiment was in Russia, where the Gorbachev government promoted co-operatives in a wide variety of economic activities. The unfortunate outcome was the formation of tens of thousands of bogus co-operatives known more for their opportunism than their commitment to co-operative values. They were forerunners of rampant capitalism at its worst, the kind of capitalism that came to characterize much of Russia's economic development in the 1990s.

In other countries, the reaction against co-operatives was initially antagonistic because they were so closely associated with the old regimes. It would take some years before the experience of the communist regimes could be put in perspective and the values of genuine co-operative enterprise fully appreciated. In the short term, therefore, organizations that were called co-operatives would be regarded at best skeptically, at worst scornfully.[238]

In reality, however, it was impossible to eliminate the co-operative impulse. Long before the communists had taken over, co-operative organizations, especially financial co-operatives, and informal co-operative activities were commonplace in central and eastern Europe. That spirit had not been extinguished; the traditions of communal activism common in the nineteenth and early twentieth centuries were still remembered. Moreover, limited institutionalized co-operative practices persisted within the communist countries, even in some of the co-operatives closely controlled by the state. Most importantly, informal co-operative activities had been widespread; they were one way that people could resist when governments intruded deeply into their lives.

Thus, while the word "co-operative" would be questionable for awhile in some countries,[239] the turn to co-operative institutions known by other names was not long in occurring. In particular, credit unions benefited from their distinctive name because it clearly separated them from other forms of co-operative enterprise. Quite quickly, therefore, they became a popular instrument for people seeking to rebuild the countries of central and eastern Europe.

While support from the church was important in fostering the development of credit unions, the most important underlying forces were nationalism and a basic desire to control economic change. For a growing number of people, credit unions were a partial answer to the question of how a new economy could be built from the ashes of the old. Frequently, too, the formation of credit unions engendered a high degree of excitement: they were part of a momentous series of changes in societies in which segments of the population had long wanted reform. Despite the turmoil caused by political disruption, the peoples of central and eastern Europe were embarking on no less than the reformulation of their societies. While outsiders might see this process as an attempt to mirror what had worked in the West, in reality it was much more subtle and complicated. Whatever ultimately emerged would be shaped by the needs, values and history of the peoples in the region. Given their adaptability, credit unions could be a significant part of that reconstruction.

Usually, the value of credit unions in societies undergoing renewal is obvious, and that was true in central and eastern Europe. The flexibility of credit unions and their basis in community are advantages for people seeking relief in a deteriorating economy and trying to find ways to shape their future. They can be safe if legislation is appropriate, a particularly important consideration when the economic infrastructure of a society is in disarray. They are responsive if they take care to establish meaningful contacts with their members or are naturally based on strong feelings of affinity.

The people of Poland, particularly in industrial cities such as Gdansk, were among the first to recognize the value of credit unions as the communist regimes started to collapse. In September 1989, groups from Gdansk established a working relationship with the World Council. A few months later, a

Credit union delegation meeting with Lech Walesa, then president of Poland, who supported the development of credit unions. From left to right: Adam Jedlinski, Grzegorz Bierecki, Al Charbonneau, Lech Walesa, Grazyna Milewski, Andrzej Krajewski and Ksyzstof Labenda. (COURTESY OF WOCCU)

Polish interest group associated with Solidaritas, the Polish nationalist movement that had long struggled with the Marxist regime, visited Irish, Canadian and American credit unions to see what their examples could suggest about how the movement might assist the development of their country. Dean Mahon from the Geneva office visited Poland, followed by a team of American, Canadian and Irish credit union technical experts in June 1990. The team visited Gdansk and Warsaw, where it encountered considerable interest in the development of credit unions. There, and in other places, team members found a good base for future development in the approximately 10,000 savings and credit associations formally and informally organized by Polish workers during the communist era. Shortly thereafter, the Foundation of Polish Credit Unions was established to promote the movement in Poland and to funnel assistance from North American credit unions, notably those credit unions with large Polish membership bases in the United States and Canada.

Other countries in the region showed interest at about the same time. In 1991, representatives from the Ukrainian government visited credit unions in Chicago. They asked

North American credit unions for assistance in developing credit unions in their country. Representatives from American and Canadian credit unions, many of them from the fifty-two Ukrainian credit unions in their two countries (with combined assets of $1,500,000,000US), journeyed to the Ukraine. Another delegation went the following year. As in the case of Poland, they found considerable interest in credit unions, a reflection of contemporary need and past experiences.[240]

In 1992 the World Council, along with the ILO and the ICA, organized regional workshops on credit union development in central and eastern Europe. These events clearly showed the rich possibilities in what had long been a wasteland for the kind of co-operative enterprise championed by the international credit union movement. Another widespread change in the decade, also present in central and eastern Europe, was the increased assertiveness of women's movements. This trend varied around the world but was particularly strong in northern industrialized countries. In fact, in some parts of the world it was resisted, partly because it was seen as another northern imposition on southern value systems. Nevertheless, the

Throughout the late 1980s and 1990s credit union supporters from central and eastern Europe travelled to Ireland, the United States and Canada to learn about credit unions. Here, interns from Lithuania visit the United States. (Courtesy of WOCCU)

women's movement became a significant factor within the international development community and consequently was integrated within most aid programmes.

In the co-operative movement generally, the increased emphasis on gender issues was a repetition of an old theme. The roots of co-operative thought and effort stretched back to eighteenth-century reform traditions, which meant being influenced, albeit in an inconsistent way, by the gender egalitarianism that existed in the Enlightenment and some early nineteenth-century reform movements. In the nineteenth century, the co-operative movement, including co-operative banking, had generally been more open to wider participation by women than were other economic organizations. That tradition was generally taken overseas by Europeans as they scattered around the world; in Latin America, for example, German immigrants provided for gender equality when they organized co-operative banks in the late nineteenth century. It was, however, a tradition that tended to fade in Latin America, as it did in other parts of the world, when the dominant managerial paradigms of the later nineteenth century and the institutionalization of co-operative banking institutions became pervasive.

Nevertheless, from the beginning, many co-operative banking organizations were at least open to the possibility of lending money to women. Moreover, when credit unions emerged in North America, women played significant roles in helping to organize them and in supporting the educational and social activities upon which they were based. They also were able to borrow in their own right from credit unions in the United States and Canada, an unusual practice in North American banking circles until the 1950s, although the extent to which they did so is not clear.

In North America, too, women were commonly the secretary-treasurers, especially in smaller credit unions, from the earliest days of the movement. During the 1970s and 1980s, women started to become managers of larger organizations at a faster rate than was happening at comparable levels within the general banking industry. More obviously, within the workforce of credit unions, women were in a substantial majority because working as "tellers" was typically a female occupation. As credit unions expanded, many tellers took advantage of opportunities to become loans officers, personnel managers and marketing experts. Arguably, it would be just a matter of time before they would hold more senior positions, but, as in the rest of the economy, the "glass ceiling" would not be easily penetrated.

Women were also becoming steadily more evident on boards of directors and in executive positions on those boards. The proportion of women holding such offices, however, was far below their percentage of membership and was not in keeping with their economic participation in credit unions. Unfortunately, too, the voice of women was largely absent at state/provincial and national levels. That situation did not start to change significantly in the 1980s, but the limitations and inherent lost opportunities implicit in their lack of representation were at least being discussed, an improvement over the past.

In some ways, it was easier and more obviously important to stress gender issues in the newer movements outside the United States, Canada and Australia. Much of the funding secured from the international development community from the early 1980s onward was tied to the development of gender programmes. This emphasis emerged largely as a result of a United Nations meeting in Mexico in 1975 which declared the next ten years as a "Decade for Women".

Subsequently, many people involved in development activities promoted programmes with a strong feminine face because of their personal commitment, but also because it made sense to do so. Estimates in the decade, for example, suggested that between 60 and 70 percent of all work done in developing countries was carried out by women, much of it unpaid or underpaid. Many of the most stable economic activities in Africa and parts of Latin America and Asia, for example, were significantly dependent upon the contributions of women.

In many traditional societies, women were also the primary savers and the key people in the success of micro-enterprises. Whether it was making batiks in Ghana, weaving in Colombia or growing rice in Asia, women's labour was essential to the production of wealth. In reality, therefore, it would be impossible to develop sound credit unions without the meaningful involvement of women. Moreover, it was clear that in many countries women were particularly drawn to credit unions: 1992 statistics, for example, showed that over 87 percent of the members of Lesotho credit unions were women, as were more than 61 percent of members in the Gambia, 60 percent in Montserrat, 55 percent in Costa Rica and 54 percent in the Philippines.[241] In many societies, too, women were the lenders, meaning that they inevitably became important employees, especially lending officers, in credit unions, since most men did not mind dealing with women to take out loans, not always the case in some northern societies.

In both developing and developed countries, women were also important as potential sources of business. A study undertaken by the Korean movement in 1987 summarizing the situation and the possibilities for credit unions, found that women were important as members of credit unions but rarely influential — or indeed visible — on boards of directors or in management groups. The study outlined the potential of attracting the attention and interest of women, and pointed to economic changes, even in rural areas, that were placing more economic power in the hands of women. It described the trend toward more education for women, one that was not being adequately recognized or compensated, noting that they represented a growing pool of well-trained people available for credit unions, either to sit on boards or to be employed as professionals. The study also found that credit unions were attractive to women for philosophical reasons, as long as someone took the trouble to explain that philosophy to them, and argued that women in more traditional families, because of rising incomes and labour-saving devices, would be able to donate time to credit union volunteer work if they were encouraged to do so.[242]

WOCCU's support for a greater role for women within credit unions picked up momentum in 1981 when it organized a forum, "Women Entrepreneurs: Access to Capital and Credit", in Copenhagen. Part of the five-year review of what the United Nations "Decade for Women" had achieved, the forum brought together women entrepreneurs and lenders for productive purposes from several countries around the world. In the same year, the World Council sponsored a seminar in Senegal entitled "Increasing Women's Access to Credit Through Credit Unions in Africa". During the remainder of the 1980s there would be many other gatherings, from Israel to the Philippines, dedicated to the roles of women in credit unions. For the rest of the decade, too, there were several mostly successful efforts to serve women better and to enlist their support for credit unions in developing countries. "Women in Development", a common approach in international development circles by the end of the 1980s, became a major emphasis in the African movement and found expression in Latin America and Asia as well. In some instances, that meant creating credit unions especially for women, such as among fishmongers in Ghana, food hawkers in Bolivia and weavers in India. In others, it meant that credit unions focused on the kinds of micro-enterprise, such as craft production, in which women were usually the workers.

The gradual opening of the door to women was a significant trend in the 1980s, at once a return to a position implicit in co-operative thought for nearly 200 years, a recognition of natural justice and an affirmation of what the shape of the future had to be.

There were other ways in which the more general trends of the decade profoundly affected the credit union experience. For a few countries with large resources of valuable commodities, such as the Arab oil-producing nations, the decade was mostly positive. Some of them could move quickly from traditional to modern economies with relative economic ease — although the social, religious and political ramifications of the change were never simple.

Most developing countries, however, had to follow much more difficult economic roads. They were confronted by situations in which an estimated 80 percent of their natural resources were unexploited, while 90 percent of the working time of people was devoted to subsistence activities, leaving little capacity for participation in the international marketplace.[243] In short, many countries had few surplus resources and were always stretched to meet citizens' fundamental needs.

They also had to contend with an unsettled and often harsh international situation. The 1980s, for example, saw a dramatic shift in how funds were channelled from technologically developed countries to the developing parts of the world. The World Bank and the International Monetary Fund, increasingly influenced by supply-side economics and

concerned about the failures of development projects in the past, began to insist upon political change. They required governments to limit rural credit schemes, to repay loans promptly and to deregulate financial markets. The result was that many southern countries were forced to restructure their economies, often at high social and political costs at the same time as they were facing changing priorities. For example, while still considering the problems of rural society, they were forced to pay more attention to the immense economic, social and political pressures emanating from cities growing at unanticipated rates. In nearly all of the southern countries, the exodus from the rural areas picked up momentum, creating unserviced slums on the margins of most major cities. All of the problems of rapid urbanization and industrialization — overcrowded housing, unsatisfactory sewage conditions, inadequate water supplies, poor health facilities, widespread unemployment, particularly among young people — that had occurred in new industrial cities since the late eighteenth century became evident in the twentieth-century context. In fact, they reached unprecedented dimensions, creating social unrest and threatening political crises; in Central America, the Philippines, Peru and much of Africa, the threat became a terrible reality.

As the pressure mounted, the capacity of political elites to deal with change was often eroded. Governments, forced to pay off mounting debts compounded by rising interest payments, had fewer discretionary funds to meet people's needs, as the international banking system insisted upon cutbacks in social services in order that external debts be paid. International pressures, from the banking community and other governments, forced reductions in protectionist policies, particularly tariffs, often with resultant increases in unemployment or decreases in rural and industrial incomes. In some countries, these shifts took the form of "structural adjustment" agreements tied to loans or other forms of financial assistance negotiated through the World Bank and the International Monetary Fund. Such restructuring could adversely affect the relatively few credit union systems that were closely tied to governments, particularly in providing programmes of rural credit. This was evident in countries such as Indonesia, the Philippines and many African nations. Ultimately, it reaffirmed the advisability of credit unions remaining aloof from significant dependence upon government relationships.

In the long run, however, credit union movements, if operated efficiently, could benefit from the retreat of government influence and the increasing privatization of financial services. Specifically, they could become important agents in the mobilization of local capital; they could be a more institutionalized and safer form of saving and lending than the informal saving and sharing systems that operated in many countries. They were also well suited, because of their history, to operate as community-based organizations independent of direct government control, especially if the legislative framework was developed appropriately. From a business perspective, all the credit unions had to do under such circumstances was to operate prudently and efficiently. That, however, was not always as easy as it might appear. Latin America was a case in point.

LATIN AMERICA

The end of the 1970s and most of the 1980s were difficult times for Latin America. Ironically, this was partly the result of the easier flow of money into the region. The fourfold increase in petroleum prices in 1973 led to the availability of extensive surplus funds in the international banking community, particularly in Europe and ultimately in the United States. More able than ever before to move money around the world, the banking community looked for economic situations promising high returns, and Latin America became a popular alternative. This meant that more funds were available for the region than at any time in recent history, and the resulting investments at first proved very profitable for the banks and for some of the elites of Latin American countries. Unfortunately, many of the investments were made without following prudent lending practices. The result was a highly overheated economy that stimulated uneconomic investments and strained government borrowing capacities.

Ultimately, the outcome in most Latin American countries was hyperinflation. The outflow of money to pay for debt ballooned to nearly $40,000,000,000 per year compared to $13,700,000,000 coming in to the region,[244] a disastrous draining of badly needed resources. Population pressures continued to be oppressive, with the numbers increasing from 347,000,000 to 414,500,000.[245] It was a bewildering period; for many, it was distressing. To make matters worse, government debtloads accumulated to facilitate the heady expansion of the late 1970s were magnified by spiralling interest rates. That debtload, in turn, became an immense burden on Latin American societies, consuming much of the capital available across the region, delimiting social programmes and narrowing the acceptable roles for government. In the end, it would be the poor, the peasantry and the middle class who would pay the greatest price for the bad decisions of the 1970s and the 1980s. It was a story different only in degree from what was happening in other parts of the world at the same time.

The economic problems led to the often painful repositioning of the Latin American credit union movement. The movement had several qualities that made it vulnerable. For example, COLAC and many of the national movements had become dependent upon developmental assistance from outside agencies and reliant upon their own capacities to serve as financial intermediaries. Put another way, they had not developed adequate dues structures to meet most of their needs. For that reason, the Latin American movement was less solidly based on the continuing financial support of its members than other regional movements, with the exception of Africa. COLAC was in a particularly vulnerable position.

To some extent, this reliance on outside funding was understandable because of the nature of the Latin American movement. It had started out essentially serving the peasants and industrial workers of the region. This highly laudable objective meant that it was difficult, even after some 2,500 credit unions had been created, to build institutions and savings programmes sufficient to finance strong national and regional organizations. The reality was that small credit unions essentially serving people with limited financial means possessed few resources with which to fund significant national and regional organizations. And yet, without such funds, the kinds of national movements desired by the credit unionists of Latin America could not be built; a strong, self-sufficient regional organization could only be a dream. It was a continuing conundrum for those responsible for leading the movement.

Moreover, the underlying financial structure of the movement did not facilitate easy growth or diverse development. Generally, and particularly in the Andean countries and Central America, the movement was built on the idea of inexpensive lending, not on the primacy of savings. In other words, while saving was not ignored, it was not the starting point of the movement.[246] What was important was that the credit union would be a source of inexpensive loans for members, with decisions often based on the reputation of the individual. This proved to be a restrictive approach; it tended to produce small credit unions serving limited needs, especially as inflation took hold.

Most Latin American credit unions built their assets almost totally from member deposits in shares, which received no interest and were rewarded only if a given credit union had a surplus at the end of the year. This very inexpensive capital, often referred to as "social capital", was then loaned out at rates up to the legal limit, normally 12 percent per annum, a particularly beneficial restriction for borrowing members when interest rates soared in the 1980s. There were no systematic efforts or obvious attractions, however, to encourage member savings beyond the desire to contribute to the common good or to qualify for loans, which were typically limited to a multiple of two or three times the amount members had in their share accounts. It was not a system oriented toward growth or toward the meeting of diverse member needs.

Moreover, loans were often extended for the purposes of survival, an understandable pattern given the nature of the memberships. Unfortunately, all too often that meant "getting by" from one week to another or one month to another. Not often enough did it mean financing opportunities for individuals and families to enter wealth-creating opportunities in small businesses or to improve marketing of whatever they were already producing. Not often enough did it help people become self-sufficient and able to control their own economic destiny.

This in turn meant that the growth of savings within the credit unions was slow. Even worse, it meant that credit unions remained locked in the provision of a limited set of services that did not meet the needs of people more involved in the marketplace. Most credit unions did not have the range of deposit accounts, chequing services and lines of credit required by people operating small business enterprises. It was a self-limiting circle.

As the problems accumulated in the 1980s, the Latin American movement started to change its emphasis. Under the leadership of its chief executive officer, Angel Castro, COLAC undertook a series of extensive analyses of the dilemmas confronting the Latin American movements, and those studies demonstrated the need for considerable change. They advocated paying more attention to savings rather than lending, primarily through the development of better savings programmes and the offering of competitive rates on deposits. They called for increased standards of care for the management of lending policies and practices, and suggested that central organizations accept an increased liquidity function so that funds could be distributed more effectively across movements. The studies encouraged even more extensive planning activities than had been carried out in the past, and called for more training and better information systems for managers to assist them in dealing effectively with risks in lending and in securing information in a timely fashion. They advocated more specialized training for elected leaders so that they could carry out their increasingly more complicated responsibilities. They argued that national federations and COLAC itself should rely upon what their systems could afford and be less reliant upon outside contributions.[247] In total, all of these changes amounted to a gradual migration to more "managerial" credit unions.

This shift was associated with a growing determination, within WOCCU and in the countries themselves, to use credit unions as engines for economic development. That meant expanding beyond the original base of peasants and urban workers to attract owners of small businesses. To some extent, credit unions had served smaller entrepreneurs in the past. In fact, it was estimated that about 10 percent of loan portfolios and 10 percent of the loans were for small enterprise development.[248] Making more such loans in a prudent fashion would have two main benefits: it would help expand the deposit base of local credit unions and, even more, it would foster the economic growth of the communities in which credit unions existed. It was becoming clearer than ever before that the health of credit unions depended upon social stability. The notion of community, already strong in the Latin American movement, was being given a broader definition. Starting in 1987, the World Council launched a major initiative in Guatemala, the Cooperative Strengthening Project, that reflected this changing emphasis. It was a rebuilding project, financed largely by USAID, and aimed at reconstructing and stabilizing the co-operative movement that was developed in the wake of considerable economic and political instability following the 1984-1986 Guatemalan civil war.

The project was undertaken by a consortium that included COLAC, the National Cooperative Banking Association and the co-operative arm of the U.S. Department of Agriculture. It used resources from all consortium members to strengthen co-operative organizations, partly through assistance for better accounting practices and the introduction of computing systems. The project helped various co-operative organiza-tions, but particularly the Guatemalan credit unions, in dealing with delinquency problems. Above all, it assisted credit unions in overcoming their reputation as "poor people's banks", a reputation that restricted their growth and the capacity to serve their communities.[249] It was the beginning of a trend that would become widespread in the 1990s.

GUATEMALA

The Guatemalan initiative helped credit unions mobilize savings from members by offering competitive savings rates on withdrawable deposit accounts. It encouraged the develop-ment of procedures that would allow better stabilization of the movement by extending financial assistance to help restore asset values and accelerate the write-down of uncollectible loans.[250] It trained credit union personnel to assess the capacity of borrowers to repay loans based on criteria beyond the size of their deposit accounts and previous repayment record. The findings, surprising to some, were that credit unions could be more aggressive in building local economies, functioning beyond their traditional role in Latin America. They could generate considerable local savings and serve groups ignored by all other financial institutions.

The success of the Guatemalan experiment was demon-strated in a University of Wisconsin 1994 study that compared saving and borrowing patterns in communities where credit unions used a more aggressive, market-oriented approach with the patterns in communities that had little or no credit union activity.[251] It found that more of the poorest households in the credit union communities had savings accounts, significantly higher levels of savings, and better access to credit. Since most of the households were engaged in agriculture and small business, where periodic access to credit was essential for success, these differences were notable.[252]

All told, some twenty credit unions were involved in the Cooperative Strengthening Project. Their total assets (allowing for inflation) increased by 126 percent between 1987 and 1992; deposits grew by 504 percent; and total capital by 443 percent.[253] According to assessments made at the end of the project, "every major area of credit union operations [had] been strengthened in every way".[254]

The success of the Guatemalan experiment encouraged the acceptance of a "new" model of credit union for the emerging movements. The old model had been characterized by low-interest shares, outside subsidies, casual loan-making criteria, poor loan documentation, underestimation of loan risks, and low levels of institutional capital. The new model required a shift from share to deposit savings, market rates on loans, capitalization of earnings, careful credit analysis, market-based business planning, and better information systems.[255] The migration to the new model was encouraged by the introduc-tion of a stabilization fund that extended assistance to credit unions as they converted their practices to the new model, and the fund remained in place as long as the credit unions adhered to the new standards.

The Guatemalan experiment was of great importance to the future of the World Council: it marked a strong commitment to the introduction of stronger, more precise and more measurable managerial practices into developing credit unions. It also required working closely with local credit unions as opposed to working through central organizations geared to the needs of populist credit unions. In many ways, the changes involved the transfer of operating practices that had proved to be successful in the more developed movements. In the diffi-cult financial circumstances typical of Latin America in the later 1980s and early 1990s, it was a promising experiment.

THE CARIBBEAN

In the Caribbean, the main challenge confronting the movement was the development of regional stability. The region was still characterized by relatively small credit unions scattered among several islands, that essentially served people of modest income; this meant that, as in so many other areas where the movement was developing, it was difficult to create the surplus funds needed to build a strong regional organization or to invest in the kind of computing systems needed to create efficiency and build accountabilities. In the 1970s, support from the American and Canadian movements had helped the Caribbean Confederation of Credit Unions achieve some stability. During the 1980s, further support from the two movements, but particularly the Canadian movement, helped the confederation create a development programme to assist local credit unions in expanding memberships and enhancing management capabilities. The effect was to push Caribbean credit unions into stronger marketing positions that were able to meet a wider range of member needs and community services. None of this was easily achieved, however, and it required remarkable efforts by a series of leaders, especially Everard Dean, who received the Humming Bird Medal from the government of Trinidad and Tobago in 1989 and was named a senator in 1992 by the president of Trinidad and Tobago for his credit union efforts.[256]

AFRICA

While the 1980s were difficult for many Latin American countries, they verged on disaster for many countries in sub-Saharan Africa. In those years, the dreams of the independence period ran into adversities caused by several unfavourable factors: shifting global economic realities; inevitable tensions as peoples long controlled by foreign masters learned the difficult arts of self-government; declining levels of economic assistance; changes in understanding of the role of the state; and harsh rules for economic performance laid down by the international banking community and northern countries, arguably in a brutal and doctrinaire fashion.

Beneath all the problems were fundamental trends of enormous complexity for governments as well as the private and co-operative sectors. Dale Majers, a perceptive WOCCU employee with all the straightforward virtues of the American Midwest, summarized many of these problems in 1990, after he had worked in the region for many years.[257] Africa had one of the fastest growing birth rates in the world, and fully 85 percent of people were of working age; 73 percent of the population was engaged in agriculture, which, because of a declining amount of arable land and the increasing use of technology, did not require as much labour as previously. The brutal truth was that there were more people than necessary in the countryside. Moreover, commodity prices were generally falling, meaning that on-farm income was actually declining. In fact, some nations had difficulty in sustaining adequate food supplies, and continent-wide food production declined in fourteen of the years between 1973 and 1989.

These demographic and economic realities placed pressures on governments and economies that could not always be contained: it was just not possible to create enough jobs to give people the chance to earn a decent living. Moreover, health and education standards in Africa were the lowest in the world, creating widespread dissatisfaction with government services. Added to all of these problems was the advent of double-digit inflation in most African countries throughout much of the 1980s.[258] The result of all these pressures was that political instability became commonplace because governments, most of which were less than a generation away from colonial status, lacked the resources and sophistication to deal with the accumulating problems.

In total, fourteen of the countries whose credit union movements belonged to ACCOSCA were evaluated as "low-income" by the World Bank because their annual per capita incomes were below $400US annually. Another eight were classified as "lower middle-income", with annual average per capita incomes of just over $710US. Moreover, the trends were not positive: the quality of life indicators declined in virtually all countries for most years between 1970 and 1990. While many regions around the world suffered amid the dislocations of the economic adjustments of the 1980s, none suffered as much or had as many fundamental problems as Africa.

African peoples survived amid this economic and consequent political turmoil in part because they continued to utilize the informal economy financed by their own indigenous financial institutions, such as *esusu* and *tontine*. Partly as an extension of those practices, they also used credit unions more regularly and in greater numbers. Between 1986 and 1991 the average annual growth in numbers of credit unions was nearly 6 percent and the increases in membership exceeded 5 percent, surpassing 5,000,000 people.[259] As in the more dramatic cases of Uganda and Tanzania in the previous decade, the movement grew because it was a last resort for many people, because governments were increasingly unable to meet their needs.

The roles that credit unions played can in part be seen in the kinds of loans they extended to their members. On average, credit unions loaned money for the following purposes: housing, 25 percent; health and education, 15 percent; social and consumer, 40 percent; and agricultural and small business, 20 percent. Agricultural and small business loans averaged $160US and mostly financed agricultural production, particularly input costs such as fertilizer. Most of the loans were unsecured, short-term personal loans with fixed interest rates. As in other parts of the developing world, they were usually based upon multiples of a member's savings balance (e.g., two or three times the value of the member's savings balance).[260] In circumstances where opportunities for borrowing were disappearing or becoming roads to lifetime bondage, one is hard pressed to imagine the cumulative benefits of these small loans to hundreds of thousands of Africans.

TOGO

While it is impossible to single out all the accomplishments in the African movements, a few that were closely associated with the World Council are instructive and noteworthy. In Togo, the movement made significant gains in the 1980s. Started in 1967, it had made steady progress largely through the work of a group of enthusiastic volunteers organized in a national promotion committee (Le Conseil nationale pour le développement des coopératives d'épargne et de crédit, or CONAUDEC). By 1983 there were 78 credit unions with 6,700 members and slightly less than $50,000,000US in total shares and savings.[261] In 1983 a five-year plan was introduced to help develop the institutional structure the Togolese movement would need for further development. Using funds from ACCOSCA, the World Council, USAID, Bread for the World (a German organization) and Crédit Mutuel, the movement converted CONAUDEC into a regular central organization and renamed it Fédération des unions coopératives d'épargne et de crédit du Togo, or FUCEC-Togo. FUCEC-Togo undertook an extensive programme of institution-building among local credit unions. Its first challenge was to provide leaders with basic management skills (for example, accounting and bookkeeping) to meet growing member needs adequately. This process was led by Chet Aeschliman, a former finance specialist and director of finance for the World Council, and before that a Peace Corps volunteer in Cameroon. The result was annual growth in savings of between 21 percent and 53 percent in the first five years of the plan, far exceeding the national growth rate of savings deposits of 2 to 4 percent.[262] In many ways it was an excellent example of how the emphasis on savings and institution-building could reap dividends.

LESOTHO

Work in Lesotho, one of the poorest countries in the world, was important because it was a generally successful effort at expanding agricultural production. In a sense, it was a contin-

An early credit union meeting in Lesotho. (COURTESY OF CUNA)

uation of a programme that went back to the 1960s, when credit unions sponsored a tractor rental system that allowed men to work their farms even while they were employed in South African mines. More directly, the work was a continuation of agricultural production credit programmes started in 1976 by the Lesotho Co-operative Credit Union League, ACCOSCA and the Global Projects Office.

The specific project started in 1985 was called Lesotho Agricultural and Institutional Support programme (or LAPIS). Working together with Co-op Lesotho, the apex organization for agricultural marketing, LAPIS emphasized the production of high-value cash crops and livestock while it strengthened local production ability and marketing capacity. It encouraged dietary change by emphasizing the production of potatoes, cabbages, apples, peaches and pears and by encouraging poultry-raising and dairying. In addition to a healthier diet, these kinds of agricultural activities also permitted greater production with minimal soil degradation than was the case in the more conventional raising of cereals. The agricultural programme encouraged the gentler dimensions of the green revolution by making more sprayers, plows, planters, tool bars, harrows and cultivators available to members, while it helped fund easier access to fertilizers and ox teams. To accommodate this significantly enlarged sphere of activity, and to ensure adequate control, many credit unions organized farm committees and hired their first trained managers.

LAPIS also fostered village-based, value-added production. One of the more interesting examples of this initiative was the development of a yarn production project. Bicycle rims were converted into spinning wheels for sixty Basotho women who were supplied with mohair. The women turned the mohair into yarn that was then exported. By the mid-1980s over 2,000 women had spinning machines and were making a significant economic contribution to their families and communities.[263] All told, the Lesotho experiment was a successful example of how special programmes in rural areas could work.

MALAWI

Another successful experiment took place in Malawi, also one of Africa's poorest nations, and a country particularly hard hit by the economic problems of the 1980s. Soaring oil prices, plummeting commodity prices, the closure of Mozambican ports, drought, mealybug infestations, a growing refugee problem, regional unrest — the list of problems was long and intimidating.[264] Moreover, because of past inefficiencies and government interference, the wider co-operative movement, which was focused on the marketing of agricultural produce, was in disrepute.

Following unsuccessful efforts by Roman Catholic missionaries to establish credit unions in the 1960s, an association of enthusiasts, most of whom were also Catholic, organized the Malawi Promotion, Education and Advisory Committee (PEAC) in 1972. PEAC succeeded in developing twenty-six credit unions by 1980. All too often, however, the committee was considered an arm of the church charged with distributing loans that came to be seen as charity and consequently were sometimes not repaid. PEAC was particularly active in rural areas, often among the very poor who, because of the charitable dimensions and the elite leadership, seldom had any strong sense of ownership.[265]

In 1980, with the help of ACCOSCA and the World Council, PEAC was converted into the Malawi Union of Savings and Credit Co-operatives (MUSCCO) and became the established apex organization for the Malawi movement. The next ten years saw considerable progress as the organization became increasingly more businesslike. It emphasized savings rather than credit, hired professional managers, increased training for elected officials, created a centralized lending facility that made somewhat larger loans available for small enterprise development, and emphasized procedures to make credit unions safe for investment. MUSCCO adopted a market-driven business approach to credit unionism that achieved significant success. It would become an important precedent for future developments within WOCCU.

SOUTH AFRICA

Perhaps the most satisfying African development in the period, however, was the creation of a movement in South Africa. At the time South Africa was still governed by the policies of apartheid, and helping people, especially black

South Africans, develop a movement took some nerve and ingenuity by credit union donors in order to ensure that the funds reached South Africa and were used appropriately. The movement was started in 1981 when Roman Catholic leaders Peter Templeton, Norman Reynolds and Sister Marie McLaughlin established four credit unions (St. Francis, St. Theresa, Mater Dei and Holy Trinity) in the so-called "black townships". By the end of the decade the number of credit unions had grown to forty, serving nearly 4,000 members. That growth was possible because of support from the Canadian Co-operative Association and the Catholic Relief Services as well as WOCCU and CUNA Mutual.[266] It was an achievement that elicited great pride in South Africa and in the North American movements as well.

Despite these positive developments, many African credit union movements encountered grave problems during the decade. Perhaps the most common problem was the difficult transition from populist organizations to organizations characterized by strong management cultures. The needs of African credit unions were many: more sophisticated savings accounts offering variable terms and different interest structures; strong management to keep delinquency rates under 5 percent; better managerial skills for daily operations; stabilization systems to help overcome problems stemming from economic trends, mistakes and, occasionally, fraud; and central liquidity facilities to maximize local credit union resources and build effectively upon the strengths that had been achieved.

Meeting these needs would require stable organizations with well-developed training and support programmes, not easy during a period of declining resources and uncertain government relations. Moreover, it was difficult because the needs were multiplying: not only did managers and employees require expanded and more complicated training programmes, not only was there a need for more extensive planning but there was also a continuous demand for the improved training of elected leaders. The role of directors and committee persons was changing as the movements developed, and there was a greater requirement for them to be better monitors of larger organizations and better prepared for the development and articulation of policies.

GHANA AND NIGERIA

The history of the Ghanaian movement is a case in point. Since its beginnings in 1955, the movement had grown steadily. The Ghana Co-operative Credit Union Association (CUA) was formed in 1968, the beginnings of a national structure. By 1976 CUA employed forty people to serve the 480 credit unions in its membership. Sustaining this level of national development, however, required considerable outside funding, since many of the credit unions were too small to provide much support for the national organization. Fortunately, throughout the 1970s, CUA was able to secure support from funding partners, most notably the Konrad Adenauer Foundation.

Then, in the early 1980s the Ghanaian economy, like most national economies on the continent, went into a tailspin, largely because of four interrelated developments. First, there was a precipitous drop in prices for such commodities as coffee and cocoa, key exports in the national economy. Second, as the economy declined, a structural adjustment programme required by the international banking community completely reversed the way in which the economy had been managed since independence; the cost in human terms was high. Third, inflation occasionally reached 30 percent and seemed to be locked into a permanent level of over 20 percent, a disastrous trend for most citizens and the spiralling national debt. Fourth, the government had inappropriate priorities — for example, the construction of showpiece highways when there were acute health and education needs. It was a combination of trends that spelled economic disaster.

Like nearly all aspects of Ghanaian society, the credit union movement reeled under the accumulating problems. In fact, it is a tribute to the leadership of the early 1980s and the basic strength of the movement that it survived the initial shocks. By 1982, the number had shrunk to 265; in one year the number of credit unions affiliated with CUA declined by 35 percent, in most circumstances an almost inevitably fatal drop for any second- or third-tier organization.[267]

As the problems mounted, the capacity of the Ghanaian leadership to respond to the continuing and deepening challenges became less effective. In particular, it was not able to sustain necessary services for the national movement and was forced to fund its declining activities from the central loan fund built up through savings from member credit unions. It was a strategy that could have only a limited life. To make matters worse, CUA discovered in 1989 that one of its accountants, now disappeared, had embezzled funds from the organization. The management crisis that resulted was resolved quickly enough, but it further undermined the already declining support of local credit unions.

Consequently, the Ghanaian movement, like other African movements buffeted by the economic and political turmoil of the 1980s, confronted a major restructuring and revitalization process as the decade came to a close. In its own case, this meant replenishing the central fund partly through grants from overseas agencies (CCA and Rabobank), partly through the recovery of some of the misappropriated funds and partly through increased support from local credit unions. It also had to undertake a significant education programme, not least for the directors of CUA, since it had become clear that their training in the 1980s had not kept pace with the needs of the organization.

In fact, the Ghanaian situation revealed how challenging it was to sustain adequate training for both management and elected leadership as credit unions adopted management cultures. All too often, elected leaders were equipped with only the level of knowledge needed to run small credit unions providing simple services essentially through volunteer labour, a level that just was not sufficient given the way the movement had grown during the 1970s. The Ghanaian turnaround would not be easy, but in retrospect it was possible because the movement had shown remarkable resiliency in the face of extremely difficult problems.

Nigeria, which had the largest movement in Africa, faced similar problems. There were between 8,000 and 15,000 credit unions scattered among its twenty-one states during the 1980s (thirty-one states as of 1991).[268] These were powerful institutions on a local level, reflecting how easily Nigerians had moved into credit unions from their long experience with *esusus*. They were also frequently integrated at local, regional and state levels with co-operatives providing consumer goods or, more frequently, marketing primary products. That rela-

tionship led to some problems, because too frequently it meant that leaders did not have the necessary training to operate financial institutions; nor were they always able to protect the financial integrity of their credit unions when the demands of the related co-operatives became too insistent.[269] Despite these problems, the movement was one of the strongest in Africa.

As with other African movements, the greatest difficulty confronting the Nigerian movement was the development of a strong national framework. Partly this was because the country itself was an artificial creation in that it was more the result of the vagaries of imperialism than the product of natural associations of people over a long period of history. Partly it was because the apex organization (the National Association of Co-operative Credit Unions of Nigeria) had not worked out a clear vision of its roles and responsibilities.[270] Somewhat like Canada and Australia, the strength of the Nigerian movement lay in local credit unions and, to some extent, state organizations; like them, the Nigerian credit union movement would require considerable time and effort to create a healthy national structure.

Looked at broadly, there were two other structural issues that inhibited the development of credit unions in sub-Saharan Africa. The first concerned legislation. The credit union movement, as it had evolved from the American experience, followed the tradition of having a separate governing piece of legislation, rather than omnibus legislation governing all kinds of co-operatives or reliance upon general banking legislation. That approach ensured inclusion of the necessary provisions for democratic control and adequate requirements for the protection of member deposits. Unfortunately, the African situation rarely reflected this preferred norm. Many of the statutes governing credit unions in Africa were very old, essentially designed with agricultural co-operatives in mind, and ignoring essential credit union attributes such as common bonds, supervisory and educational committees, and different kinds of savings accounts. They typically imposed reserve requirements necessary for the sound operation of agricultural co-operatives but impossible for most credit unions.[271]

The second, and related, issue concerned fixed limits for interest rates on loans, a policy adopted in Africa, as in other newer credit union regions, because of what had been a practice in the early history of North American credit unionism. In the early years of the American and Canadian movements it had been customary to charge 1 percent per month on the diminishing balance of a loan, an attractive rate for North Americans in the relatively stable interest rate situation of the 1920-1955 period, especially for people who could not secure loans elsewhere or only from lenders who charged exorbitant rates. That practice, which also conformed with a general understanding of co-operative principles as enunciated by the International Co-operative Alliance, was taken outward from North America by credit union organizers in the 1950s and 1960s. In the process, the practice became elevated into a principle in some places, and was an unfortunate development when interest rates on deposits and on loans in the marketplace often exceeded 20 percent.

Ironically, at the same time as the practice was being adopted elsewhere, it was being jettisoned in the United States, Canada and Australia as interest rates became more variable beginning in the late 1950s. By the end of the 1960s most credit unions in the three countries had moved away from the practice, although some smaller credit unions continued to follow it. The majority of credit unions moved to competitive interest rates on deposits so that they could continue to attract funds when interest rates were rising and also develop the more complex investment and lending instruments requested by their members.

The reasons for this gap in practice between the established and the developing movements are not too hard to understand. Some North American credit union organizers, when they went overseas, carried with them perspectives somewhat out of step with what was happening in their own countries. They were advocates of populist credit unions and appreciated the direct accountability of smaller credit unions. Naturally enough, too, they preferred simple calculations easily carried out by people with limited training (the same reason why the practice had been popular in the United States and Canada a generation earlier). As long as there was interest rate stability, the idea of a simple 1 percent a month made considerable sense. Unfortunately, such stability was far from being the norm by the 1980s — in Africa and many other parts of the world as well. The resulting dilemma can be seen in the case of

Tanzania. In 1991, the Tanzanian government introduced legislation that centred individual savings and credit co-operatives in rural communities and provided them with their own national organization. It also significantly improved the auditing system for the country's credit unions. These positive steps, however, were undermined by the system of interest rates imposed by the new act. Interest on loans was limited to 12 percent although the going rate in other Tanzanian financial institutions was 30 percent or higher. At the same time, the credit unions could only pay between 1 and 5 percent on deposits, while the competition was regularly paying over 20 percent. The cumulative result was a credit union system that was stronger, but a system still handicapped in what it could accomplish or undertake.

UGANDA

The statutory limitation on interest rates was only one of the ways in which governments could adversely affect the development of credit unions. A more extreme example occurred in Uganda, where the political instability created by Idi Amin's regime in the 1980s rocked the credit union movement. In 1988 the economic costs of that regime's mismanagement were reflected in a devaluation of the nation's currency. The last two zeros were simply eliminated, and a special tax of 30 percent was imposed on whatever remained. Thus, a person with the equivalent of $1,000 was left with ten dollars and that amount was subject to a special three dollar tax, leaving only seven dollars. The consequences, disastrous for individuals and families, were not much better for financial institutions either.

The impact of this devaluation on the country's struggling credit union movement was devastating, and it is a tribute to its leadership that it coped as well as it did. Across the country, responsible leaders made the hard decision to freeze operations when necessary. Many credit unions became the heart of local economies, entering into a wide range of activities to assist members and their communities. In one instance, a credit union took over a brick-making business to preserve employment for its members. In others, they operated or assisted in the operation of marketing businesses, again so members would have some income. In several instances, they accepted and made payments in kind rather than insisting upon cash. It was a resilient movement that served its members well under particularly trying circumstances.

The Ugandan situation was a very dramatic example of how government actions or ineffectiveness could threaten credit union movements. More commonly, the problem was just an inappropriate set of government policies or inadequately prepared public servants. In fairness, though, and in contrast to the rather facile view some North Americans had of the problem, it must be appreciated that finding the appropriate roles for government was extremely difficult. For example, in many countries the literacy level was still low, particularly in rural areas, meaning that leadership could fall to a small group that might abuse its power. That kind of situation posed serious challenges for the administering public servants, especially when there was a significant involvement of local political leaders. The point was that in such circumstances, the government had to be prepared to step in and assume responsibility in the interests of the general membership. In other words, although the preference of North American advisors was for as much independence from governments as possible, some support was almost invariably required, especially when credit unions were in the formative stage.

The history of the movement in Swaziland demonstrates this point. Started in 1966, the Swaziland movement had gone through a burst of organizational activities in the early 1970s, by which time some thirty credit co-operatives were organized. Despite those promising beginnings, however, the movement steadily declined. From the perspective of a WOCCU consultant in the mid-1980s, a principal reason for the decline was the lack of effective support from government officials. In fact, one such official admitted: "We started to ignore Savings and Credit Co-operatives because we did not have the knowledge of credit union management that we [could] share with members. Most of us, to save ourselves from embarrassment, did not come to the societies' assistance when it was needed most".[272] Government relations was one of the most perplexing issues confronting the African movements in the 1980s: it was not an issue that could be resolved easily or quickly, nor was it an issue that only affected Africa.

The World Council and ACCOSCA found the situation within the African continent challenging, to say the least. The sheer size of the continent, when coupled with the particular problems of the decade, made progress difficult. Nevertheless, WOCCU continued to work closely with USAID in several African projects. In 1986 it negotiated a five-year, $2,100,000US programme for Lesotho to develop credit unions in rural areas. It also had significant projects in Togo focused on institutional development, in Cameroon on small-enterprise development, and in Malawi on strengthening the central support system. WOCCU also assisted the ACCOSCA office in Nairobi in developing its training programmes. The by-now classic problem confronting ACCOSCA was that it had far too few resources to meet the demands for training and assistance from its member organizations. The pressures became so great that ACCOSCA, with encouragement from the World Council, began to change its approach.

In the past, ACCOSCA had emphasized the creation of a regional superstructure, a natural emphasis given the way in which funding had been attracted, and the direction of orthodox development thought in the 1970s and early 1980s. In some ways, however, it had placed too great pressures on the national movements, few of which could afford to meet their own needs, let alone those of a regional organization. Most seriously, the regional structure did not readily enable credit union members to appreciate the need for them to accept responsibility for the stability and future of their pan-African organizations. In fact, the long history of outside loans and grants had tended to create dependence rather than independence; they had allowed leaders to underestimate the importance of establishing sound credit unions at a local level. Only rarely had the approach been able to provide the technical support that local credit unions increasingly required.

Consequently, as the 1990s opened, more attention was given, as in some parts of Latin America, to supporting promising local credit union groups. The changed priorities were evident in Plan Africa 2000, a co-ordinated effort to work with local credit unions to emphasize safety and soundness in their operations through strengthening institutional frameworks, expanding the range of products offered to members, and improving services. It was a slower approach, one obviously aimed at creating credit unions with stronger management cultures rather than more effective populist traditions. Its great virtue was that it offered the long-term benefit of building stability upward from strong local credit unions rather than downward from central organizations precariously funded by donors and whatever financial activities they could manage to undertake.

In a way, the shift to local credit unions was symptomatic of much that was occurring in Africa itself. The visionary ambitions of the independence period were giving way to narrower, more realistic, expectations; the shift to more local, more mundane matters in credit unions echoed that change. The role of the state, once so prominent, was diminished, the result of external pressures, weak political institutions, inadequate economic infrastructure, and insufficient expertise. For credit unions, this meant widely variable government support and an echoing emphasis on building stronger, more self-reliant local institutions.

The best hope for Africa lay in the emerging new generation that was evident by the 1980s, people who were better trained than previous generations and more able to manage increasingly market-oriented economies. In credit unions, that development was apparent in the growing numbers of young professionals serving on boards or working as paid employees. The decade of the 1980s had been immensely difficult , but the solutions to these problems, as in most co-operatives facing problems, were being found within its own people. Ultimately, the same would be true for Africa itself.

ASIA

In contrast to Latin America and Africa, many Asian movements experienced remarkable growth and development as the 1980s progressed. The economies of several countries flourished, and a significantly larger percentage of national populations enjoyed a greater share of the national wealth. The political situation in many countries stabilized, and liberal democratic political cultures became more evident.

In 1985, WOCCU started a three-year programme aimed at expanding the movement in regions where no credit unions existed. In that same year, a small movement in India joined the World Council, bringing to four the number of affiliated countries in South Asia; the others were Bangladesh, Pakistan and Sri Lanka. Contacts were also made with interested groups in Nepal. It was the beginning of serious efforts in a subregion of immense size in terms of geography, population and complexity of issues, one that was as intimidating as any region in the world.

At the same time, the more established movements, such as those in Korea, Hong Kong and Thailand were moving into the second stage of development, and establishing more effective managerial credit unions, the stage at which they would create strong, more self-sufficient national organizations. For their benefit, ACCU organized seminars on technological changes, interlending and stabilization funds.

SRI LANKA

In the 1980s the Sri Lankan movement, (called SANASA, an abbreviation of the Sinhalese name for the national organization, *Sa*kasuruwam Ha *Na*ya Gancidenu *Sa*mupakara Samithi) achieved remarkable success, although growth often stretched human and financial resources to the limit. The movement fashioned its own philosophy out of Sinhalese history, Buddhist thought, Antigonish influences and optimistic pragmatism, all based upon the deep village traditions of Sri Lanka, traditions that included many spontaneous co-operative activities, notably in the planting and harvesting of crops. Committed to the mobilization of savings that would largely remain in the community, SANASA attracted a remarkable amount of support in all parts of the country.

The SANASA movement was also remarkable in its abiding commitment to serving the needs of the genuinely poor. Most other movements over time had weakened in that commitment but the Sri Lankan movement, in large part because of the leadership of P.A. Kiriwaneniya, never wavered.

Until 1984 the Sri Lankan movement emphasized promotion and education; between 1984 and 1990 it became increasingly concerned with expanded training and the creation of central institutions, and from 1990 onward with the strengthening of financial capacities. Because of the nature of Sri Lankan communities and a strong commitment in

SANASA to democratic structures, the primary societies were limited to about 600 members, with most of them below the limit. These local organizations, numbering some 6,000, with more than 700,000 members by the late 1980s, developed a series of institutions to bring credit unions together on local, district and "cluster" levels. The entire movement placed great emphasis on member involvement and worked hard at bringing out members to monthly and annual meetings, and to other gatherings.[273] Every three years SANASA held a national congress that attracted between 150,000 and 200,000 people in the stadia of larger cities and were major social occasions as well as business meetings. Most dramatically, perhaps, SANASA brought the Sinhalese and Tamil peoples together, despite the divisions that split the country so tragically during the period. In fact, SANASA became the largest social movement in the country, and one of the strongest grassroots movements in co-operative circles around the world.

THE PHILIPPINES

Another particularly dynamic movement in Asia existed in the Philippines, a country of remarkable diversity. In the 1980s the Philippines had a population of 60,000,000 divided among 111 ethno-linguistic groups scattered across 3,000 islands. Its significant social, economic and political cleavages were most apparent to the outside world during the 1980s in the political unrest associated with the end of the Marcos regime. The co-operative movement generally was much affected by these divisions. For example, there were important differences between rural and urban co-operatives, including credit unions. There were powerful ethnic dimensions most obviously manifested in co-operatives serving Moslems and tribal communities. The movement was divided into two groups: those co-operatives close to the government of the day and those that were closer to reform groups opposed to the government.

The World Council affiliate in the Philippines, the Philippines Federation of Credit Cooperatives Incorporated (PFCCI), was originally closely tied to the government, but in the early 1980s began to assert a greater degree of independence. It endorsed the operating principles adopted by WOCCU in 1983 and paid more attention to training programmes, emphasized the importance of financial autonomy, and increasingly focused on rural credit unions. The World Council worked carefully with PFCCI on these initiatives and provided some funding.

At the same time, the Canadian movement began to work with the National Federation of Co-operatives (NATCCO), an unaffiliated co-operative movement with an interest in credit unions. The strong association with co-operatives was more acceptable to Canadian than to American credit unionists, a reflection of the different traditions of the two countries. NATCCO was also more deeply rooted in ethnic credit unions, which were particularly responsive to rural situations and associated with reform political movements. The Canadian initiative caused some tensions between the two North American movements and demonstrated the necessity for more collaboration and exchanges of information between established movements involved in supporting credit union movements in the same overseas country, especially in countries where political tensions were pervasive.

KOREA

The regional movement in Asia that grew most rapidly in the 1980s and early 1990s was in Korea. During the 1970s the Korean movement had expanded rapidly, from 792 credit unions in 1973, to 1,467 by the end of the decade. During the 1980s and early 1990s, the number of credit unions did not change substantially, but the increase in members and assets was remarkable. In 1983, the movement possessed 1,000,000 members and nearly $740,000,000US in assets; by 1992 there were nearly 2,800,000 members, with over $7,729,000,000US in assets. The movement had the highest penetration rate (9.31 percent of the population) of any Asian credit union movement, and possessed nearly 80 percent of all the credit union assets in the region.

At the local level, Korean credit unions were well integrated into their communities. Many of them provided community halls and schools as well as free libraries and medical care. They expanded the kinds of services they provided to their members to include a wide range of deposit accounts, from shares to "self-help" deposits to educational and demand savings accounts. They also developed their own lending programmes based on multiples of savings accounts and the character of borrowers.

This growth was accomplished in Korea despite adverse economic conditions and some deregulation of the financial industries in the early 1980s. It was made possible by the restructuring of the Korean movement in 1980, which provided a greater degree of co-ordination and integration. Fifteen leagues were established throughout the country to organize credit unions, sponsor training programmes, finance research and carry out interlending activities. The National Credit Union Federation of Korea (NACUFOK), organized in 1973, became larger and more powerful as the 1980s progressed.

NACUFOK provided a wide range of services to member leagues and their member organizations. It carried out national promotional campaigns, represented the movement to government, advised local credit unions on management issues, and set national standards. NACUFOK was an aggressive organization that provided strong direction to the national movement, in part because it had a close but independent relationship with the government. Its stabilization fund, established in 1984, was responsible for the "stay-healthy" activities of the movement. It provided insurance services for the movement, most of them through CUNA Mutual. All told, NACUFOK possessed as much influence within its movement as any other national organization within the international movement.

Above all, the Korean movement paid greater attention to the training and preparation of board members, especially managers. Its national training centre, which graduated over 31,000 people between 1981 and 1992, served the needs of elected leaders, managers, supervisors and staff. The educational system was characterized by considerable breadth as well as technical specialization. All told, the strongly entrenched educational programmes provided coherence and a set of common experiences and helped to explain why there was such unity of purpose and common understanding within the movement, no small reason for its success.

In total, while the credit union movement was challenged by the economic boom that swept much of Asia in the decade, it also benefited remarkably from it. The result overall was a period of credit union growth that rivalled what the United States and Canada had experienced in the 1950s and 1960s. Initially, the Asian movements focused considerable effort upon building credit unions in rural areas; with over 80 percent of the Asian population living in the countryside, it seemed appropriate to do so. Conferences were organized on the theme of rural credit, and most Asian movements developed special programmes to reach farming families. The movements in Sri Lanka, the Philippines, Thailand and Indonesia made particularly strenuous efforts to reach rural villages and families, generally with good success. Increasingly, though, they were challenged by urban growth. At a rate few had expected, Asian cities began to expand. In particular, the main industrial cities of the "four tigers" boomed as industrialization proceeded at an unprecedented rate. Thus, by the end of the decade, several movements, most notably in Korea and Indonesia, rekindled their efforts in urban centres among both employee and community groups. The result was a truly remarkable period of expansion, even though cumulatively the regional movement reached less than 1 percent of Asia's vast population.

Some movements were limited in their growth because they targeted only a small section of the community. This was true especially in countries where the movement was still primarily serving Christian populations. In Bangladesh, Japan and India, for example, the movement remained strongest among small Christian minorities. While these movements undoubtedly served their parish groups well, it was clear that more work had to be done to bring the possibilities of the movement to the attention of the majority groups. In Bangladesh, the reorientation of the movement was the responsibility of the credit union league that had been formed in 1978 following a visit by Augustine Kang and Andrew So. Visits by Somchit Varangkangyubol and Robby Tulus in the early 1980s further helped stimulate the adoption of a wider perspective. In 1984 the league began the process of upgrading the management capacities of the existing credit unions, almost all of which were parish-based, and the process of reaching out to the wider community.[274] Although progress was slow, it was steady throughout the remainder of the decade.

Augustine Kang also played a significant role in helping to promote the credit union alternative in China. In March 1992, Kang led a workshop in China, which sparked the formation of two credit unions, the first co-operative community banks formed in the country since those developed by Christian missionaries in the 1920s.

Amid the growth of the 1980s and early 1990s, ACCU made steady progress, attracting funds from USAID, the Australian movement, the Irish movement and the Canadian movement, either for its own work or that of national movements. It operated a continuing series of workshops and training sessions and released a remarkable range of publications. Like the other regional organizations, however, ACCU was confronted by the challenge of finding all the resources it required, even when some of its member organizations were prospering. More than the other confederations, ACCU was operating in a region of immense size, variety and complexity.

Augustine Kang (left) and Robby Tulus, two of the most prominent early leaders of the Asian credit union movement. (COURTESY OF WOCCU)

In fact, it arguably possessed two kinds of movements: more pragmatic movements in Sino-Asia and more philosophical movements in Indo-Asia. Bringing these two groups together in common cause was not easy.

Despite these problems, in many ways, the Asian movements of the period were among the more exciting in the world. In several countries they were developing at unprecedented rates, more than adequately reflecting the growth of the region. The Asian movements were also particularly innovative. Indonesia offered interest-free loans for health emergencies and successfully supported co-operative entrepreneurship. Thailand effectively sustained production and marketing services. Sri Lanka supported remarkably active committees on agriculture, women and youth. Malaysia developed innovative branch network systems, a model worthy of consideration elsewhere. Korea moved quickly and easily into managerial credit unions, advanced technological systems and a powerful national structure, all developments that had created far greater tensions in other societies.

The Asian movements were also confronting problems fairly typical of movements in other parts of the world. They had a growing need for professional managers, which some of them, as in the case of Korea, sought to fill through their own extensive training programmes. They were well aware that they needed a more "scientific" style of management that could reduce uncertainties, use new tools for gathering and analyzing information, and adhere to steadily more demanding government regulatory requirements. Asian credit unions also required better trained volunteers able to make the transition from the "hands-on" approach typical of populist credit unions to the directional role of directors in managerial credit unions. They needed strong directors to help create a separate place for credit unions in their societies and to ensure that legislative frameworks were appropriate.

In pursuing their legislative objectives, the Asian credit unions sought distinctive credit union legislation that would protect the voluntary nature of board members, define the role of government appropriately, promote the formation of equity, and facilitate member commitment. Unfortunately, in too many countries these qualities were not honoured because credit unions were administered under general co-operative acts devised essentially for the implementation of directed government policies. While the 1980s and early 1990s had generally been good to most Asian movements, there was still much to be done.

THE PACIFIC
FIJI

Among the islands in the Pacific, Fiji remained the most important movement, although it encountered serious challenges, some of which emerged from a temporary crisis in leadership. In 1984 Father Ganey died, and his death left a void; like a giant oak he had cast a large shadow that made it difficult for a new generation of leaders to develop. Moreover, his passionate commitment to small credit unions, in essence those with populist cultures, had helped create a movement of 114 credit unions, many of them essentially uneconomic in very small communities. Unfortunately, the consequences of that preference were not well appreciated: the result was that many credit unions were hard pressed to provide the services members required, to train enough leaders, and to create adequate resources for the league.[275]

By the mid-1980s the movement was facing serious difficulties in moving either to a structure that could realistically sustain populist credit unions or to one that absorbed much of the culture of managerial credit unions. Carlos Matos was sent to Fiji under the Volunteers in Overseas Cooperative Assistance (VOCA) programme, an organization that arranged for American volunteers with co-operative backgrounds to work with co-operatives in developing countries.

Matos's report included recommendations similar to those made in many other credit union studies of the period. It focused on expanding technical competence so as to cope with the advent of computerized systems, the need for more administrative skills, increasingly complicated accounting procedures, and the desirability of, if not requirement for, sound planning. It was a typical interpretation of the problems common in emerging movements in the period.

During 1986-1987, the Fijian movement was further disrupted when droughts reduced sugar industry incomes and helped lead to the devaluation of the Fijian dollar. A

Fiji Police and Prisons Credit Union in Suva. (COURTESY OF CUNA)

military coup in 1987 further weakened the economy, at least in the short term. In the attendant crisis the Police and Prisons Credit Union, one of the stronger financial institutions in the country, played a significant role in helping to stabilize the economy.

PAPUA NEW GUINEA

In Papua New Guinea the movement encountered problems in the 1980s. It entered the decade with about 300 loans and savings societies and a federation serving the needs of 105,000 people, most of them in rural areas. Unfortunately, training was inadequate and managerial expertise insufficient. Many rural societies had to be closed in the later 1980s, and the number of credit unions shrank to twenty, most of them in Port Moresby. The Bank of Papua New Guinea assumed temporary control of the movement in 1989; with government assistance, the bank restructured the movement and, despite the difficulties, encouraged its expansion, particularly in the metropolitan areas. Australians, notably Ken Miller, played a helpful role in the resuscitation of the movement, largely through funding from their own Credit Union Foundation. The turnaround was quick, but painful.[276]

Despite the problems in these movements, leaders from the Pacific were still interested in pursuing the possibilities of greater collaboration. They were encouraged because several credit union organizations from outside the Pacific were playing important roles in fostering development in the region. The Australian Federation was particularly active in Papua New Guinea, Fiji, the Solomon Islands and Tonga. The New Zealand Credit Union League assisted the movements in Tonga and the Cook Islands. The Hawaiian Credit Union League extended support to credit unions in American Samoa, Guam and Kwajalein. CUNA, through the CUNA Foundation (today called the National Credit Union Foundation), was involved, as was CUNA Mutual and the Canadian Co-operative Association. Perhaps a federated entity could bring all these efforts together within an effective regional programme.

In 1990 a formal meeting was held in Fiji to consider setting up an Oceania confederation. Seven island movements participated, but it was agreed that the time had not arrived for its creation: the islands were too scattered and their movements were too small to make a full-fledged confederation feasible. The costs of forming such organizations prematurely were now well understood by the international movement. On the other hand, everyone recognized the need for forging a more systematic approach to development among the islands, and it was agreed to meet more regularly. Participants also agreed to work with development partners to better ensure the economic viability of the existing credit unions, especially in Papua New Guinea, Fiji and Tonga. A second agreement was to arrange for greater support for beginning movements in the Solomon Islands, Vanuatu and Kiribati.[277] It was a cautious approach, but one that reflected what had been learned and what was desirable in helping new movements at the start.

IRELAND

In Ireland, a similar pattern of increased concern for soundness was evident in the 1980s and 1990s, even though the movement continued to make remarkable progress: by 1992 it had over 500 credit unions, more than 1,320,000 members (more than a 41 percent penetration of the Irish market), and assets of over $4,000,000,000US. Part of the concern over soundness was the flip-side of the Irish emphasis on democracy and volunteerism. Among the northern national movements, the Irish movement arguably possessed the deepest commitment to populist traditions. The role of the volunteer was pervasive, and the league operated in a particularly open and democratic way. Its board was heavily involved in the league's daily operations and held frequent and lengthy meetings. Although they worked through an extensive network of committees, the league directors had a burden that was extensive and demanding. By the end of the 1980s, the limits of direct democracy (i.e., daily management by elected leaders) had arguably been reached, even for people as committed as the Irish credit union leaders.

In 1989, the Irish movement appointed a planning committee to review how well the movement was prepared to meet anticipated future needs. The committee raised basic structural,

John Nicholson, president of the World Council, gives a special award to Nora Herlihy for her work on behalf of credit unions during a WOCCU meeting in Dublin. (COURTESY OF CUNA)

technological and funding issues, leading to the appointment of consultants, Price Waterhouse, to analyze the current situation. In July 1992, the company delivered a report that called for the extensive restructuring of the national movement. In essence, Price Waterhouse proposed a set of reforms that would make the Irish movement more like those in the U.S., Canada and Australia. Their report called for the appointment of a chief executive officer; previously, there had been no senior managing officer, and the president, board and committees were expected to provide executive leadership. It recommended a clearer separation of board/management responsibilities, more focused annual meetings, the appointment of an audit committee rather than an elected supervisory committee, an enhanced training department, new marketing and information technology departments, an improved budgetary process, and an expanded set of services to local credit union members.

The Price Waterhouse report was a fundamental challenge to the Irish movement. On the one hand, it demonstrated how a well-meaning democratic impulse had created inefficiencies

Whenever the World Council has a forum, its leaders meet with important figures from the host country. Mary Robinson, then president of Ireland, welcomes the credit union international leadership to the forum in Cork in 1994. (COURTESY OF WOCCU)

that were increasingly unacceptable. There was no doubt that change was necessary, and that would be challenging; for some, it would be disturbing. On another level, the report was controversial because it raised, directly and indirectly, the issue of how to ensure apparent and real democratic control within credit unions dominated by managerial cultures. It was — and is — one of the most difficult problems within the credit union experience. The North American and Australian answers to the problem generally had produced weakened democratic systems, most obvious in the low participation rates for elections, although they had retained the protections afforded by annual elections and accountability mechanisms. The challenge facing the Irish movement, therefore, was to see if it could retain the sense of deep member/volunteer involvement and ownership as they embraced some of the elements of corporate control and direction.

In its international activities, the Irish movement was always a generous, enthusiastic and independent participant. In 1980, the league formally entered into international development work, especially in Africa. It was a popular initiative within the Irish movement, and local credit unions have been generous and involved participants in the overseas programme ever since. In 1989, so as to qualify for matching funds from the Commission of the European Communities, the Irish movement incorporated the ILCU International Development Foundation to assume responsibility for its overseas work. The foundation was involved in around twenty projects annually, most of them small and of the "people-to-people" variety, as opposed to funding technical experts. They served movements in several African countries as well as Malaysia, Sri Lanka and the Caribbean. The Irish movement also sponsored visits by many credit union leaders from the developing movements; they were particularly useful visits because of the emphasis within the Irish movement on volunteer involvement and small credit unions, a populist emphasis similar to that found in most developing movements.[278]

UNITED KINGDOM

The movement in the United Kingdom had a mixed experience during the 1980s and early 1990s. It faced severe legislative problems in two respects, both of them emanating from the Credit Unions Act passed in 1979. First, the common bond qualifications were more stringent than in other countries, inhibiting the development of community credit unions as they were commonly formed elsewhere. The Registrar of Friendly Societies, the government office responsible for credit unions, administered the common bond provision in a particularly narrow fashion, thereby slowing down, if not inhibiting, the development of credit unions. Second, the amount a member could invest in the credit union was limited to £5,000 or 1.5 percent of a credit union's total shareholding, whichever was greater. This provision severely limited the size to which credit unions could grow, as did the limit on loans.

Unfortunately, the British movement was also restricted by a division between two national organizations. The National Federation of Credit Unions (NFCUL) emerged in the Greater London area in 1964, organized by credit unions in Highgate, London and Hove. The federation possessed a strong tradition of volunteerism. It made slow progress and placed great emphasis on the autonomy of credit unions in the selection of insurance services. Much like some groups within the Canadian and Australian movements, NFCUL wanted to develop its own insurance programme rather than automatically affiliating with CUNA Mutual. It was also drawn to the Raiffeisen movement in Germany, rather than to North American credit union circles, for much of its inspiration and ideology.[279]

The Association of British Credit Unions Limited (ABCUL) was formally created in 1975, although its roots, like NFCUL, stretched back to the 1960s. Based in Lancashire, ABCUL was a member of the World Council from its earliest days and enjoyed support from the Irish League. It was a more aggressive organization than NFCUL and, by the end of 1980, had fifty credit union members, many of them from the Midlands, and a growing number from Scotland and Northern Ireland. During the mid-1980s, the league expanded rapidly, fostering the creation of more than a hundred credit unions.[280] The league was particularly aggressive in requesting that the government change the governing legislation for the movement in the United Kingdom. It played a key role in achieving limited reforms in 1989, even though the govern-

ment was not comforted by the movement's internal problems and continuing divisions.

ABCUL was a strong supporter of CUNA Mutual, which was generous in providing funds for its operations, as was the World Council at different times. In fact, on two or three occasions ABCUL would not have survived without support from the North American organizations. By the later 1980s, however, the league was working hard at eliminating its dependency on American support, which was not easy, given the size limitations imposed by the legislation and resulting from the division of resources in the national movement. It would not be successful until the middle of the following decade.

Despite its problems, the British movement grew steadily, in the process exhibiting many of the trends evident in other national movements. For example, there was "a flight to size", 20 percent of the credit unions accounting for 70 percent of the membership and 88 percent of the assets. Similar to other movements, too, the British movement achieved much of its early successes among public servants, especially in Scotland.[281] It had taken time and the beginnings had been difficult, but the British movement had become solidly established by the early 1990s.

The more developed movements in Australia, the United States and Canada experienced fundamental changes during the 1980s and early 1990s. They were buffeted by regulatory changes that reduced the barriers between different kinds of financial industries (for example, insurance, savings and investment) and opened national markets to new financial organizations, including some from other countries. In Australia, too, the federal government chartered fifteen new banks, thereby altering the environment within which credit unions had to survive.

In all three countries, credit unions faced competition that was organizing in different ways — for example through bankcards and electronic banking. Their market in personal loans was undermined by the widespread if expensive use of credit cards. The technological changes that had started to revolutionize the workplace in the 1970s, particularly the work-place of financial institutions, did not abate; they gained momentum. Such changes challenged the three credit union movements to their roots, partly because they demanded considerable initiative and unity from the three movements if they were to stay in the race. Nor would the resulting debates be tranquil, largely because a significant number of credit unionists doubted whether it was appropriate to compete at all. This series of challenges tended to polarize advocates of populist and managerial cultures. It was not a simple debate because it divided two or more groups of dedicated people with somewhat different visions of how the movement should develop. Coping with fundamental change within organizations is always difficult and it can be painful.

The largest Australian credit unions were closed-bond, employee-based credit unions; in that way the Australian movement was similar to the American. There were, however, several larger community-based credit unions that tended to pull the movement out into the general financial markets; in that way the movement was more akin to the Canadian. The larger community organizations were particularly pressured to develop more services and technological capacity; they were joined by some of the larger closed-bond credit unions whose members were demanding more extensive financial services. The resulting drive for increased managerial skills, new technologies, marketing programmes and new financial "products" among a minority of larger credit unions contrasted with the large number of (usually) smaller credit unions that wished to retain strong member bonds, along with important and traditional roles for volunteers. That division, which did not neatly coincide with state boundaries or type of credit union, became an important characteristic of the movement in the 1980s, as in a way it had been earlier.

In the end, and as was the case in the United States and Canada, the most powerful forces were aligned behind the position that credit unions should enter into the mainstream and use democratic structures, community connections and pooled resources to create an alternative financial system. Many individuals led the transition of the Australian movement from a populist to an essentially managerial culture. In the 1980s, in particular, these individuals included Ken Miller, Reg Elliott, who had become manager of the Association of New South Wales Credit Unions Limited in 1977, Bill Howe, Steve Birt and Peter Timmins, who became the manager of the Australian Federation of Credit Union Leagues in 1979. They also became the most prominent representatives of Australia in the deliberations of the World Council, bringing with them a concern for the business efficiency of the international movement.

In reality, however, the divisions within Australia, like similar divisions in the United States and Canada, were exaggerated by the debates they engendered and by the pressures of what were difficult competitive situations. The ultimate issue was rarely as it was presented: a cruel choice between "niche" activities on the margins of economic influence, and slavish imitation of banks. The issue was more complicated: how to equip elected leaders so they could retain the primacy of social and human concerns over simplistic balance sheet calculations; how to prepare managers and directors who would be proud of the distinctive organizations they helped lead. In short, the Australians, like their counterparts in North America, were wrestling with the same issues as their Irish colleagues.

In its international activities, the Australian movement was increasingly important. In addition to the significant roles played by such leaders as Bill Howe, Peter Timmins, David Dinning and Ken Miller within WOCCU, the movement was vitally important to the development of credit unions in the Pacific region, particularly because of the help it gave movements in the nearby islands. In the early 1980s, the movement joined the Australian Council for Overseas Aid through its foundation in order to qualify for matching funds from the Australian government international development programmes, which allowed them to play an even greater role than in the past.

In the United States and Canada, the inflationary trends that started with the economic boom and rising costs of petroleum in the early 1970s continued to gather momentum. These trends redistributed wealth, undercut the capacity of governments to meet the needs of their citizens, and created unprecedented levels of peacetime public debt. Increasingly for credit unionists, the 1950s and 1960s took on the aura of a golden age when credit unions could make easy progress; the world they were working through in the 1970s and 1980s was fundamentally different.

In the United States, the economic trends forced a higher degree of regional and national integration for credit unions.

Many credit unions and state organizations pooled resources as never before in order to offer more services to members. Networking became increasingly more obvious at the national level as organizations sought to learn from each other and to benefit from economies of scale. The national movement helped state and local organizations to introduce automatic teller machines, an alternative to the "brick and mortar" that had previously measured growth. It organized a national information centre, NARCUP, as the credit union system became more and more a family of integrated national organizations.[282]

All of these developments helped credit unions cope with the immense problems created as interest rates soared to over 20 percent early in the decade. In fact, the capacity of the American movement to deal with the pressures was remarkable testimony to its managerial skills and the "insulation" against general economic trends provided by the generally pervasive closed-bond structures.

The move toward a stronger national credit union system was also evident, albeit in less direct form, in the growth of corporate credit union centrals and the expansion of the U.S. Central Credit Union. While they were strongly committed to state priorities, the corporate centrals inevitably were drawn into joint activities and were increasingly interested in a more cohesive national approach. By the early 1980s, for example, forty-two centrals were linked together electronically through a common database system, a powerful force in its own right for the cause of greater cohesion. At the same time, CUNA encouraged the trend toward greater integration by developing a multi-purpose information system intended to serve all credit union organizations in the movement. Despite all the economic pressures and declining margins, the American movement grew steadily during the 1980s and 1990s.

While it is clear that much of the driving force behind the American developments emerged from managerial imperatives, it would be incorrect to think that the American movement was slipping easily into a near-bank niche in the marketplace. In fact, it carried out a long process of soul-searching throughout much of the decade as leaders and members sought to retain the idealism, more obvious and perhaps easier to sustain, in the movement's formative period. That search played a key role in the World Council's quest for operating principles in the early 1980s, and the need to establish the "credit union difference" was emphasized in the important work done by CUNA's Planning Committee during the mid-1980s under the leadership of Joe Perkowski. The American commitment to broader purposes and service for the poor, however, was best demonstrated in the formation of numerous credit unions serving the needs of low-income Americans and poorer communities.[283]

On a more disquieting note, the 1980s and early 1990s witnessed growing efforts by the competition within the United States to make credit unions subject to federal income tax. Through an effective lobbying campaign, the movement was able to withstand these pressures, although the task was becoming increasingly more difficult. Almost as alarming was the growing tendency, in many other countries as well, for the regulatory officials to group credit unions in the same category as other financial institutions. In the United States, for example, that trend was evident in the move to bring together all the deposit insurance funds within the financial industries. Propelled by the bad experience of the funds supporting savings and loans organizations and the banks, it threatened to disrupt one of the pillars upon which the American movement had been built.

The Canadian movement was even more deeply affected by the economic changes of the 1980s. Although it continued to grow, a testimony to its capacity to meet important needs, especially mortgage lending, several provincial movements faced serious problems. In general, the difficulties emanated from mismatching of rates between deposits and loans, an inherited but faulty conviction that growth would resolve most problems and an inadequately trained leadership. The movement reacted aggressively to the problems by increasing managerial efficiencies, improving information systems, hiring more qualified experts, and developing better training programmes for directors. In the process, the credit union movement distanced itself somewhat from the general co-operative movement, most obviously in the restructuring of the Canadian Co-operative Credit Society into Credit Union Central of Canada. Close ties were maintained, though, in lobbying and overseas development activities and in the revitalization of co-operative initiatives on a regional/provincial basis.

Like the American movement, the Canadian movement experimented widely with technological innovation. In some ways, it led Canadian financial industries in forging the development of a national electronic banking system, guided by such individuals as Norm Bromberger and Brian Downey. It was a difficult process because it required bringing together all the provincial organizations and, more challengingly perhaps, most of the larger credit unions.

The cumulative impact of all these changes in the most developed movements was an increased commitment to the sound management of credit unions. In turn, this concern with carefully developed policies, prudent administration, cost effectiveness and well-qualified people affected the way in which the international movement developed. In many ways, the move toward a greater emphasis on sound business practice in the developing world echoed what had been learned in the three older established movements and in Korea.

This relationship between the developed and developing movements highlights the way in which the World Council, in effect, was a broker for credit union practices throughout the world. By the early 1990s WOCCU had become a complex organization dealing with a wide range of interests in over seventy countries. It had been forced to grow far beyond the goals envisioned in the later 1970s, even if economic and political trends were limiting the possibilities.

The remarkable accomplishment of the World Council in this period was its capacity to adjust to change. The economic, political and social changes of the 1980s created immense challenges in all parts of the world. WOCCU entered the 1980s solidly based on the development ideology of the time, an approach that emphasized regional and national priorities, one that had been shaped by the conventional thinking of the Cold War. It entered the 1990s with a changing emphasis on more solid and more local growth. It was learning how to exist in societies where the role of the state was being revolutionized and the capacity of national governments to control their destinies was being eroded. It was learning how to make the adjustment from an age of ideological divisions to an age of ideological conformity, a particularly difficult challenge for any co-operative organization.

Al Charbonneau was chief executive officer of the World Council throughout the period. Along with many others, particularly board leaders like John Nicholson and Alex Gracie from Canada, Bill Howe and Ken Miller from Australia, Everard Dean from Trinidad and Tobago, Charbonneau was greatly concerned with promoting a genuinely international perspective within the World Council; not least, he insisted upon expanding the capacity of the World Council to speak with people around the world in a growing number of languages.

Charbonneau worked very hard at expanding the World Council's relationship with similar organizations. He successfully negotiated an increasing collaboration with the Desjardins movement in Canada, and he promoted stronger ties with financial co-operatives in Europe. Along with the presidents of the day he travelled tirelessly within the national movements, building consensus, lobbying governments, and encouraging sound growth. An ebullient and resourceful leader, Charbonneau did much to bring about a higher sense of cohesion within the international movement.

During the 1980s the presidency of the World Council was shared by people from a steadily widening group of countries. At the start of the period the president was John Nicholson, who helped lead the World Council through the difficult reorganization period. He was followed in 1984 by Rocael Garcia, a native of Guatemala and the first president of the council to

Al Charbonneau making a speech in Lesotho. (COURTESY OF WOCCU)

come from a developing part of the world. A lawyer by training, Garcia had been active in the Latin American movement since the early 1970s, serving on the boards of the Co-operative Agricultural School in Chimaltenango, Guatemala, and on FECOLAC, the regional educational foundation.[284]

Garcia was followed in 1986 by Joseph Cugini from the Rhode Island movement. Alex Gracie, who had played an instrumental role in stabilizing the national Canadian movement during one of its most divisive periods, became president in 1988; he was followed by Joe Perkowski in 1991. Although originally from Michigan, Perkowski had been CEO of the U.S. Federal Employees Credit Union in Minnesota since 1977. As a Polish-American, he paid particular attention to the possibilities in central and eastern Europe and helped in the formation of the Foundation for Polish Credit Unions. Perkowski also played a key role in the development of the People to People programme.

Despite all the problems of the decade, the movement continued to make significant strides around the world. Between 1984 and 1992, the number of affiliated societies almost doubled, from 38,500 to 71,500; the number of

The Board of Directors of the World Council, 1987, included many of the most important international leaders of the decade. Back row, left to right: Joseph Cuigini, Paul Herring, Les Tendler, Michael Sang Ho Lee, Edilberto Esquivel, Alhaji Saiyadi Ringim, Denis J. McLeary, Milton Sprowl. Front row, left to right: Joseph Perkowski, Everard Dean, Bill Howe, Marvin Cottom, Alex Gracie, Augustine Murray. (COURTESY OF WOCCU)

members increased from 55,750,000 to 92,300,000; and assets increased from $113,770,000,000US to $463,870,000,000US. Even allowing for the fact that some of the growth came from new member organizations and that inflation distorted the assets figures somewhat, the growth was remarkable. The World Council shared some of the credit for the enthusiasm, skill and diligence that made the expansion possible.

In many ways, the World Council was a difficult organization to describe or to explain. Simplistically, it was a few offices in the credit union complex in Madison with a few other offices in some other parts of the world. In reality, it was an immense network of social capital led by fewer than forty permanent staff, embracing hundreds of paid officers, most financed by funds from development agencies, and thousands of volunteers from more than seventy movements. It was driven ultimately by the power of the credit union idea, even though that idea was being transformed in many contexts. The balance sheet was never simple, and traditional accounting methods told only part of the story.

The Executive Committee of the World Council, 1988. From left to right: Al Charbonneau, Pastor Yawo Agbi-Awuna, Al Williams, Alex Gracie, Joseph Perkowski, Augustine Murray, Everard Dean. (COURTESY OF CUNA)

Chapter Eleven

A Long Look at the Present
1992-1997

If we stay the same and we are unaware of the changes taking place in the environment in which we are operating, then our credit unions eventually will die.

David Dinning

We may not know what the final answers are or will be. But we are collectively facing the uncertainty of an era of change with creativity and bold action. And our answers will be appropriate as long as they are based upon a basic premise — that whatever we do must be measured in terms of its impact upon the most important link in our chain of relationships, the individual credit union members.

Chris Baker

THE WEATHER CO-OPERATED. A VIBRANT SUN AND BLUE skies crowned the mountains and the sea that make Vancouver one of the most attractive cities in the world. The conference hotel jutted out into the water, its mock sails seemingly full to the wind, while tankers, cruise ships and fishing vessels hourly changed the vista. Over 2,000 delegates from nearly all member countries were gathering for the 1997 forum of the World Council of Credit Unions. It was the largest and, from some perspectives, the most successful gathering ever held by the World Council. The global reach of the movement was apparent in the variety of dress worn by delegates and by the rich diversity of art and curios they brought for the charity auction. It was audible in the different languages and accents overheard in meetings and during breaks, meals and entertainment. The event was also a happy occasion, a hallmark of WOCCU gatherings, perhaps most evident in the credit union tours and home visits arranged by local credit unionists in what has become one of the World Council's most valued traditions.

It is not easy to place such contemporary events in perspective. Nor is it easy to make judgments on the recent history of the World Council. The patterns in the present are always difficult to grasp. The preoccupation with daily events, the demands of personalities, the crises that distort our views of the world, the stresses that are the norms of any organization's life, the incessant demand for immediate attention to matters that are less important than they appear to be — such pressures cloud a longer view. Understanding what is really important is never easy. It is especially difficult in a movement that spans the world and tests any observer's ability truly to think globally.

Yet, there are a few easy generalizations that can be made. The most obvious one is continuing growth. The delegates attending the Vancouver meeting represented a movement active in eighty-five countries. Statistically, these national movements represented 36,244 credit unions serving 89,685,210 members; their assets totalled $379,334,156,511US.[285] Growth was slowing in many parts of the world, but the levels that had been achieved were remarkable. Any of the few people in attendance who had also been present at the CUNA 1954 meeting when the international programme was launched must have been amazed. Even taking into account the uncertainties around a few of the national statistics, they represented a remarkable achievement. Roy Bergengren's face would have beamed.

The growth also indicated considerable strength. Despite the adversities and challenges of the 1980s, the established movements in the United States, Canada and Australia had made remarkable progress, reaching asset levels of $300,287,000,000US, $32,600,000,000US and $10,800,000,000US respectively. They were serving 63,790,000 members in the United States, 4,100,000 in Canada and 2,900,000 in Australia. These three countries had been joined as mature movements by Korea, which was serving 4,711,000 members through 1,671 credit unions with $19,700,000,000US in assets, and by Ireland, which had 532 credit unions with nearly 2,000,000 members and $4,680,000,000US in assets.

Strength, however, is not simply a matter of size. There were numerous smaller movements that proportionately or comparatively were doing as well, by various measures, as those with the most impressive numbers. Movements such as those in Malawi, Togo, Sri Lanka, the Philippines, Guatemala, Belize, Costa Rica and Fiji, for example, were serving their members and communities with efficiency and care. They were responding well, often to very difficult challenges. Others, such as those in Ireland, Dominica, Montserrat, Jamaica, Trinidad and Tobago, were serving more than 40 percent of the populations in their countries. Similar percentages could be found in some regions, such as Saskatchewan, within national movements. Most importantly, buried within the statistics were the remarkable accomplishments of the tens of thousands of credit unions that were pillars of their communities, centres for economic activity, and voices of social concern. No set of global statistics could completely capture their kind of economic and social power. The calculations of accountants provide valuable insights, but there are other measurements of effectiveness.

Another indication of strength is the degree to which the movement is still reaching out to new people. The continuing capacity of the established movements to attract new members and, at least in the case of the community development credit union movement in the United States, to serve low-income people, demonstrates that the limits have not yet been reached. The continuing expansion in the developing movements, and the growth in central and eastern Europe, and the promising beginnings in China show that the days of credit union crusading are not over.

One other kind of strength, albeit one often hidden by the very debate it engenders, is the sheer diversity of the international movement. It was not difficult, even in the courteous and friendly atmosphere of the gathering in Vancouver, to hear vigorous, even heated, discussions about issues that inevitably flow from the dynamics of credit unions: different viewpoints from those who visualize the movement in one or other of the streams within the broad co-operative heritage; disagreements with and among those who see credit unions as manifestations of specific contexts and those who are content to see them as convenient institutional houses for limited purposes. There were intense debates over how to treat members and serve communities; over the proper relationship with the state; over what kind of regional, national and international structures are needed; and, most commonly, which managerial systems were most effective with which kind of credit union. There were discussions about how to reinforce the kind of institutional culture that was deemed to be best, and reflections on what it meant as credit unions and their movements went through different stages. They were the kinds of issues one always finds at credit union gatherings.

Such disagreements might lead an outsider to question the cohesion of the movement. The reality, however, is that such debates emerge naturally and consistently enough from the dynamics of credit unionism. When faced openly and creatively, as Chris Baker mused in 1984, they can be as much a source of strength as of weakness. They allow credit unions to serve a wide range of members and to ensure a continual search for better ways to do so. They naturally propel credit unions into new activities and new institutional frameworks. Indeed, denying such debates because of a belief that one's credit union or one's movement has achieved near perfection or because such debates appear unseemly, or because of a fatal preference for "group-think", is to throw away the pragmatic experimentation and open attitude that have contributed so much to the survival and expansion of the movement.

The arguments, of course, also reflected the kind of challenges that confront the international movement. Many of those challenges inevitably end up at the door of the World Council. Since 1954 WOCCU and its predecessors have been heavily engaged in development activities. It has developed a considerable staff of permanent employees and a much wider group of consultants and practitioners scattered around the world. It has built an extensive programme reaching out to sister co-operative organizations and development assistance organizations. Much of that activity has been based on grants, mostly from USAID but also from CIDA, MISEREOR, the Catholic Relief Services, Rabobank and CUNA Mutual Insurance. A growing pool of funds was being raised from foundations, notably in the United States but also in Canada, Australia and Ireland. The problem was that support from national governments was declining amid the economic reorientation of the 1980s and the end of the Cold War competition that, for many, had justified international development programmes. The altruism and, arguably, the far-sightedness that could be found in the 1960s and 1970s lost vitality in the 1980s as even the richest countries looked inwards and, all too often, created virtue out of self-centredness.

Chris Baker, who succeeded Al Charbonneau as chief executive officer in 1993, was therefore faced by the fact of declining income and the challenge of identifying new sources of funding. The World Council was unable to escape coping with "leaner and meaner", that mantra of so many businesses amid the economic swings of the 1980s and 1990s. The result was the reduction of staff in 1994 and again in 1996-1997, the closing of the Geneva office and the narrowing of objectives that necessarily followed. In fact, by 1997 the World Council had reduced its spheres of activity to two: trade association and international development, in essence its core activities.

These changes were driven by a concern that credit unions in some parts of the world were not developing rapidly or effectively enough. The development arm of the council would be charged primarily with helping movements improve the performance of their credit unions. The increased emphasis on

Christopher E. Baker, chief executive officer of the World Council, 1997.
(COURTESY OF WOCCU)

trade association activities was the result of increasing pressures for the World Council to provide leadership in the consideration of such matters as "taxation, uniqueness of credit unions, legislation, field of membership, use of the Internet, status of development of new credit unions, existence of rival associations, regional legislation, new types of services, different delivery systems, guaranteed systems, safety and soundness and capitalization".[286]

This more directed approach was developed through considerable discussion led by Chris Baker and involving the CEO advisory committee and consultations at the 1996 annual meeting. It also involved extensive deliberations by the board of directors, even though the board at the time was going through considerable transition because of the sudden passing of its president, Gus Murray from Ireland, and its vice-president, Al Williams from the United States. They were distinguished credit unionists who had provided excellent leadership for both their local and national movements as well as the World Council. Tod Manrell from British Columbia became president; an optimistic and confident leader, he had been the longest serving president at both Credit Union Central of British Columbia and Credit Union Central of Canada. Manrell was well qualified and well suited to provide leadership in a time of significant change.

On the development side of its work, WOCCU's emphasis in the 1990s, even more than in the past, was on the importance of savings as opposed to credit. The reason for that emphasis was not hard to establish. The international development community for the previous twenty-five years or so had tended to place its priorities on expanding credit, with mixed results. In some instances, borrowers had become dependent on credit; in others, the loans were never repaid. Too often, the expansion of credit inflicted long-term debt on the poor. Moreover, moneylenders had not disappeared: they survived by providing sustained, long-term borrowing services, albeit often at exorbitant rates. Usury, that perpetual villain in credit union circles, had not been wrestled to the ground.

Tod and Irene Manrell, 1997. (Courtesy of WOCCU)

The evolving World Council perspective was well summed up by Lucy Ito, WOCCU's regional manager for Asia and the South Pacific, in a 1995 briefing paper in which she eschewed a "do-gooder" approach and reaffirmed the importance and dignity of self-help. She called for the creation of credit unions that, while they might not be "liked" as much as some would prefer, would be secure places to save and access savings. They would provide timely, continued and appropriate amounts of credit, and possess the elements of permanence: for example, sound management and well-trained directors. For Ito, credit unions must have the ability to survive and, equally, possess the "survival instinct".[287]

Ito's point was, in part, a criticism of the past emphasis on low-cost loans as opposed to the encouragement of savings and the granting of fairly priced loans that would allow credit unions to grow through their own efforts. Ito argued that the growth of credit unions in some parts of the world had slowed in part because often, the rates they paid on deposits were too low. She charged that management was not always sufficiently professional and that policies designed for personal lending (for example, lending limits restricted to low multiples of deposits) restricted the ability of credit unions to lend to small business borrowers. From her perspective, this weakness in serving the needs of small businesses or micro-enterprises undermined the capacity of credit unions to contribute to the sound and permanent economic development of communities.

Ito, of course, was promoting the "new" model of credit unions that had evolved through the work of, among others, Brian Branch in Latin America, Chet Aeschliman, Dale Majers in Africa, and her own efforts in Asia. It flowed from the practical leadership provided by Chris Baker and David Dinning, who served the World Council in Madison from 1994 to 1997. In essence, the model called for the adoption within developing movements of a much more complete management culture. Services would be driven by the demand of members, meaning that credit unions had to expand savings opportunities for members and develop more flexible but prudent lending practices. They would create a wider range of savings accounts, de-emphasizing the traditional role of share accounts, as had happened in the American, Canadian and Australian movements. They would offer lines of credit and differential interest rates. They would allow members to withdraw their deposits more easily, and they would upgrade management so that members could be assured of the security of their funds.

This approach can be seen as an extension of what had worked so well in the United States, Canada, Australia and, increasingly, Ireland and Korea. In that sense, it was an example of an easily missed truth: the established and developing movements were bound together and profoundly influenced each other; what happened in one, particularly in the larger movements, usually flowed to the rest.

Inevitably, the new approach would sharply influence all spheres of activity — member relations, community connections, state relations, structural ties and, of course, management practice — over which credit unions have some control. For some, it ran the risk of ignoring or downplaying the role of democratic structures and social concerns. It could equally be argued, however, that it was establishing the framework within which all of those dimensions of credit unionism could be more effectively pursued. Just as in the United States, Canada and Australia, the shift to more managerial cultures elsewhere could be an end in itself, or it could be the means to accomplish even more. Which eventuality prevailed depended upon how leaders and members viewed the process and took advantage of the possibilities.

There were organizational consequences that flowed from the new emphasis. To some extent, it marked a bonding of like-minded credit union pragmatists around the world, people who were primarily committed to making credit unions effective as financial institutions. They were not as concerned as earlier leaders had been with the development of new credit unions; they were more interested in stabilizing existing organizations at the local level and then building outward by meeting the needs of growing memberships. Their commitment to large programmes, to dwelling on the needs of national and confederation organizations, did not run as deep.

Where does the new model fit within the long view of the history of credit unionism? One answer is that it places a priority upon self-reliance and self-responsibility, two concepts that echo through the history of community-based co-opera-

tive banking. Another response is that the new realities reflect the continuing strength of certain aspects of the American credit union model. That model, influenced in its early days by the business acumen of Edward A. Filene and steadily increasing managerial competence over the years, has always stressed economic viability. It has consistently paid close attention to member benefits within the prudent capacity of credit unions to provide them.

The "new credit union", however, was not just the American model, as it had developed over the decades, writ large. For example, in many parts of the world, the bonds of association were community, not workplace, religious affiliation or ethnic identity. That broader association, as it had done in Canada, Ireland, Sri Lanka, Colombia and Ghana, to mention only a few countries, would create its own set of priorities.

Considered in perspective, however, the emphasis on better management practice and efficiency is a two-edged sword. It can drive credit unions into a relatively comfortable niche of small deposit-takers serving the people whom the other financial institutions would just as soon ignore. It can also provide the most prudent way to meet member needs, sustain democratic control and cultivate community health, three of the most powerful dimensions of credit union activism since the beginnings of the movement. It will inevitably hasten the pace of debate as credit unions and their movements go from the formative to the managerial period, as they shift from populist to managerial cultures.

In the sphere of membership the new credit union means maximizing relationships, both in the sense of having members use as many services as possible and in steadily deepening their sense of ownership and their willingness to invest. It is a much more subtle kind of relationship, one based on careful understanding of member needs and wishes, one that does not rely as much on spontaneous and incidental connections. In terms of democratic process, it means finding ways of steadily increasing a member's sense of ownership and participation, not an easy achievement, given that credit unions as financial institutions have needs for confidentiality, and discipline in conducting financial affairs means having clear policies that are essentially not negotiable. But it can be done, especially if one does not define democracy in too limited a fashion. Just as importantly, it means ensuring that directors can fulfil their democratic responsibilities. In addition to being able to understand the business as it grows increasingly complex, directors must have the competence to provide general direction and approve key general policy decisions. The need for director training, therefore, increases as credit unions grow larger and more complex. It is not enough to ensure that they possess certain kinds of expertise — for example, in accounting, marketing and human resource development.

Put another way, as management cadres grow more specialized and complicated, they need to remember that the broad social and economic purpose is a shared responsibility with the board and therefore requires joint training and planning sessions that are not just exercises in managerial manipulation. The relationship between management cadres and boards of directors is never more difficult or more important than when credit unions become more complex; preserving appropriate democratic procedures is never more challenging.

In the sphere of community relations, it means a much more careful assessment of community needs and a recognition that credit unions rely upon healthy communities for their own survival. It means reaching out to more segments of the community than was previously the case. All of these needs are tall orders. They have profound implications for the structures of credit unions. They will likely mean a gradual de-emphasis in the formation of credit unions except in those parts of the world where they essentially do not exist or among classes of people they do not yet serve. This will likely mean more mergers and more pooling of resources. On an international level, it will probably mean increasing collaboration and co-ordination with different kinds of co-operative banking movements, and perhaps a blurring of the inherited differences. It will mean a gradual changing of relations with governments as credit unions transcend the traditional boundaries of state, province and nation.

Ultimately, therefore, the two-edged sword raises the perpetual question at the heart of credit unionism and all co-operative endeavour: for what purpose? In an interview

in 1996, Paul Hebert, veteran of credit union debates, struggles and institutional transformations, gave one of the best answers:

> Unless you leave something behind that is permanent and will act as an agent of change for people, the heck with it, you are just spinning your wheels.[288]

A long view of credit unions suggests that the international movement is up to meeting the criteria of permanence and activism stressed in Hebert's comment. Their ability to do so is implicit in the dynamics that have typified the activities of credit unions and credit unionists around the world for nearly a century. Wise stewards will recognize the usefulness of those dynamics and will nurture them assiduously. Ultimately, if one is to judge from history, they can also look forward to enjoying their benefits.

The Board of Directors of the World Council, 1998-1999. From left to right: Christopher E. Baker (chief executive officer), Gary Plank, Melvin Edwards, Gerry Foley, Robert McVeigh, Dennis Cutter, Alan Parry (president). (COURTESY OF WOCCU)

READING A BOOK LIKE THIS REMINDS ONE OF THE fact that the world of credit unions and financial co-operatives is an ever-changing kaleidoscope — that what we see in our own backyards is but a part of a much larger, changing whole. This book helps us to identify and come to a better understanding of the men and women of vision, the creative spirits, who have breathed life into what we all too often take for granted in many national movements today. It also reminds us that, in many parts of the world, the pioneering days of credit unions are still evident: that the credit union idea is still largely unknown to many people, and that the challenges of achieving stability still confront many movements, not all of them new.

Ian MacPherson has done an excellent job of weaving a tapestry from the many strands of historical experience which merge together in our international credit union system. He makes our past more coherent and understandable. In doing so, he sets the essential groundwork for us to be able to look into the future.

In this age of daily changes, the problems — and the solutions — of yesterday will surely not be the same as those of tomorrow, but that is nothing new. Each generation of credit unionists has had to define the particular responses to the challenges confronting it. Raiffeisen, Schulze-Delitzsch, Desjardins, Filene, Bergengren and our other trail-blazing pioneers designed systems that worked in the environments of their day. And so must we.

What are those challenges and what trends can be foreseen in our movement in the future? A worthy epilogue to a book such as this must at least outline these, in order that the links joining the past to the present and to the future can be appreciated.

CENTRALIZATION

A continuing theme throughout the history of credit unions has been the working out of relationships between local and central institutions. There are natural and understandable tensions. Credit unions necessarily and appropriately are reflections of local pride and capabilities. They have been built by people concerned about maximizing local influence and meeting local needs. They do not easily transfer control to other organizations, even those that they partly own.

Yet there is always a need for collaboration among credit unions for the common good, and today that need is growing. Without strong links among them, credit unions will not be able to achieve their full potential — in fact, some may not even survive. The future will see a growing need for increasing collaboration between existing credit unions and between older and newer movements. There will have to be greater discipline, more co-operation, more planning and more integration. Without these, our strengths would fade away in a new environment which is far more competitive than ever before. Lasting success will require efficiencies of scale; in most credit union movements this will mean levels of operation which cannot be obtained without redesigning the way in which we provide services to our members.

CHANGES IN SERVICE DELIVERY STRUCTURES

There has never been a time when credit unions were not being transformed by technology and evolving management systems. The changes resulting from these transformations during the last fifteen years have been dramatic. If anything, that trend will become even more important. Electronic systems, for example, have significantly altered what credit unions can — and must — do with the funds they gather. But can anyone predict with confidence where technology will lead us in the next decade? How can we anticipate the kind of international financial system that we will have in the early twenty-first century? All we can know is that the delivery systems used by credit unions in the next twenty years will be dramatically different. What we have seen in the last fifteen years is just the beginning. But one thing that we can be sure of is that the costs of future technological innovations will be very high. The day of going it alone is rapidly coming to a close.

Credit unions throughout the world will have to struggle to achieve the kind of delivery systems that will best benefit their members. They will have to find ways to fund expensive new delivery systems in conjunction with others. Yet the biggest challenge which we will face will be that of constantly reminding ourselves that the structures of credit unions are not ends in themselves; they are servants of member needs.

As credit unions continue to become more complex organizations, their need for new technology will require people with new and different kinds of skills and expertise. This, too, is not new. As history readily shows, the kinds of people who work in credit unions change significantly whenever technology evolves. The numbers of well-trained and highly educated staff members will only increase; staff turnover will be high; and the need for senior management and boards of directors to understand the best purposes of technology will not abate.

CHALLENGES OF CAPITALIZATION

Credit unions are concerned about the responsible management of money. They are democratic institutions in which the rights of persons are paramount. That means that capital is viewed as a servant and its claims are always weighed against the claims of members, employees and communities. There is rarely an end to the needs for capital, but there are always questions about how it should be attracted and how it should be used. How credit union leaders and members respond to those questions will be of increasing importance in the years ahead. The margin for error in issues around capital is steadily growing narrower.

The needs for capital are particularly evident in movements where the demand for expensive technology is pressing. That has led to considerable experimentation with different ways to raise necessary capital. Most of this experimentation has been done in the conventional way, through associations and joint ventures among credit unions where the ultimate control rests with members through traditional control structures; some of it, by placing increasing emphasis on other organizations or outside investors, has threatened the basic autonomy of the organization. There may be room for partnerships with other organizations, particularly other kinds of financial co-operatives, but we will be facing a very large challenge in making sure that such partnerships are established on terms that ensure continuance, autonomy and member control.

CHALLENGES OF GLOBALIZATION

As this book demonstrates, understanding the full international movement is a daunting task. There are so many movements, so many different needs, so many underlying philosophies, social movements and political systems. Understanding what credit unions mean to people in so many different cultural contexts and within such varying economic conditions requires considerable opportunity and years of experience.

And yet, there is enough commonality in purpose and sufficient mutual agreement on the nature of the credit union that an international movement does exist. There are enough people willing to accept that there is value in diversity that the international movement actually possesses a remarkable advantage. Unlike many other institutions that are just beginning to become acquainted with the realities of many parts of the globe, credit union people have been involved for fifty years. We possess networks, understand local situations and have experiences that others do not. It is an advantage we should use more creatively.

At the same time, there are aspects of globalization that should give us pause. The financial industries have moved remarkably fast to take advantage of rapidly advancing financial systems. They have prospered by the remarkable freedom capital has gained to roam the world with comparatively limited and decreasing control by government.

One of the greatest challenges confronting credit unions internationally is to respond to the rapid expansion of the international financial industries. There are some advantages in size that credit unions, for the foreseeable future, will not possess. Nor will they as easily be able to close out operations that are less profitable. Credit unions are tied to communities and are restricted by what the legislation and the memberships deem to be appropriate ways to invest deposits and build assets.

These limitations have made it very difficult for many in the credit union world to focus upon the true challenges implied by the globalizing trends of the present and future. Many credit union leaders believe that they need to limit their focus to the local and domestic economic environment but in doing so, they overlook the fact that these no longer operate in isolation from other competitive forces. They may be right in that the challenge is not one that needs to be responded to today, but if we fail to project into the future soon, we are likely to find that the financial world has passed us by and we can no longer compete effectively in a highly networked globalized economy.

SELF-SUFFICIENCY, VIABILITY AND STANDARDS OF PERFORMANCE

Ultimately, the primary responsibility of all credit union leaders, from the local to the international level, must be to work for the viability of their organizations. Their first duty is to pay careful attention to the governing policies and customary business practices of their organizations. They must ensure that adequate reserves are maintained, that loans are extended prudently, that technological changes are introduced at the appropriate time and that necessary education and training programs are ongoing. They are unrelenting tasks that sometimes require making difficult decisions. They are tasks that earn their greatest rewards when members are well served and appreciate the values which credit unions embrace.

Credit unions, therefore, must always struggle with enhancing their standards of performance. This is true of a credit union in a small, rural village in Latin America or Africa; it is equally true in a large, multi-branch credit union in California or New South Wales. Improving performance in credit unions means careful monitoring; it means ensuring that employees are well trained; it means adoption of the appropriate technology; it means the continual upgrading of boards of directors through continuous training and careful recruitment. It means staying in touch with member needs, either through the informal linkages typical of small, newer credit unions or the more sophisticated member-analysis systems of larger credit unions. It means the prudent allocation of surpluses so that stability is always assured. It is an essential responsibility of elected officials and management: indeed of all those involved in credit unions. The future of many of the newer credit union movements will depend upon the degree to which they are able to respond to these challenges.

RETAINING/REDEFINING CREDIT UNION UNIQUENESS

Throughout the history of credit unionism there has been an understandable need to keep in mind the ways in which credit unions are unique. Given that they function in the marketplace and that they must become complex organizations to effectively respond to member needs, they can often appear to be the same as other types of financial institutions. That problem has become particularly evident in the more established movements, within the largest and most modern credit unions.

This perception, however, is nearly always misleading. As long as the basic legal framework provides for member control, and as long as credit unions have strong ties to their communities and provide effective services to their member-owners, then credit unions will be shaped by forces different from those that move private financial institutions.

And yet, credit union leaders must work hard at retaining and explaining their organizational differences. They must continuously project these in their advertising and their contacts with members. They must resist attempts by regulators to make credit unions mere carbon copies of other financial institutions. They must cultivate and build upon their associations with their communities. They must celebrate the roles played by volunteers and ensure that volunteers do indeed set the key policies. They must cultivate a sense of pride in credit union distinctiveness among employees.

One of the most significant challenges faced by credit unions in the next ten years will be that of redefining themselves. In order to speak clearly to governments and others in our rapidly changing environment, we need to restate our principles which may have been made unclear by the passage of time. We need to define ourselves in terms of this new environment in ways that will continue to make it evident that credit unions do indeed continue to be unique.

KEEPING PURPOSE CONSTANT

In pursuing the restatement of our values we must be careful to "keep purpose constant". One of the burdens — but also one of the values — of history is that it creates a sense of long-term purpose. The essential initial role of credit unions over the years has been to serve people, frequently of lower economic status, not served well by existing financial institutions. It has done so through encouraging economic democracy, helping people to work through collective enterprises concerned with individual well-being.

From the beginnings of community co-operative banking in the 1850s down through the history of credit unionism, a common theme has been the dream of people controlling democratically the economy that shapes their lives. That dream has most obviously been realized, albeit in limited ways, at the local level, in credit unions which have been built on member service and community responsibility. The chief task that awaits us all is how to expand on those local bases to make credit unions more powerful forces in the affairs of our countries, regions and indeed, the world. That challenge has been implicit, sometimes abundantly evident, in the movement from the beginning, clear in the work of Desjardins, Filene and Bergengren and fundamental to those who have shared the dream of an international movement. The purpose has always been constant: the full scope has yet to be realized.

Christopher E. Baker
Chief Executive Officer of the World Council
Madison, Wisconsin

ENDNOTES

1. For the latest history of the international co-operative movement, see Johnston Birchall's valuable study, *The International Co-operative Movement* (Manchester: Manchester University Press, 1997).

2. D.S. Tucker, *The Evolution of People's Banks* (New York: Columbia University Press, 1922), pp. 20-27.

3. G. Aschhoff and E. Henningsen, *The German Cooperative System* (Frankfurt am Main: Fritz Knapp Verlag, 1966), p. 21.

4. For somewhat fuller descriptions of the spread of co-operative banking see H.W. Wolff, *People's Banks: A Record of Social & Economic Progress* (London: King & Son, Ltd., 1919), pp. 147-158.

5. *Ibid.*, pp. 346-383.

6. "La Caisse étudiante Desjardins: une école d'apprendissage", *World Reporter* (January 1993), p. 16.

7. *Annual Report of the Massachusetts Commissioner of Banks* (Boston: State Printers, 1909), p. iii.

8. "Alphonse Desjardins", *The Bugle* [official publication of the Credit Union League of Alberta] (October 1948), p. 8.

9. "The First American Credit Union", *World Reporter* (Quarter II, 1979), p. 2.

10. J.C. Moody and G.C. Fite, *The Credit Union Movement: Origins and Development, 1850-1980,* 2nd. edition (Dubuque: Kendall/Hunt Publishing, 1984) p. 27.

11. *Ibid.*, p. 29.

12. *Ibid.*, p. 27.

13. For a fuller discussion of his trip, see Moody and Fite, pp. 29-31.

14. *Annual Report of the Commissioner of Banks*, 1909, p. iv.

15. *Ibid.*, pp. ii- iii.

16. "Credit Unions", Filene Papers, May 3, 1936, CUNA Archives.

17. Jay to Desjardins, March 3, 1909, Copp 6420 1909. CUNA Archives.

18. J.L. Snider, *Credit Unions in Massachusetts* (Cambridge: Harvard University Press, 1939) p. 7.

19. *Ibid.*, p. 7.

20. *Ibid.*, pp. 6-7.

21. See J.G. Knapp, *The Rise of American Cooperative Enterprise, 1620-1920* (Danville: Interstate Publishers, 1969), p. 141 and footnote 37, p. 473.

22. Moody and Fite, p. 29.

23. For a wandering but useful description of the Boston 1915 project, see G.W. Johnson, *Liberal's Progress* (New York: Coward-McCann, 1948), pp. 98-115; for a brief summary, see Moody and Fite, p. 27.

24. Johnson, p. 106.

25. The Russell Sage Foundation, with which Filene was long if argumentatively associated, was organized in 1907 to investigate living conditions in the United States, especially among poor people. It had a long association with the credit union movement.

26. Moody and Fite, p. 28.

27. This summary is adapted from Moody and Fite, p. 37.

28. D. Molvig, *Staff Training and Recognition Program* (Dubuque: Kendall/Hunt Publishing, 1995) p. 9.

29. "Filene the Peacemaker", Saskatchewan Credit Union League, undated. Copy in CUNA Archives.

30. Filene's range of interests was remarkable. Fascinated by the problem of how to communicate over the barriers of language, a problem that had to be resolved if international peace was to become possible, Filene played an instrumental role in devising the first system for simultaneous interpretation so that truly international conferences could be held. He conceptualized the solution, hired technicians to make the idea a reality, and donated the necessary equipment, called "hushaphones", or Filene silent translators, to the International Labour Office. Source — a speech by Lillian Schoedler at the Joint Meeting, November 1954, p. 3, Filene Papers, CUNA Archives.

31. "Interest Rate Saga", *World Reporter* (January, 1986), p. 16.

32. Roy F. Bergengren, *Cooperative Banking: A Credit Union Book* (New York: The Macmillan Company, 1923), pp. 78-84.

33. The North Carolina experiment was the subject of much study and controversy. See Bergengren, 1923, pp. 171-223.

34. The account of the MCUA is based largely on Moody and Fite, pp. 51-59.

35. *World Reporter* (Quarter I, 1979), p.1.

36. Roy F. Bergengren, "Filene Memorial Address", CUNA Archives.

37. The term "scientific management" was coined by Louis D. Brandeis to draw attention to Taylor's work. Brandeis believed that Taylor's work would ultimately benefit workers as well as employers.

38. When one reflects on Taylorism and its relationship with the labour and co-operative movements, one becomes aware of a remarkable irony: arguably the first individual to undertake serious time studies was Robert Owen, regarded in the United Kingdom as the founder of the trade union movement and a key forerunner of the co-operative movement.

39. Edward A Filene, speech to the California Credit Union League, 1936, as quoted in *The Bridge* (September 1941), p. 203.

40. Roy F. Bergengren, "God Gave Us Men", Part III, Chapter V, p. 7, and Part IV, Chapter III, p. 4, unpublished manuscript, CUNA Archives.

41. *Ibid.*

42. Roy F. Bergengren, *Credit Union Little Book* (Suva: School of the Pacific, 1964), Chapter VII.

43. Roy F. Bergengren and T. Doig, *The War and After: A Sixth Credit Union Book* (Madison: Credit Union Extension Bureau, 1942), p. 43.

44. *Ibid.*, Chapter VII.

45. "Co-operative Credit in Ontario", *The Canadian Co-operator*, (January 1931), p. 11.

46. Louise McCarren Herring, "Sharing the American Dream", in *Sharing the American Dream, A Second Look*, p. 33.

47. Series of articles in *The Bridge* (September 1946 to January 1947).

48. For a description of the Antigonish movement, see A.F. Laidlaw, *The Campus and the Community: The Global Impact of the Antigonish Movement* (Montreal: Harvest House, 1961).

49. *Ibid.*, pp. 74-75.

50. Bergengren actually received his first enquiry from Nova Scotia in 1925 when A.B. Macdonald, then working for the Department of Agriculture, wrote asking for advice on a credit union act being debated (it was not passed) in the provincial legislature. See Bergengren, *Crusade: The Fight for Economic Democracy in North America, 1921-1945* (New York: Exposition Press, 1952), p. 87.

51. Bergengren, "God Gave Us Men", Part IV, Chapter III, p. 6.

52. *The Bridge* (March 1947), pp. 8-10.

53. *Ibid.*, p. 10.

54. Moody and Fite, p. 152.

55. Interview with Paul Hebert, November 11, 1996.

56. *The Bridge* (April 1942), p. 77.

57. Mark A. Van Steenwyk, "Cooperatives in the Philippines: A Study of Past Performance, Current Status And Future Trends" (May 1, 1987), USAID Document for Contract No. AID 492-0249-C-00-6098-00, p. 3.

58. *The Bridge* (February 1, 1948), p. 8.

59. *Asian Credit Union Development Memo,* (Bangkok: Association of Asian Credit Unions, 1963), p. 253.

60. *Staff Training and Recognition Programme* (Dubuque: Kendall/Hunt Publishing, 1995), p. 6.

61. Bergengren and Doig, p. 71.

62. *The Credit Union Yearbook*, 1958, p. 22. The assets, however, grew from $322,600,000 to $434,600,000, an increase of more than 33 percent, one indication of the increased earning power of members, the limited opportunities for purchasing consumer goods, and the return of full employment — as well as increased opportunities for overtime.

63. *Ibid.*, p. 22.

64. *Ibid.*, p. 23.

65. *The Bridge* (February 1946), p. 10.

66. "Preliminary Statement for Cooperative Review Group", (August 8, 1961), WOCCU, 800062.

67. *The Bridge* (May 1946), pp. 18-19.

68. Interview with A.A. Bailey, October 4, 1996.

69. *The Bridge* (July 1948), p. 148.

70. *Ibid.*, p. 149.

71. *World Reporter* (October 1974), p. 6.

72. Interview with A.A. Bailey, October 4, 1996.

73. *Ibid.*

74. *Ibid.*

75. The author is indebted to Everard Dean for providing a draft of a history of the Trinidadian credit union movement, "Historical Background and Summary of Development Efforts of the Credit Union Movement in the Caribbean". Most of the description of the "T&T" movement is based on that draft.

76. "50 Years of Service in T & T", *Trinidad Express* Newspapers Ltd. supplement (March 31, 1996), p. 5.

77. *The Bridge* (January 1948), p. 15.

78. *The Bridge* (October 1947), p. 3.

79. *The Bridge* (August 1946), p. 3.

80. Mark A. Van Steenwyk, "Cooperatives in the Philippines".

81. Subsequently, the Association of Credit Union League Executives (ACULE).

82. *The History of ACULE: "Creating Leadership Through Cooperation", 1942-1982* (Madison: Association of Credit Union League Executives, 1982), p. 9.

83. As quoted in Jack and Selma Dublin, *Credit Unions in a Changing World: The Tanzania-Kenya Experience* (Detroit: Wayne State University Press, 1983), p. 51.

84. Moody and Fite, p. 239.

85. Roy F. Bergengren, "The World Needs Credit Unions", *The Bridge* (April 1954), p. 11.

86. The books were, respectively, *Asia and the Awakening East* and *North of Malaya*.

87. Roy F. Bergengren to Agnes Gartland, November 12, 1953, Bergengren Papers, WOCCU.

88. *Ibid.*

89. Bergengren, "The World Needs Credit Unions", p. 12.

90. Roy F. Bergengren to J.C. Howell, November 14, 1953. Bergengren Papers, WOCCU, file: CORR 6350, 1953.

91. Father McIver worked in credit union development from 1945 onward, in the Dominican Republic, Guyana and the Philippines. From 1975 to 1979 he taught at the Coady International Institute. Even after retiring, at age 71, he went to Kwazululand to carry on organizing credit unions. The author is indebted to Jim Murphy for supplying background on Father McIver's career.

92. "10:10 p.m., May 15, 1954", Bergengren Papers, WOCCU, file: CORR, 7029, 1954.

93. C.E. Murphy to A.A. Bailey, undated, WOCCU, 800062, file: Memoranda World Extension Department, 1962.

94. *Ibid.*

95. *Ibid.*

96. Speech by Olaf Spetland, March 15, 1958, p. 3. WOCCU, 800062, file: Correspondence Africa & South America. A.A. Bailey 1966-67.

97. *The Credit Union Yearbook*, 1957, p. 29.

98. *World Reporter* (Winter 1977-78), p. 1.

99. Interview with A.A. Bailey, October 4, 1996.

100. *Co-operatives in the Caribbean: An Introduction* (Kingston: National Union of Co-operative Societies, 1994), p. 50.

101. *Ibid.*, p. 54.

102. G. McEoin, *Agent for Change: The Story of Harvey (Pablo) Steele* (Maryknoll: Orbis Books, 1973), p. 55.

103. A.A. Bailey, "Confederation — The Need for and Goal of Confederation", undated paper in author's possession. Approximate date (from internal references) 1968 or 1969. Provided by the Caribbean Confederation of Credit Unions.

104. Interview with A.A. Bailey, October 4, 1996.

105. The World Extension Department, "Five Year Credit Union Development Program", p. 19. WOCCU, 800061, file: Five Year Credit Union Development Program, The World Extension Department.

106. *The International Credit Union Yearbook*, 1963, p. 29.

107. *World Reporter*, (May 1974), p. 1.

108. "Credit Union Development Around the World", IC Special Committee on Cooperatives, WOCCU, 800062.

109. ACOSCA Africa Cooperative Savings and Credit Association, *Ten Years Toward Self-Reliance, 1968-1978* (Nairobi: ACOSCA, 1978), p. 4.

110. *Ibid.*

111. Carlos. M. Matos, "A Credit Union Program for Fiji: In Pursuit of Self-Reliance", June 1984, p. 6, WOCCU.

112. *Credit Union Magazine* (September 1963), p. 7.

113. *Asian Credit Union Development Memo* (Bangkok: Association of Asian Credit Unions, 1993), p.14.

114. *Ibid.*, p.155.

115. R.W. Tulus, "Country Report — Indonesia", *A Glimpse into the Asian Credit Union Movement* (Seoul: Asian Confederation of Credit Unions, 1981), p. 117.

116. For a description of Russell's co-operative work, see Henry Summerfield, *That Myriad Minded Man: A Biography of G.W. Russell — A.E.* (Totawa: Rowman and Littlefield, 1975), pp. 88-94.

117. A. Culloty, "Nora Herlihy: Irish Credit Union Pioneer", (December/January 1991), p. 9, article provided by Irish Credit Union League.

118. Nora Herlihy, "Before the Dawn", p.8, article provided by Irish Credit Union League.

119. *Ibid.*, p. 10.

120. Information provided by Irish Credit Union League.

121. *The International Credit Union Yearbook*, 1963, p. 42.

122. *Ibid.*, p. 47.

123. Statistics are based on *The Credit Union Yearbook*, 1955, p. 3 and *The International Credit Union Yearbook*, 1963, p. 1.

124. J.O. Shipe to A.A. Bailey, December 31, 1968. WOCCU, 800062, file: Correspondence Africa & South America. A.A. Bailey.

125. *World Reporter* (August 1973), p. 7.

126. A. Marble, "Co-operatives and the AID Program", July 14, 1965, WOCCU, 800061, file: CUNA/AID Correspondence.

127. *World Reporter* (November 1972), p. 4.

128. "Problems Facing the Overseas Activities of the World Extension Department, April 26, 1961", WOCCU, 800061, file: CUNA World Extension Department. Reports.

129. WOCCU, 800061, file: Five Year Credit Union Development Program, The World Extension Department.

130. A.A. Bailey, "Confederation".

131. Moody and Fite, p. 241.

132. *Credit Union Magazine* (April 1963), pp. 4-15.

133. *Credit Union Magazine* (July 1964), p. 4.

134. *Ibid.*, pp. 4-6.

135. "Report", WOCCU, 800052, file: Colombia — Correspondence 1964-1965.

136. H. Wegner, "The Colombia Credit Union Program", p. 5, WOCCU, 800052, file: Colombia — Correspondence 1964-1965.

137. Interview with Paul Hebert, November 10, 1966.

138. *World Reporter* (May-July 1976), p. 5.

139. *Ibid.*, p. 9.

140. *World Reporter* (August 1973), p. 8.

141. *Annual Report, CUNA World Extension Division, 1962-63*, p. 2. WOCCU, 800061, file: CUNA World Extension Department. Reports.

142. Report by Eleanor R. Jacob, p. 1, WOCCU, 800052, file: Evaluation of the Directed Production Program in Ecuador, 1972.

143. *Credit Union Magazine* (May 1965), pp. 4-12.

144. Interview with Percy Avram, February 24, 1997.

145. Transcript of speech by Jack Vaughn to the International Symposium, Toronto, May 31, 1982. Personal files of Chris Baker.

146. Interview with Gordon Hurd, Madison, Wisconsin, December 9, 1996.

147. Fortunately, the traditional American concerns about the efficacy of credit unions in rural areas were fading. During the 1950s community credit unions in the United States had shown that they could work with farming members effectively. In Canada, too, rural credit unions, especially on the Prairies were commonplace. And, in any event, most of the Peace Corps volunteers were unaware of the traditional concerns about rural credit unions in the American movement.

148. The writings on over-reliance on government-to-government aid are voluminous. For a thoughtful critique from a "friend" of developmental assistance — and an experienced practitioner — see R.L. Oshins, "A Nation-Based Approach to Developmental Assistance", *International Development Review*, 1963, pp. 6-15.

149. WOCCU, *The International Credit Union Yearbook*, 1971, p. 5a.

150. C.E. Murphy to A.A. Bailey, undated (but apparently from late 1966), WOCCU, 800062, file: Memoranda World Extension Department.

151. Dates are from *Ten Years Toward Self-Reliance*, pp. 4-6.

152. *Credit Union Magazine* (November 1968), p. 5.

153. WOCCU, *The International Credit Union Yearbook*, 1971, p. 5a.

154. A.A. Bailey, "Confederation".

155. J. Hermanns, "MISEREOR: A Portrait", *World Reporter* (Quarter 1, 1979), p. 2.

156. C. Purden, *Agents for Change: Credit Unions in Saskatchewan* (Saskatoon: Modern Press, 1980), p. 240.

157. "Credit Unions in Tanganyika", pp. 3-9, WOCCU, 800064, file: Final Report on Tanganyika.

158. Interview with Jack and Selma Dublin, May 25, 1996.

159. The author is indebted to Jack and Selma Dublin for helping him to understand some of the foregoing issues involved in developing credit unions in many parts of Africa. See their valuable book, *Credit Unions in a Changing World*.

160. See Ottfried C. Kirsch and Fred V. Goricke, *Scope and Impact of The Credit Union Movement in Selected African Countries* (Mainz: 1977).

161. *Ten Years Toward Self-Reliance*, p. 8.

162. *A Glimpse into the Asian Credit Union Movement* (Seoul: Asian Confederation of Credit Unions, 1981), pp. 87-88.

163. *Ibid.*, p. 91.

164. J. Collins, "One Step at a Time: A Brief History of Hong Kong Credit Unions", *World Reporter* (May-June 1975), p. 5.

165. *Ibid.*, p. 125.

166. "Country Report — History of the Credit Union Movement in Thailand", *A Glimpse into the Asian Credit Union Movement*, pp. 123-24.

167. *Ibid.*, pp. 294-95.

168. "History of the Credit Union Movement in New Zealand", unpublished manuscript provided by the New Zealand Association of Credit Unions.

169. C. Smith, "Credit Unions in New Zealand", in N. Runcie (ed.), *Credit Unions in the South Pacific — Australia, New Zealand, Papua and New Guinea* (London: University of London, 1969) pp. 208-210.

170. *World Reporter* (August-October 1977), pp. 3-4.

171. There was, of course, a reason the bank supported an employee credit union: under its charter, it could not lend to employees, except housing loans at low return. It did not particularly want its employees borrowing from other financial institutions, and so it accepted the credit union as a poor second choice. Based on comments received from Ken Miller, February 12, 1997.

172. "Credit Unions Down Under", *Credit Union Magazine* (June 1965), p. 42.

173. Gary Lewis, *People Before Profit: The Credit Union Movement in Australia* (Kent Town: Wakefield Press, 1996), p. 43.

174. *Ibid.*, pp. 338-339.

175. G.A. Arbuckle, "Economic and Social Development in the Fiji Islands Through Credit Unions", in N. Runcie, (ed.), *Credit Unions in the South Pacific*, p. 101.

176. Carlos Matos, quoted in "Fiji's Credit Union School" by Suzanne Bisset, *World Reporter* (Quarter III, 1978), p. 2.

177. *Ibid.*, pp. 2-3.

178. *Ibid.*, p. 3.

179. "Credit Union Victory in the United Kingdom", *World Reporter* (Quarter II, 1979), pp. 1 and 6.

180. Statistics are based on *The International Credit Union Yearbook* for 1963 and 1970.

181. See *Short History of the Caribbean Movement: Early Beginnings, Achievements* (Barbados: Caribbean Confederation of Credit Unions, 1987) for more information on the Caribbean movement.

182. They were Canada, Bolivia, Brazil, British Honduras, Colombia, Ecuador, Panama, the Netherlands Antilles, Peru, Jamaica, Trinidad, Australia, Fiji, the Philippines and Ireland.

183. Interview with Paul Hebert, November 10, 1996.

184. For a thorough discussion of this complex issue see Lewis, *People Before Profit*, pp. 67-85.

185. Interview with Rod Glen, April 1980.

186. A.A. Bailey to J.O. Shipe, November 29, 1965, WOCCU, 800062, file: Memoranda World Extension Department 1962.

187. "A Three Year Development Project for Credit Union Development in the Less Developed Countries", p. 3, WOCCU, 800061, file: Developing Countries — Financial Management.

188. A.A. Bailey, "Confederation".

189. C.E. Murphy to A.A. Bailey, undated (probably late 1966). WOCCU, 800062, file: Memoranda World Extension Department 1962.

190. In the midst of the intense and sometimes vicious debates between CUNA and CUNA Mutual supporters in the 1950s, Glen was frequently called a communist, though in fact he belonged to the Co-operative Commonwealth Federation, a social democratic party that in those years spent much of its time and energy combatting the Communist Party. Someone within the American movement nevertheless reported Glen to the FBI. The result was that he was investigated by the Royal Canadian Mounted Police and threatened with denial of entry into the United States. The attack was halted by the intervention of the Member of Parliament from Glen's home town of Nanaimo. The MP made a public issue of the charge and Glen never did have difficulty entering the United States. The bitterness and mistrust nevertheless remained in some circles in the United States through the 1960s and 1970s. Interview with Rod Glen, April 1980.

191. All statistics are from the annual reports of the World Council of Credit Unions.

192. *A Report on the Planning Committee Meeting of the World Council of Credit Unions*, (Madison: WOCCU, 1971).

193. Jack and Connie McLanahan, *Cooperative/Credit Union Dictionary and Reference* (Richmond, Kentucky: The Cooperative Alumni Association, 1990), p. 293.

194. *World Reporter* (November-December 1975 and January 1976), p. 8.

195. Statistics are based on *The International Credit Union Yearbook*, 1963 and 1973 and *The World Council of Credit Unions Statistical Report and Directory*, 1978-1979.

196. *A Report on the Planning Committee Meeting*, p. 5.

197. For a fuller treatment of the Australian movement see Lewis, *People Before Profit*.

198. *The International Credit Union Yearbook*, 1971, p. 2a.

199. *World Reporter* (November-December 1975 and January 1976), p. 6.

200. Interview with Dale Magers, October 25, 1996.

201. Adapted from the approach advocated by Alexander F. Laidlaw. See "The Great Co-operative Debate", *World Reporter* (Quarter IV, 1978,), p. 4.

202. Harry W. Culbreth, Position Paper, "Role of Cooperative Finance in Developing Agriculture and Cooperatives in Developing Countries", WOCCU, 800108, file: Co-operatives and Developing Countries. Also "Support for Credit Union Development by the Agency for International Development", WOCCU, 800061, file: Credit Union Growth in Developing Countries.

203. *World Reporter* (May-July 1976), p. 8.

204. One of the leaders of the Antigonish movement in the 1940s and 1950s, Laidlaw had a substantial interest in developing co-operatives overseas. In 1957-1958 he chaired a Royal Commission in Ceylon (Sri Lanka) that helped stimulate growth within the credit union/co-operative movement in that country.

205. A. Castro, "The COLAC System", Part II, *World Reporter* (Quarter IV, 1982), p. 4.

206. "How a Million-Dollar Grant Multiplies its Impact", *World Reporter* (May-July 1975), p. 6.

207. *World Reporter* (May 1975), pp. 5-6.

208. *World Reporter* (Quarter II, 1980), p. 1.

209. Rymel Serrano Uribe, "Report on COLAC", Minutes, WOCCU Board of Directors, March 16, 1972, p. 13.

210. *World Reporter* (May 1974), pp. 1-4.

211. Rymel Serrano Uribe, "Resume of Report on Latin America Credit Union Movement", Minutes, WOCCU Board of Directors, February 1977, p. 2.

212. Rymel Serrano Uribe, "Credit Unions in Latin America", *World Reporter* (May-July, 1977), pp. 1-2.

213. Uribe, "Resume of Report", p. 2.

214. Lual A.L. Deng, "African Savings and Credit Cooperatives: A Baseline Survey of Institutional Development in Ghana, Ivory Coast, and Zambia", March 1976, WOCCU, file: ACOSCA.

215. Based on *The International Credit Union Yearbook*, 1971 and *The World Council of Credit Unions Statistical Report and Directory*, 1982-1983.

216. *Ten Years Toward Self-Reliance*, p. 3.

217. C. Aeschliman, "Strengthening of National, Regional and Local Credit Union Structures". WOCCU, national files: Cameroon — Project Reports.

218. A.A. Bailey, "World Extension Department", CUNA, *Annual Report*, 1970, pp. 4-5.

219. *Ibid.*, p. 5.

220. *World Reporter* (Quarter II, 1979), p. 2.

221. *World Reporter* (Quarter IV, 1979), p. 5.

222. For a concise, critical examination of *ujamaa* see Gavin Green, "Rural Credit and Marketing Systems in Tanzania: A Twenty-Five Year Perspective", *Rural Development in Practice* (August 1988), pp. 14-15.

223. *A Glimpse into the Asian Credit Union Movement*, Foreword, p. iv.

224. *Ibid.*, p. v.

225. *Asian Credit Union Development Memo*, (Bangkok: Association of Asian Credit Unions, 1993) p. 88.

226. *Short History of the Caribbean Credit Union Movement*, p. 10.

227. "Credit Union Victory in the United Kingdom", *World Reporter* (Quarter II, 1979), pp. 1 and 6.

228. *World Reporter* (Quarter IV), p. 3.

229. World Council of Credit Unions, *International Annual Report, 1979/1980*, p. 6.

230. Interview with Rod Glen, October 28, 1979.

231. "Support for Credit Union Development by the U.S. Agency for International Development", May 1, 1980, p. 1, WOCCU, 80061, file: Credit Union Growth in Developing Countries.

232. Interview with Paul Hebert, November, 11, 1996.

233. *Overview Analysis of the World Council of Credit Unions* (Madison: WOCCU, 1980), p. 2.

234. *Credit Unions: A World of Progress, Supplement*, p. 75.

235. *Overview Analysis*, p. 3.

236. Chris Baker, "Congratulatory Speech from WOCCU", Tenth Anniversary, Asian Confederation of Credit Unions, 1981, p. 1.

237. Birchall, *The International Co-operative Movement*, p. 117.

238. See *ibid.*, pp. 117-225, for one of the best brief discussions on the restructuring of central and eastern Europe.

239. The negative attitude toward co-operatives was not universal. In Romania, for example, where co-operatives had a history stretching back to the 1850s, co-operative societies had been able to withstand the more extreme intervention in their affairs by the Marxist government. As the switch to a market economy took place, the existing co-operatives were able to evolve more readily into a conventional co-operative bank. See COPAC, "The Credit and Consumer Cooperatives of Romania — A Return to the Free Market Economy", *Perspectives: Monthly News for the World Council of Credit Unions* (October 1991), p.1

240. *Perspectives* (November 1993), p. 2

241. *Perspectives* (April 1994), p. 3.

242. National Credit Union Federation of Korea, "Women's Involvement in Korean Credit Union Movement: A Case Study", WOCCU, file: Korea.

243. H. Allen, "The Great Co-operative Debate", *World Reporter* (Quarter III, 1978), p. 4.

244. *COLAC 1990s: The COLAC System Development Strategies* (Panama: COLAC), p.16.

245. *Ibid.*

246. Much of this description is based on a particularly cogent paper by Angel Castro, "The Importance of Savings and Credit Functions of Primary Co-operative Financial Institutions in Latin America", IVth International Raiffeisen Co-operative Seminar, September 21-25, 1987, pp. 61-77, WOCCU.

247. For a more complete summary of this trend toward more managerial credit unions, see *ibid.*

248. John H. Magill, "Credit Unions: A Formal Sector Alternative for Financing Micro-enterprise Development", September 1991, unpublished report, p. 13, WOCCU.

249. *World Reporter* (January 1989), pp. 28-29.

250. D. C. Richardson, B.L. Lennon and B.A. Branch, "Credit Unions Retooled: A Road Map for Financial Stabilization", (Madison: WOCCU Research Monograph Series, Number 1, March 1993), p. 1.

251. B. Barham and S. Boucher, "Credit Unions in Guatemalan Financial Markets: Helping to Meet the Needs of Small Scale Producers", (Madison: WOCCU Research Monograph Series, Number 6, November 1994).

252. *Ibid.*, pp. 3-4.

253. Richardson *et al*, p.1.

254. Richardson *et al*, p. 2.

255. Richardson *et al*, pp. 3-4.

256. Everard Dean, "Historical Background and Summary of Development Efforts of the Credit Union Movement in the Caribbean", draft of a history.

257. Dale Majers, "The African Credit Union Movement: An Overview", January 1990, WOCCU, file: (Africa) ACOSCA.

258. *Ibid.*

259. "African Credit Unions as Cooperatives: Achievements, Potential and Developmental Issues", December 1992, unpublished report, p. 3, WOCCU.

260. *Ibid.*

261. G. Almeyda de Stemper, "The Role of Credit in Development Projects: The Credit Union Movement in Togo", *American Review of Money, Finance and Banking* (Volume 1, 1987), p. 30.

262. *Ibid.*, p. 33.

263. Interview with Dale Majers. For a more complete description of the Lesotho experiment, see Hayward Allen, "Lesotho: An African Microcosm of Macroeconomic Development", 1985, unpublished paper, WOCCU, file: Lesotho.

264. " 'The Malawi Experience': A Case Study of Partnership in Development for the SEEP Network Workshop on Institutional Development in the Small Enterprise Sector, May 22-25, 1990", WOCCU, file: Malawi, 1990.

265. *Ibid.*, pp. 5-7.

266. South African Credit Union League, 1991 Annual Report, pp. 5-6.

267. Deng, "African Savings and Credit Cooperatives", pp. 17-18. CUA, in effect, was a third-tier organization, in that local credit unions were organized in chapters on a geographical basis; the chapters served as a second tier in many respects and were the organizing units for CUA.

268. The actual number of credit unions or savings and thrift co-operatives in Nigeria never seems to have been established satisfactorily during the period. The lack of reliable national data was in itself a reflection of the weakness of the national organization; it is also indicative of how credit unions were built upon indigenous financial institutions, most of which were not registered and, in fact, resisted any attempt at government regulation.

269. "A Summary of the Nigerian Credit Union Movement", WOCCU, file: Nigeria, 1990.

270. *Ibid.*

271. C. Mandizha, "African Co-operative Laws: Change is Urgently Needed", *World Reporter* (January 1988), pp. 10-12.

272. Mebratu Tsegaye, "Assessment of Savings and Credit Co-operatives in Swaziland, Summary Report", p. 3. WOCCU, file: Swaziland, 1983-89.

273. "Sanasa: An Introduction to Thrift and Credit Cooperatives in Sri Lanka", unpublished report, International Co-operative Alliance Library, Geneva.

274. "History of the Credit Union Movement in Bangladesh", WOCCU, file: Bangladesh.

275. Carlos M. Matos, "A Credit Union Program for Fiji: In Pursuit of Self-Reliance", June 1984, p. 21, WOCCU Archives.

276. 1995 Regional Workshop Forum, Fiji, p. 29.

277. "Credit Union Development in the South Pacific", South Pacific Credit Union Development Conference, December 7-9, 1992, WOCCU, file: COLAC.

278. A. Murray, "Looking to the Next Century: The Irish League of Credit Unions International Development Foundation Ltd.", *World Reporter* (May 1992), pp. 16-17.

279. *Credit Unions in Great Britain: A Review of the Years 1979-1995* (Registry of Friendly Societies, undated), pp. 19-21.

280. *Ibid.*, pp. 16-19.

281. P. Bussy, "Credit Unions in Great Britain 1994-95", in *The World of Co-operative Enterprise* (Oxford: The Plunkett Foundation, 1996), pp. 193-199.

282. Address by Tony Schumacher, International Symposium, Toronto, pp. 5-6.

283. John Isbister, *Thin Cats: The Community Development Credit Union in the United States* (Madison: Center for Cooperatives, University of California, 1994).

284. *World Reporter* (Quarter III, 1984), p. 1.

285. WOCCU, *1996 Statistical Report*, p. 4. There were some major shifts in international statistics during the late 1980s and 1990s because the Ghanaian statistics were not always available. Since they represented between 15,500 and 16,000 credit unions and nearly 3,000,000 members, their inclusion or exclusion could dramatically affect the international statistics. They were not included in the 1996 calculations.

286. *Annual Meeting Book*, Regional Educational Conference and Annual General Assembly, Port-of-Spain, Trinidad, June 1996, p. 18.

287. For example, see Lucy Ito, "Poverty Alleviation: The Role of 'Credit' Institutions vs. the Role of Financial Intermediaries", ACCU Regional Workshop, Colombo, Sri Lanka, May 25-29, 1995, p. 2.

288. Interview with Paul Hebert, November 10, 1996.

ENDNOTES TO CHAPTER HEAD QUOTES

Chapter One

A. Quoted in J. Burns, "Luzzatti: Italy's Credit Union Pioneer", *World Reporter* (Quarter III, 1981), p. 4.

B. Quoted in "The Credit Union: Christian Social Leadership in Action", May 18, 1958, WOCCU, 800108.

Chapter Two

A. "Remarks at Blue Hill Neighbourhood Credit Union", May 13, 1934, Filene Papers, CUNA Archives.

B. "Statement of May 19, 1937", Filene Papers, CUNA Archives.

Chapter Three

A. May 1954, when asking the board of CUNA for the formation of an international programme.

B. "1954 — Year of Challenge", Bergengren Papers, WOCCU, file : CORR 6330 1953.

Chapter Four

A. Speech made in late 1950s, WOCCU, 800062, file: Correspondence Africa & South America. A.A. Bailey 1966-67.

B. *Credit Union Magazine* (January 1963).

Chapter Five

Immediate Past President, CUNA International, *Proceedings of the International Conference on Cooperative Thrift and Credit,* Kingston, Jamaica, October 3-8, 1966.

Chapter Eight

A. "Report of the Planning Committee", WOCCU, 800108, file: WOCCU, 1971.

B. "Outgoing Managing Director Andrew So's Report, 1974", *A Glimpse into the Asian Credit Union Movement.*

Chapter Nine

A. "The Challenge Awaits", *World Reporter* (Quarter III, 1978).

B. "Credit Union Membership and Savings Growth: An Overview", *Papers Presented at the World Council of Credit Unions First International Credit Union Forum,* Panama City, August 20-25, 1984.

Chapter Ten

A. *Development of a National Credit Union Movement,* June 1987.

B. *COLAC 1990s* (Panama).

Chapter Eleven

A. 54th Annual General Meeting, Jamaica Co-operative Credit Union League, May 1995, *Credit Union News* (June 1995).

B. "Report of the Chief Executive Officer", *Annual Meeting Book,* 1996, Regional Educational Conference & Annual General Assembly, Port-of-Spain, Trinidad, June 23-26, 1996.

INDEX